W9-BGL-631

YES!
YOU CAN
OWN THE
HOME
YOU WANT

YES!
YOU CAN
OWN THE
HOME
YOU WANT

GARY W. ELDRED

643.12
EL24Y

JOHN WILEY & SONS
New York • Chichester • Brisbane • Toronto • Singapore

This text is printed on acid-free paper.
Copyright © 1995 by Gary W. Eldred
Published by John Wiley & Sons, Inc.

All rights reserved. Published simultaneously in Canada.

Reproduction or translation of any part of this work beyond
that permitted by Section 107 or 108 of the 1976 United
States Copyright Act without the permission of the copyright
owner is unlawful. Requests for permission or further
information should be addressed to the Permissions Department,
John Wiley & Sons, Inc.

This publication is designed to provide accurate and authoritative
information in regard to the subject matter covered. It is sold
with the understanding that the publisher is not engaged in
rendering legal, accounting, or other professional services. If
legal advice or other expert assistance is required, the services
of a competent professional person should be sought.

Library of Congress Cataloging-in-Publication Data

Eldred, Gary W.
    Yes! You can own the home you want / Gary W. Eldred.
      p. cm.
    Includes index.
    ISBN 0-471-09946-5 (cloth) ISBN
  0-471-09978-3 (paper)
    1. House buying I. Title.
  HD1379.E433 1995
643'.12—dc2095-1371

Printed in the United States of America
10 9 8 7 6 5 4 3 2 1

FOREWORD

Owning a home, along with steady employment and obtaining an education, are the components of the "American Dream." These goals are what most people consider necessary for long-term financial security. Of these, home ownership often is regarded as the most difficult to achieve. However, those who choose owning over renting consistently report that it is worth the sacrifice and effort required to buy a home.

Although some renters truly are barred from buying by financial constraints, a large majority of renters are passing up a great opportunity to own simply because they believe—mistakenly—that they can't afford to buy. In many cases, the perception most renters have of buying is far more arduous than reality.

Speaking as a real estate professional and on behalf of the NATIONAL ASSOCIATION OF REALTORS®, my message to anyone considering buying a home is this: Buying a home may be *easier than you think*. Indeed, in this new book, home ownership advocate Gary Eldred explains dozens of techniques and strategies that — regardless of your present circumstances — can help you move up from renting to home ownership. Just as important, keep in mind that *you don't have to go it alone*.

Although your home buying process may at times seem overwhelming, an experienced real estate professional can guide you through each step—from choosing the type of home that suits your needs to explaining various types of home financing possibilities.

It's best to be as calm and objective as possible when you decide to make an offer on a house. However, finally locating a place that says "home" to you is an exciting and emotionally charged experience. A real estate practitioner can help you make the decision that is right for you, providing service that is quick and efficient. Remember, real estate professionals spend their days looking at homes; comparing neighborhoods; and evaluating schools, special services, public transportation, and, in general, the quality of life a community can provide.

Once you've decided to enlist the help of a professional, it's important to find the right one. When selecting a real estate agent, consider asking the following questions: How long have you held a license? Have you earned any professional designations? Are you a full-time practitioner? How familiar are you with this area? Take the time to find the agent who best fits your needs. Trust me: It's time well spent.

Another tip: When selecting a real estate professional to assist you, be sure to work with a REALTOR®. REALTORS® are members of the NATIONAL ASSOCIATION OF REALTORS® and are bound by a strict Code of Ethics. Your peace of mind and the most important investment of your future are at stake. It's in your interest to seek the best home buying assistance available—the service of a REALTOR®. You deserve nothing less.

GILL WOODS
President
NATIONAL ASSOCIATION OF REALTORS®

AUTHOR'S NOTE

Throughout the past 20 years, the most frequent complaint I've heard from renters is this: "I wish we could have bought a home years ago." Next, these renters often have added, "But we really didn't have the money to afford the home we wanted." If this is what you think, you need to think again.

During this past year, thousands of Realtors, mortgage lenders, home builders, and not-for-profit housing groups, as well as hundreds of federal, state, and local government agencies, have joined a national initiative to assist at least 10 million more individuals, families, and alternative households to become homeowners by the year 2000. "This initiative," says U.S. Department of Housing and Urban Development Secretary Henry Cisneros, "will spark a dramatic expansion of home ownership to include millions of families and individuals who today barely dream of becoming homeowners."

In announcing this initiative at a White House "Home Ownership Event," President Clinton said, "I want to thank again all of the people here from the private sector who have worked with Secretary Cisneros on this initiative. Our home ownership strategy will not require more legislation. It will not grow the federal bureaucracy. It's 100 specific actions that address the practical needs of people who are trying to build their personal version of the American Dream . . . [especially those families] who have historically felt excluded from home ownership. . . ."

What's included in these 100 specific actions? Virtually everything you can think of to make home buying and home financing easier: innovative low- (and no-) down-payment mortgages; lower closing costs; advanced information technology; more flexible qualifying standards; more liberal qualifying ratios; ways to overcome blemished credit; home buyer counseling; mortgage bond money; mortgage credit certificates; "fixer-upper" financing; special financing from new home builders; and much, much more. All of these strategies and techniques and dozens of others are discussed in this book. Also, please see Appendix I.

In one of my previous books, *The 106 Common Mistakes Home Buyers Make* (John Wiley & Sons, Inc.), I emphasized that "continuing to rent is the greatest mistake of all." Now, relying on the knowledge contained in this book, a committed Realtor and loan advisor, and a positive "can-do" attitude, you can easily avoid making this mistake. I'm confident that with our new national private–public strategy to expand home ownership, if you want to own your own home, you can own your own home.

If you have any questions whatsoever about home buying, choosing a Realtor, or home financing, **please give me a call at (800) 942-9304 (extension 20691).** I would very much like to hear from you. Good luck, and I wish you the best as you move toward this all-important goal.

Gary W. Eldred

CONTENTS

INTRODUCTION
YOU CAN OWN THE HOME YOU WANT

"We couldn't believe it," exclaimed an enthusiastic Jennifer Wirtz. "Last month we looked at the same home we had really wanted several years ago. It had just come back on the market. The earlier asking price had been $239,000, and the sellers wouldn't budge. It's new listing price was $198,000. We got it for $187,500. Even better, our payments will be $600 less than if we had actually been able to afford the home several years ago."

"Better still," said their Realtor, Ebbie Kaufman, "the reality is that even with our area's relatively high housing prices, first-time home buyers like the Wirtzes can get into home ownership almost as cheaply as they can rent."

In the Denver, Colorado, suburb of Englewood, Anita Fowler, age 27 and a nurse at a nearby clinic, just bought her first home. She got a great three-bedroom, two-bath brick bungalow for just $78,700. "The home needs more than a little T.L.C.," Anita said, "but with my talent for decorating and design, I know I'll be able to increase its value. I just feel so lucky to get it. My Realtor learned the home was coming onto the market, telephoned me, and then got my offer accepted even before it went into the Multiple Listing Service (MLS).

"I've been wanting to buy for several years," Anita admitted. "Yet I was uncertain about the economy and whether homes were still a good investment. Now I know I made the right decision. The Denver housing market has really recovered from the severe downturn we felt after the energy bust. Besides, you can't believe how good it feels to come home to your own home. I liked the condo I was renting, but my heart is now in my home."

A NEW CYCLE BEGINS

For the past two years, newspaper and magazine articles all across the country have reported great opportunities for first-time home buyers. "First-time home buyers are leading the market—lower mortgage rates and home prices are turning renters into owners," reports *The New York Times*. "Deals too good to last," writes *U.S. News & World Report*. A *Parade* article spotlights "the very best deals" in a dozen different cities throughout the United States. Another article in *The New York Times* says, "Low interest rates and a large inventory of unsold homes are making it possible for many first-time buyers to enter the housing market for the first time in years."

Sales data from the National Association of Realtors (NAR) confirm *The New York Times* reporting. The NAR says that during the past 12 months, first-time home buyers have accounted for nearly one-half of the sales of existing homes. A just-released survey, *Who's Buying Homes in America*, by Chicago Title, found the same thing. Virtually everyone agrees that due to increasing incomes and lower interest rates, homes in most areas of the country have become relatively more affordable than they were throughout most of the 1980s and early 1990s. In fact, all things considered, the most recent Affordability Index calculated by the NAR shows home affordability at a near record high. Many renters who had been sitting on the sidelines have now gotten into the game.

DO YOU STILL FEEL LEFT OUT?

Unfortunately, though, far too many renters still aren't joining in. "Sure, in our area monthly mortgage payments are more affordable than they were a few years ago," report Joyce and Bill Hampton. "But there's still no way we can buy the home we want. We don't have enough for a down payment. Besides, we're not so sure owning makes economic sense anymore. We've seen magazine articles warn against buying. A lot of experts say renting is cheaper. Homes are not the sure-fire investments they once were."

Sam Sloan, age 49 and a long-time resident of Honolulu, has given up on buying in Hawaii. "We do not own a home here, and both my wife and I work," says Sam. "We have tried seriously to get the home we want and we can't afford it. Could we buy a house? Absolutely. Could we buy a house we like? Absolutely not."

Patty King, age 34, is an attorney who has lived in Seattle for the past eight years. Patty put off buying. She had believed she would be married by her mid-30s. Home buying would come after marriage. She now says, with regret, "I wish I had bought earlier. But I can't really get excited about buying now. It's a big psychological roadblock to know many of my friends bought their homes some years back at much lower prices. Even worse, interest rates aren't as low as they were a year or two ago."

Broderick Perkins, a newspaper columnist in the San Francisco Bay area, urged his readers to, "Give your home-buying budget one last desperate squeeze—or wait until the next recession." But then he adds, "This advice comes from a savings-poor renter who is still years away from a down payment. If I could get into the market, I'd be at the front of the line."

* * * * *

During the past two years, nearly 7.5 million Americans have been able to move up from renting to home ownership. But millions of other renters are holding back. Many believe they can't afford to buy. Some believe they can't afford to buy the home they really want. Some believe they missed their chance to own when prices were lower or when interest rates hit their 25-year low in the fall of 1993. Now they believe it's too late. A large number believe that renting costs less than owning or that homes no longer stand out as a good investment.

With lingering concerns over affordability, the costs of renting versus owning, job security, and potential appreciation, it's little wonder the U.S. Census Bureau recently reported that fewer Americans under age 45 now own their own homes. During the past 15 years, even as home buying has actually become easier, the percentage of home owning Americans age 35 to 44 has fallen from 72 percent to 66 percent. For Americans age 25 to 34, the percentage of those who own dropped from 52.3 to 42.9 percent. And for adults under age 25, homeowners account for just 15 percent of all households. These significant reductions are the first long-term drops in home ownership we've experienced since the 1930s. Unfortunately, some experts believe these numbers could get worse.

Harold Quinley, of the international market research firm Yanklevich, Skelly, White, Clancey and Shulman, has found through his firm's work that many Americans in their 20s and early 30s "are convinced they may never own a home because they believe they grew up in harder economic times than those who came before them. They expect things will be tougher for them in the future." Even though these younger Americans still highly value home ownership, "many won't even try to own a home unless they are somehow persuaded the trade-offs are worth it. They feel no urgency to buy."

ARE YOU UNCERTAIN ABOUT OWNING?

If you're like many renters today, you may be fence sitting. On the one hand, you may realize that favorable home prices and lower interest rates have made home ownership easier than it was throughout the 1980s and early 1990s. On the other hand, you may believe you still can't afford to own, that ownership is not as good an investment as it used to be, or that our country's economic future makes home ownership too risky and uncertain.

If in some ways you can identify with these feelings, this book will help you decide whether now is the time for you to own. Moreover, if you're similar to the great majority of renters I've met in my real estate classes and Stop Renting Now!™ seminars, I'm convinced that home ownership will prove possible, desirable, and profitable for you. The benefits of owning are worth the investment. In my experience, I have found large numbers of renters who regret not buying. In contrast, few homeowners ever regret their decision to own. And as history points the way to our future (as it always has), three or four years from now those renters who chose to continue renting will surely look back with regret on the opportunities they missed today.

Even more important than helping you decide to own, of course, this book shows you the many ways you can get into home ownership—even if you think you can't. You may not be able to start immediately with your ideal home. Few people do. But the best way to make progress toward this life goal is to get into some type of home ownership as quickly as possible.

Consider for a minute Sam Sloan, the long-term Hawaii resident quoted several pages back. He and his wife have rented all their adult lives because they believed they couldn't afford the home they wanted. But could they have afforded some type of home? As Sam said, "Absolutely."

Yet, after having rented in Hawaii for the past 20 years—during a period when median prices climbed from $60,000 to $300,000—are Sam and his wife any closer to their goal of owning the home they really want? Unfortunately, they are not. By failing to get started in home ownership years ago, Sam and his wife are now further from their ideal home. On the other hand, if in earlier years they had relaxed their requirements and bought an affordable home, today they would be much closer to their ideal. If there's any lesson the past has taught, it is this: Don't pass up home ownership today just because you can't yet afford your ideal home.

DON'T POSTPONE: YOU CAN OWN

When I began to offer *Stop Renting Now!*™ seminars, I was surprised at the age group of many who signed up. Often as many as one-half of the class were over age 40. (I had expected nearly everyone who attended would be in their mid-20s to early 30s.) As I talked with these older renters, I learned that, strictly speaking, "unaffordability" had not blocked their road to home ownership. Instead, their complaint was, "We could never afford the home we wanted."

One woman I clearly recall illustrates this point. I will call her Anne Lange. At the time I met her, Anne was age 44. She had lived in the San Francisco Bay area since graduating from the University of California–Berkeley more than 20 years earlier. "Why didn't you buy?" I asked Anne.

"I never saw anything I liked that I could afford," she replied. "After growing up in a four-bedroom, two-bath house with a floored attic, a finished basement, an upstairs and downstairs, and a half-acre lot, I could never adjust to the two-bedroom, one-bath cottage that was within my budget."

"But 20 years ago, those two-bedroom, one-bath cottages were selling for just $30,000 to $45,000. They're now selling for $225,000," I said. "Had you bought after college, you would have nearly 80 to 90 percent equity in the property. You could easily have traded up to something much better."

Anne lamented, "That's water over the dam. The question is how can I stop renting now?"

After I reviewed Anne's finances, one thing became obvious. Anne spent too much money for clothes, travel, her car, and eating out. I suggested to Anne that she change her spending habits. Through careful financial planning, Anne could find an extra $300 to $500 per month to invest in a home. Next, I told her that since she wanted to stay in the East Bay, she should consider Emeryville, a small city next to Berkeley just 15 minutes from downtown San Francisco. This city had a great first-time buyer program that offered modest home prices, very low down payments, and below-market interest rates. I was sure some changes in Anne's budget, when linked to Emeryville's first-time buyer program, could move Anne into home owner-ship.

Anne responded to my suggestion, "Emeryville! Who wants to live in Emeryville?" (As it turns out, quite a number of first-time home buyers in their 20s and early 30s. They know that a good way to get started in home ownership is to find an affordable community—so much the better if the community also makes special first-time buyer financing available.) Anne, though, still wanted to own in the Berkeley hills where many of her friends from college now lived. Try as I might, I couldn't persuade Anne to see that her best chance to get a home in the Berkeley hills was first to buy somewhere else more affordable. Continuing to rent would push her goal further beyond reach.

Having failed to persuade Anne to get started in home owner-ship in Emeryville or some other affordable community, I next suggested various affordability strategies such as shared equity, co-ownership, value creation, and other proven techniques. (These techniques are discussed in later chapters.) With the right affordability strategies and techniques, I believed Anne—like most other renters—could probably extend her range of affordability to the home she wanted. But Anne responded, "I don't want to get into any of those things. I don't understand them."

Anne saw her home buying problem as a problem of *afford-ability*. In truth, though, like Sam Sloan and his wife, as well as millions of other renters, Anne was really blocked from home ownership by two critical shortcomings: (1) her *attitude* and (2) her *lack of education* concerning alternative ways to buy and finance a home.

In some ways, many of us are like Anne or Sam. We avoid committing to a plan because we resist options that we don't fully understand as well as those that don't fit our idealized self-image. But this lack of commitment leads to self-defeat. So please, don't needlessly give up on home ownership. Don't postpone buying because you "can't afford the home you really want." Even if you have looked at homes and believe they are priced out of reach, your real problem may be attitude and education—not unaffordability.

Regardless of the obstacles you think you face—down payment, monthly payments, credit record, job history, discrimination, you name it; regardless of whether you live in a high-priced area, or an area with low-to-moderate home prices—I'm sure there's a financial strategy or combination of strategies that can make ownership *possible* and *profitable* for you. Don't end up like Patty King, Anne Lange, Sam Sloan, or millions of other renters who now wish they had bought years ago. Don't hold back, like Broderick Perkins, because you think you need a pile of savings for a down payment. Don't let market realities defeat you. Meet them. Accept difficulties as a challenge to your imagination, creativity, and self-discipline. If you want to become a home-owner, don't simply hope for your ideal home. Don't wait for someday. Plan your progress toward home ownership now. Few things in life give more satisfaction than working toward and achieving a desired goal—especially the goal of owning your own home.

HOME PRICES ARE GOING UP

Once you have developed the attitude and education to buy, you still might question whether you should buy. Or perhaps you may question whether now really is the time to invest in a home.

Admittedly, *buy now* stands as one of the most frequently heard clichés in real estate. Yet within recent memory, we have seen home prices decline in the oil and gas states (Texas, Oklahoma, Colorado, and Louisiana). We've seen overbuilding depress home prices in Arizona and Florida. We've watched the raging bull markets of Southern California, Washington, D.C.,

New York City, and New England turn into corralled sheep. With these market experiences still vivid in our memories, it's no wonder many media experts have popularized the idea that renting costs less than owning, or "Buy a home if you want a place to live, but don't mistake it for a bank account with a white picket fence."

The facts, though, don't support these pessimistic conclusions. Although local markets will vary, on the whole we are about to see another round of appreciation in home prices. Portland, Oregon; Boise, Idaho; Seattle, Washington; Austin, Texas; and Denver, Colorado are just five recent examples of fast-appreciating markets that will be followed by other cities throughout the United States. Like most investments, home prices move in cycles—sometimes up, sometimes down. Unfortunately, most people incorrectly base their forecasts on whatever has happened recently. If home prices are galloping ahead at 10 to 15 percent a year, the predominant forecast will be for home prices to continue running at that pace. If home prices are declining, stable, or showing slow growth, most people will color the future bleak.

Yet a brief glimpse of history shows that home price trend lines don't extend from the past to the present as straight, smooth, and constant. They look more like the ragged peaks, plateaus, and valleys of a range of mountains. And mountain climbers always go through a series of ups and downs as they steadily move to higher and higher levels. The same is generally true for home prices.

Over time, home prices have always risen to higher levels, even though at any given time, price levels will depend on the peaks, valleys, and plateaus of supply and demand. So to reasonably forecast where home prices are going requires us to map out the future path of supply and demand—not simply to project the present into the future. What does this map show? Growing demand and constricted supply.

DEMAND FOR HOME OWNERSHIP IS UP

Population and incomes in the United States are increasing. More than one million immigrants a year are moving to the United States. Looking back over the past 20 years, interest rates are still relatively low. The use of many special financing programs, strategies, and techniques is being expanded to increase the number of first-time home buyers and try to turn around falling rates of home ownership.

In fact, the largest provider of mortgage funds in the country, the Federal National Mortgage Association (Fannie Mae), has just pledged one trillion dollars to finance homes for low-to-average-income individuals and families. In addition, President Clinton has pledged his administration's support for new and expanded initiatives to promote home ownership. The economy is firmly on a path of sustainable growth. All these supply and demand issues point to growing demand for homes.

On the other hand, home building has been depressed. The 1986 Tax Reform Act made the construction of new apartments far less profitable. As a result, during the early 1990s new apartment construction dropped to its lowest level since 1940–1944. Environmental rules and regulations that restrict subdivision development are becoming more severe. Lumber prices have shot up. Government taxes and permit fees on new homes are climbing higher. All of these factors point to higher costs and fewer new homes.

As much as ever, the facts today support home price increases in the future. During the past three years, I have visited or researched housing markets throughout most of the United States and some cities in Canada. Every market I have studied reveals major opportunities. Without question, home prices in parts of the country did experience a recessionary lull. Cutbacks in defense spending, the fall of oil and gas prices, corporate restructurings, and the bankruptcy of many financial institutions did depress home prices. But these downturns create opportunity, for recessionary lulls are followed by economic recovery.

You may recall that from the mid-1970s to the early 1980s, much of America's heartland was written off as the so-called "Rust Belt"—an area supposedly in perpetual decline. Yet today, cities like St. Louis, Chicago, Milwaukee, Indianapolis, Cleveland, and Columbus stand out for their healthy local economies and healthy housing markets. Since those earlier dark economic days, home prices have nearly doubled in most of these major cities.

Interestingly enough, Pittsburgh—once thought to be the premiere Rust Belt city—is now a thriving community that was ranked as one of the best cities to live in in North America by a recent edition of the *Places Rated Almanac*. The term "Rust Belt" has virtually disappeared from media consciousness. Likewise, during the past year or two, most so-called "Oil Belt" cities have shown strong gains in their local economies and housing markets. Similarly, New England, metro Washington, D.C., California, Florida, New Mexico, and Arizona are displaying many signs of emerging strength.

Beyond the general and specific economic expansions that can be expected during the coming three to seven years, nearly every U.S. and Canadian city offers good opportunities in selected neighborhoods that will experience above-average rates of appreciation. And as always, bargain properties, motivated owners, fixer-uppers, and other opportunities are available to savvy home buyers.

Whatever you eventually decide, you owe it to yourself not to passively accept the popular notions that renting costs less than owning, a home is no longer a good investment, or even worse, that standard excuse, "We'd like to own but we can't afford it." As a rule, *now is the time to buy* is more than a cliché. It stands as historical fact. During the past 50 years, *buying now* has almost always proven better than buying later. While over time renters have piled up rent receipts, owners have built wealth.

Of course, every rule has its exceptions. Major layoffs in your community, plant closings, or overbuilding can sometimes temporarily pull home prices down from earlier peaks. Sometimes high mortgage interest rates also can make buying more difficult. On the other hand, during times when interest rates are relatively low, when home prices are stable or slowly increasing, when inventories of unsold homes are higher than normal, and when the economy is on a path of growth, owning can present extraordinary opportunities.

In other words, even though *buy now* has proved itself a reliable (though not infallible) rule to follow, some times clearly seem better than others. The facts show we are going through one of those times. Not only is ownership more affordable, but the odds are nearly certain that your home will prove to be your wisest investment. Experience shows that no other investment can beat the emotional and financial returns of owning your own home.

As much as ever, economic forecasts strongly indicate that now really is the time for you to develop the attitude and education necessary to achieve home ownership. With a positive "can do" attitude, knowledge of your home buying possibilities, and a Realtor who's committed to helping you achieve this important goal, I'm confident you can own the home you want.

1 ATTITUDE + EDUCATION = HOMEOWNER

Two years ago Jim and Nancy Lopez became engaged. "At the time," says Jim, "we were like most other couples we know in their early 20s. We planned to begin married life just renting an apartment. We even talked about some complexes where it might be fun to live. We didn't even consider buying."

But fortunately for Jim and Nancy, that's not where their ideas stopped. One day, a month or so after their engagement, Nancy casually remarked, "Wouldn't it be great if we could own our own home instead of renting an apartment?"

"At first, we joked about it," admits Jim. "But then, almost at the same time, we both said, 'Why not?' From that day forward, we made up our minds. We geared nearly everything we did toward this goal."

"I picked up a second job waiting tables," Nancy chips in. "And even though Jim had a pretty good job, he made extra money cutting grass and trimming hedges. Once we decided to own, we were able to save $150 to $200 per week. We stopped eating out in restaurants and buying new clothes. We put off buying a new car. We had thought about moving in together before we got married, but we both decided to live with our parents. That decision alone really kicked up our ability to save. We also knew we would have to apply for some type of home financing. So Jim and I both paid close attention to our student loans and car loans. We made sure we paid all our bills before their due dates."

Instead of gifts and an expensive wedding, Jim and Nancy asked relatives and parents to contribute to their "home improvement" fund. "It's hard to believe," says Nancy, "but with savings and gifts, we accumulated more than $20,000 in less than two years. Along with this money and a special State of New York low-interest-rate mortgage, we were able to come back from our honeymoon this past June to our own $160,000, three-bedroom townhouse. I hate to say it, but several of our friends are green with envy."

"Everything—market slowdown, lower interest rates, special financing, and our parents' help—came together for us," says Jim. "We were really fortunate."

Without a doubt, Jim and Nancy were fortunate. Yet they're not taking credit where credit is due. Things didn't just "come together" for them. Luck and good fortune didn't get them a home. Instead, they made things happen. They started with the attitude, "We're going to own, not rent." Once they fixed that belief in their minds, they were able to find ways to move toward their goal of home ownership.

ATTITUDE MAKES THE DIFFERENCE

As the experience of Jim and Nancy Lopez shows, the first step to home ownership does not begin with money, a credit record, a job, or any of the other requirements typically associated with qualifying to buy. The first step begins with *attitude*. Once you develop the necessary "can do—will do" attitude, all other home buying requirements tend to fall in line.

You might find it surprising that a book on home buying should focus on the importance of attitude. But what you think you can achieve will determine what you actually can achieve. Mary Kay Ash, founder of Mary Kay Cosmetics, says, "By changing your attitude you can change your life."

Mary Kay knows what she is talking about. Not only has she built one of the most successful business organizations in the world, she has inspired thousands of women to reach beyond the self-limiting beliefs that blocked their lives. In fact, among women earning in excess of $100,000 per year, more work with Mary Kay Cosmetics than with any other company.

Dr. Robert Schuller, the well-known minister, inspirationalist and best-selling author, reminds us, "People don't fail to achieve their goals because they lack intelligence, ability, opportunity, or talent. More importantly, they don't get what they want because they don't give their problems all they've got." Dr.

Schuller goes on to point out, "Nobody has a money problem. First of all, it is always an idea problem."

In contrast to Jim and Nancy Lopez, many renters who could own their own home never develop a "can do—will do" attitude. Without this attitude, they fail to generate a plan to get the home they want. Remember Anne from the introductory chapter. She wanted to live in the Berkeley hills. To her own grief, however, Anne focused her thoughts almost exclusively on her home buying problem. In contrast, Jim and Nancy Lopez focused their thoughts on *solving* their home buying problem.

Over the years, I have taught thousands of students in college classes, real estate seminars, and professional education courses. I have found that only one primary difference sets apart those who best manage to reach their goals from those who never quite seem to get what they want. That difference is attitude.

DEFEATIST ATTITUDES BLOCK
POSSIBILITY THINKING

In my real estate classes and *Stop Renting Now!*™ seminars, I frequently meet renters who say they want to own a home. But they fail to change their spending habits, they fail to save, they fail to plan. Why? Because they are intentionally shortsighted? No! It's because they don't believe they will ever be able to afford the home they want. So why not drive a nice car and live in a comfortable or conveniently located rental? I have witnessed this frustrated attitude among people earning $17,000 a year—and even among some making $70,000 a year. In far too many instances, these renters could become owners if they realized how their attitudes actually blocked them from the financial planning and education that would help them achieve home ownership.

DEFEATIST ATTITUDES: THREE EXAMPLES

First comes Sarah, a forty-something divorced mother with a nine-year-old daughter. Sarah writes as a journalist for one of the largest newspapers in the country. She exudes wistful nostalgia and loss of future. To Sarah, owning the home she wants ranks right up there with other "impossible dreams." Next we will listen to Thomas, who tells us that because he is a $46,000-a-year family man, home ownership lies beyond his means. Third, we hear the complaints of Lee and Mary, a $70,000-a-year two-income couple. This northeastern couple believes that home prices and down payment requirements have shut down their chance to own the home they want.

Sarah's Lament

Now listen to Sarah as she contrasts her unforgiving past to what she sees as her unpromising future.

> For many of us, coming of age in the '60s was not personally tumultuous. The '60s were fun. It was the '80s that became tumultuous: childbirth, divorce, adventures in dating. Spending too much money on silk things, health clubs, and therapists whose personal problems dwarfed my own. To tell the truth—and at this point, why not?—I've just been too busy to notice that my life was half over until it occurred to me that I will probably die without achieving two important things I always took for granted: one, an enduring relationship with a great guy, and two, a house with more than 1,000 square feet. . . .
>
> Those who postponed buying a home and missed out didn't realize the window would close. . . . Consequently, there are two types of baby boomers—haves and have-nots—who will probably remain haves or have-nots for the rest of their lives.

My guess is that nearly all of us from time to time share Sarah's beliefs that we've missed the boat. We didn't act when we should have acted, and now it's too late. Sarah is certainly not alone in her feelings. But when feelings like these overwhelm all others, shake them off. Bring into your mind Dr. Robert Schuller's advice, "When you've exhausted all possibilities, remember this: You haven't."

Sarah forgets to ask herself how she might change her attitudes and her life. She forgets to explore the possibilities that are available because she has foreclosed their existence. As motivator Lester Brown says, "If you keep doing what you're doing, you're going to keep getting what you're getting."

Sarah needs to change her attitudes and beliefs. For as long as she believes the housing "window" is closed, she will never open her mind to how she might change her life to get the home (and great guy) she wants. With Sarah's excellent talent for writing, maybe she could earn extra money writing a book. Maybe she should pursue co-ownership as a single mother, Sarah is part of a growing number of women in similar circumstances. As you will see in later chapters, Sarah clearly has options. Yet first she must look for them. Then she will learn that the window of opportunity for home ownership has been reopened.

Thomas's Critique

A widely published newspaper columnist recently wrote a piece urging readers to "take advantage of today's home market and the lowest interest rates in 18 years." In a letter to the newspaper, Thomas criticized the columnist for presenting such a "rosy picture." Here are Thomas's critical remarks:

> I would like to point out a flaw in the rosy picture painted by the article "Picture Improves for House Market." . . . [The columnist] fails to tell how an average family earning $46,000 per year is supposed to come up with a 20 percent down payment on a $175,000 house. Counting closing costs and reserves, a prospective homeowner needs to save $46,500.
>
> Families who are average save less than 5 percent of their income. This would require at least 20 years to come up with the necessary cash. Even if they saved 10 percent of their annual income, it would still take 10 years. [The columnist] finished [his article] by saying "the housing market hasn't been this friendly in a long time." To borrow the old saying: With a friend like this, who needs an enemy?

When a student of mine showed me Thomas's critique of the columnist, I simply shook my head. I asked myself, "How could someone who reads the real estate section of the newspaper (the section where the columnist's original article had been published) still believe that home buying requires a down payment of 20 percent?" Of course, after briefly reflecting on the question, I knew the answer. When Thomas read the paper, he had been preprogrammed to see only the past negative news of "unaffordability." His defeatist attitude blocked other, more positive facts from entering his consciousness. Another way to describe this tendency is *conceptual blindness.* Once we adopt a specific world view, we ignore or reject any new ideas or facts that don't fit within it.

All of us prefer internal consistency. Those who lock in the idea "I can't afford to own" simultaneously lock out the possibility of owning. Here are some ideas and topics that Thomas could have discovered had he regularly read the real estate section with a positive attitude:

- The paper carries national columnist and real estate attorney Kenneth Harney. Mr. Harney is always bringing to light new and improved alternative home finance plans. Harney also frequently shows first-time home buyers how to overcome affordability obstacles by looking for fixer-uppers.

- The paper also carries highly respected national columnist Robert Bruss. Mr. Bruss is the country's leading proponent of seller financing and lease options. His columns frequently discuss these low-cash-down possibilities.

- The paper carries many builder advertisements that feature all kinds of low-down-payment (even no-down-payment) incentive plans.

- Union Bank, in conjunction with a local community home buyers program, was at the time offering a 3-percent-down-payment program for first-time buyers who earned less than $69,000 per year. This same program also offered a long-term subsidized after-tax fixed interest rate of 5.5 percent. The bank was promoting seminars to educate the public about this program. (I attended one of these seminars. It was excellent. The loan officers, Realtors, and other professionals present really tried to help the people who attended. I might add that, as in my own *Stop Renting Now!*™ seminars, the ages of attendees ranged from the mid-20s to perhaps the late 50s.)

- In addition to lender seminars, various Realtors in Thomas's market area were advertising and sponsoring home buyer educational seminars. These seminars could have helped Thomas learn how to become a homeowner and stay within his budget.

- The newspaper had recently reported that, according to research by the California Association of Realtors, one-half of the first-time buyers in California (where Thomas lived) paid less than $170,000 for their homes and placed down $20,000 or less. The *median* down payment was about 10 percent of the purchase price.

I might further point out that Realtor surveys typically overstate median prices and down payments. This overstatement occurs because Realtor data often omit many types of transactions (discussed in later chapters) such as lease options, employer assistance, contracts-for-deed, foreclosures, auctions, seller mortgages, private sales, nonprofit organization activities (e.g., Habitat for Humanity), and VA/FHA nonqualifying assumptions. Moreover, the cash down does not necessarily come from the cash savings of the buyers. As many as 50 percent of first-time buyers rely on gifts or loans from parents, relatives, or friends. "Sweat equity" is another good way to get around an out-of-pocket cash down payment. Investor contributions through shared equity programs also can reduce the actual cash required of home buyers.

My purpose here is not to criticize Thomas for his mistaken belief. I just want to emphasize how attitude can block education. With a changed attitude and a sense of possibilities, Thomas and his family could get on the right track toward home ownership. More than money, Thomas needs ideas.

Lee and Mary's Complaints

As a last example to illustrate the hurdle raised by defeatist thinking, let's go over the (perceived) down payment difficulties of Lee, age 34, and his wife Mary, age 27. Lee thinks that he and Mary must come up with $25,000 in cash to buy a home in the $140,000 to $180,000 price range. Lee and Mary earn $70,000 per year. Here's what Lee says:

> A house on a small lot in the area we want costs from $140,000 to $180,000. That means we need a down payment of at least $15,000. And then closing costs and points will add another $7,000 or so. I don't know any of my friends who has $25,000 in the bank.

Notice how negative thinkers frequently exaggerate their difficulties. Here Lee stretches $22,000 ($7,000 + $15,000) up to $25,000. Recall that in the last example Thomas complained that savings at the average rate would require at least 20 years to come up with the necessary cash. (Thomas ignored the fact that people who save for a house typically save at rates far in excess of the average rate. He also left out of his calculations the interest,

dividends, and capital gains that savings and investments produce.)

But clearly, Lee and Mary, with an income of $70,000 per year
and no children, are in far better objective shape than Thomas.
With careful financial planning, they should be able to save
$22,000 within 12 to 24 months. (Remember Jim and Nancy
Lopez?) But what does Lee say? He justifies the couple's lack of
savings by referring to friends who also have failed to save.

Life always gives us models with which we can identify.
Defeatist thinkers prefer to identify with negative models. Positive thinkers look for positive models. Most families in the United
States earn far less than $70,000 a year. In fact, most first-time
home buyers earn between $25,000 and $40,000 per year. Many
earn no more than $15,000 or $20,000 per year. Lee should look
to those first-time home buyers who have successfully bought
homes, especially buyers (like Nancy and Jim Lopez) who earn
substantially less than Lee and Mary. Renters who want to own
should ask: How did others save? How much did they save? What
price did they pay? What financing techniques did they use?
Where did they buy?

Moreover, if Lee and Mary would look to the experience of
those who have bought, they would find their own beliefs
mistaken. They do not need $25,000 or even $22,000 to buy a
home at the low- to mid-point of their price range. They require
no more than $15,000 in savings. And with a loan from friends
or family, an assumption of a VA mortgage, private mortgage
insurance, a new FHA loan, a community home buyer program,
a builder incentive program, a lease option, shared equity, or
sweat equity, they could easily buy with less than $10,000 in
savings.

Even more than Sarah or Thomas, Lee and Mary could
overcome their obstacles to owning through a change of attitude
and enhanced knowledge of home buying possibilities. Lee and
Mary should recall the saying attributed to Henry Ford: "Whether
you believe you can or you can't, you're nearly always right."

SELF-TALK AND NEGATIVE ATTITUDES

In his excellent book *What to Say When You Talk to Yourself,*
Dr. Shad Helmstetter writes, "You will become what you think

about most. Your success or failure in anything, large or small, will depend on your programming—what you accept from others, and what you say when you talk to yourself." In years of study, research, and counseling clients, Dr. Helmstetter has found that as a matter of habit, most of us swamp ourselves with negative self-talk. Yet we seldom realize how negative self-talk programs our subconsciousness. Through "can't do" self-talk, we actually set ourselves up to fail. Here are just a few familiar examples:

- I can't remember names.
- It's just no use.
- I'm too clumsy.
- I'm no good at math.
- I never have enough time.
- I'm too shy.
- I never know what to say.
- I'm just too disorganized.
- I'm always running late.

Is it likely that someone who programs himself or herself with these messages will change for the better? Dr. Helmstetter doesn't think so. He says, "The more you think about anything in a certain way, the more you will believe that's the way it really is." And naturally, "the more you believe that's the way it really is," the less likely it is that you will alert your mind to look for improvement.

Home buying naturally falls under the same general principles. As we saw with Sarah, Thomas, and Lee and Mary, negative self-talk discouraged them from looking for opportunities that would help them progress toward owning the homes they wanted.

Now give yourself a self-talk quiz. Do you find any of these ideas running on a treadmill in your mind?

- Prices are too high; I can't afford to buy.
- I'll never be able to afford a home.
- I hate budgets. I can never stick to them.

- We should have bought earlier; interest rates are heading back up.
- I'll never be able to come up with the cash necessary to buy.
- There's no way we can cut our spending. We're going without now.
- Homes are no longer a good investment.
- The world is full of haves and have-nots. I'm a have-not.
- Renting is cheaper than owning.
- There's not anything out there we like that we can afford.
- I don't have good credit.
- I've got too many bills.
- Our generation has it tougher than those who came before us.
- None of my friends can buy.
- It's too late. People who bought earlier were lucky.
- I've never considered buying. I hardly know the first thing about it.
- I don't know any Realtors who work with first-time buyers.
- Sure, I would like to buy *someday*.
- I don't have a college degree. I'll never be able to make the money I need to own.

The list could continue. You can probably add a few excuses of your own. It's all too easy to get caught in this self-defeating cycle. To a certain extent, negative reporting by much of the media programs us to hold negative beliefs. Then negative beliefs begin to screen out positive facts or information. Only the negative comes through. Seeing only the negative, we begin to hold our negative beliefs ever more tightly. They comfort us. Eventually, we see only what we have come to believe.

People who get caught up in this self-defeating cycle cannot see their possibilities because they screen out all facts that don't agree with their beliefs. Even worse, they close their minds to potential. To break this cycle, you must force yourself to consciously take note of each negative thought or belief that acts to cut you off from the future you want. Hook up an imaginary electrode to your mind. Give yourself a jolt every time you let negative thoughts short-circuit your problem-solving abilities. Whenever such thoughts occur, grab your mental channel selector. Switch to a different program. Every statement in the list of negative examples may contain an element of fact, a bit of truth. None of them reflects all of the facts, nor the whole truth.

When you switch to other channels, you bring in a new picture, a picture that brings other facts and knowledge to your attention. More important, when you learn to switch channels and search for more positive pictures, you remind yourself that you control your own destiny. You may not be able to control the events and conditions of the world, but you can control how you respond to them.

REPROGRAM YOUR SELF-TALK TAPES

How do you gain control and respond effectively? By reprogramming. First, erase all negative self-talk tapes that you keep replaying. Then record over them with positive self-talk. When you erase your self-constructed limits, you replace them with possibilities. To illustrate: closely read the following questions. What are your possibilities? Don't worry if you can't answer all of these questions now. You will be able to by the end of this book. But I do want you to get started thinking.

- What are six ways I can save more?
- What are six ways I can cut my spending?
- What are six ways we can increase our income?
- What kinds of home finance plans allow us to buy with little or nothing down?
- What are four ways we can overcome our credit problems?
- Who can serve as role models for us?
- Who do I know who can recommend a Realtor who works with first-time buyers?
- What leading economic indicators are positive?
- What types of home finance plans permit lower monthly payments?
- Where are the lower-priced up-and-coming neighborhoods?

- Where and how might we find bargains?
- What kinds of home finance plans would suit someone with my earnings and credit history?
- What techniques are available to make home buying easier?
- Where can I find a no-qualifier or easy-qualifier home finance plan?
- How can we persuade the sellers to offer financing?
- Where can we find below-market interest rates?
- What state, local, or federal special-assistance home buying programs are available?
- Who could I get to help us buy: parents, family, friends, investor, employer, co-owner?
- Which mortgage lenders are offering 3 percent-down first-time-buyer loans?
- What new home builders have low- or no-down-payment home finance plans?

You see, all problem solving begins with questions. Yet it's only when you accept the idea of possibilities that you can come up with the questions to ask. Others who merely settle on preprogrammed conclusions not only won't ask questions, they will unwittingly overlook the choices they do have. That's why becoming a homeowner requires jolting yourself out of false, limiting beliefs. Once you erase these beliefs, your more positive attitude alerts the mind to hunt down and lasso facts, knowledge, and experiences that lead to opportunity. Josh Billings, the celebrated 19th-century American humorist, used to joke, "I fear not the things I don't know, but rather the things I think I know that just ain't so."

Many tenants stuck in rentals believe they are blocked from home ownership. They believe they can't save, they don't have adequate cash for a down payment, they can't qualify for a mortgage, or housing prices or monthly payments have climbed beyond their reach. They believe nearly all their problems in some way can be spelled **M-O-N-E-Y**. These would-be homeowners underestimate their own potential.

As you read the following chapters, don't sell yourself short. Ask questions. Engage your mind. Make notes. Highlight ideas that can work for you. Reflect on your possibilities. Review available choices. Create alternatives. If you want to own your own home, my years of real estate experience tell me you can own your own home. It all begins by letting go of negative, self-limiting beliefs. Through education, you can reprogram your attitude with a "can do—will do" list of possibilities.

2 MASTER THE BASICS OF HOME AFFORDABILITY

Like many young first-time home buyers, Rick and Joyce Lawson recently discovered the great variety of ways to finance a home. Joyce says:

I couldn't believe all the different loans the lenders were offering. It reminded me of a mortgage cafeteria with every lender coming up with its own menu. At first it was mind boggling. In the end, though, we really did okay.

Rick and I were short of cash. To make matters more difficult, we graduated from college just two years ago. We didn't make a lot of money. But we do expect our incomes to grow. Our Realtor helped us find a lender who offered just what we needed.

Our closing costs were low. The lender let our parents pay some of the down payment. And with an adjustable-rate mortgage, our monthly payments are a lot lower than they would have been with a fixed-rate. As it turned out, we were able to afford our first-choice house in our second-choice neighborhood.

In shopping for their home, Rick and Joyce Lawson learned that today's world of home finance can confuse even the most experienced home buyer. On the other hand, they also learned that thousands of lenders and a multitude of mortgage loan products mean more opportunity. Quite likely, 10 to 15 years ago, many younger renters could not have qualified to buy the home they wanted. But as the Lawsons learned, thanks to lower interest rates and the revolution in home finance, now they are able to own their own home. And so can you.

THE BASICS OF AFFORDABILITY

To stop renting and become a homeowner, you'll need to answer two basic questions: (1) How much *cash-to-close* (down payment, closing costs, incidental expenses) can we raise? And (2) How much mortgage money can we borrow? To illustrate this basic approach to affordability, we will use a conventional fixed-rate mortgage. To start, here are the primary features of this type of home finance plan:

- You pay the loan back in equal monthly payments over 30 years. The period of repayment is called the loan term.
- Most lenders require a 20 percent down payment. With the standard fixed-rate mortgage you can typically borrow just 80 percent of your home's purchase price. Sometimes, a 20 percent down payment is referred to as an 80 percent *loan-to-value ratio*. (A 10 percent down payment would produce a 90 percent loan-to-value ratio.)
- Throughout the 30-year term, the loan interest rate and monthly payments remain *fixed*. If your monthly mortgage payment, with principal and interest, equals $800 on the day you take out your loan, it will remain at $800 until the day you make your last payment.
- When you take out a standard 30-year fixed-rate mortgage, *closing costs* amounting to 2 to 8 percent of the amount you borrow typically must be paid. These costs go for expenses like loan application fees, mortgage origination fees, property appraisal, title insurance, transfer taxes, and a property survey. (Normally buyers and sellers split these charges. Exactly who pays how much of these closing costs should be decided when you negotiate your purchase agreement with the sellers. Also, some mortgage lenders are now offering "no cost" home loans.)

Due to its relatively high down payment and monthly payments, most first-time home buyers do not use the standard 30-year fixed-rate mortgage. However, we begin with this basic type of home finance plan because it provides a benchmark of affordability. You can use it to compare with other home finance techniques.

Calculating Affordability

To calculate how much mortgage money a lender will let you borrow, the lender first looks at your gross monthly income. Then it takes a percentage of your income and qualifies you for your monthly mortgage payment based upon this housing cost ratio. The affordability calculations in this example have been simplified to illustrate basic relationships. Chapter 9 tells you in much greater detail how you can best qualify for the home financing you need.

To begin, let's say your household's gross income totals $3,800 per month. If your lender uses a qualifying (housing cost) ratio (percentage) of .25 (25 percent), this lender would permit you to spend up to $950 (.25 × $3,800) a month for your mortgage payment (principal and interest). Next, to figure out how much money this amount of payment permits you to borrow, refer to Table 2.1.

This table shows how much money you have to pay back each month for every $1,000 you might borrow at a variety of corresponding interest rates. If the market interest rate for a 30-year fixed-rate mortgage is 9.5 percent, you would have to pay $8.41 per month for each $1,000 of your original mortgage amount. If interest rates are at 8 percent, your payment per $1,000

TABLE 2.1
Monthly Payment Required per $1,000 of Original Mortgage Balance*

Interest (%)	Monthly Payment	Interest (%)	Monthly Payment
2.5	$3.95	7.5	$ 6.99
3.0	4.21	**8.0**	**7.34**
3.5	4.49	8.5	7.69
4.0	4.77	9.0	8.05
4.5	5.07	**9.5**	**8.41**
5.0	5.37	10.0	8.77
5.5	5.67	10.5	9.15
6.0	5.99	11.0	9.52
6.5	**6.32**	11.5	9.90
7.0	6.65	12.0	10.29

*Term = 30 years.

of borrowings would run $7.34 per month. If rates are at 6.5 percent, you would need to pay back $6.32 per $1,000 per month.

Considering that we're assuming you can qualify for a mortgage payment of around $950 per month, at an interest rate of 9.5, 8.0, or 6.5 percent, you could borrow $112,960, $129,428, or $150,316, respectively.

9.5%

$$\frac{\$950}{\$8.41} = \$112.960 \, (\times 1{,}000)$$

8.0%

$$\frac{\$950}{\$7.34} = \$129.428 \, (\times 1{,}000)$$

6.5%

$$\frac{\$950}{\$6.32} = \$150.316 \, (\times 1{,}000)$$

Or, if we look at it through a reciprocal perspective, we can say a 30-year mortgage of:

- $112,960 at 9.5% requires a payment for principal and interest of $950 per month;
- $129,428 at 8.0% requires a payment for principal and interest of $950 per month;
- $150,316 at 6.5% requires a payment for principal and interest of $950 per month.

These figures show clearly how lower interest rates can dramatically boost your borrowing power and housing affordability (see also Table 2.2).

Next, to figure the approximate price of the home you could buy if you had 20 percent for a down payment and, say, 4 percent of the amount borrowed to pay closing costs, divide the permissible mortgage amount by .80 (the loan-to-value ratio). Using an 8 percent interest rate, the monthly payment of $950, and the corresponding mortgage amount of $129,428, you could buy a home worth $161,785 ($129,428 divided by .80)—providing you had a total cash-to-close of $37,534 (and, of course, an acceptable credit record):

	Purchase price	= $161,785
less	Down payment @.20	= 32,357
equals	Amount borrowed	= $129,428
	Closing costs @.04	= $ 5,177
	Down payment	= $ 32,357
	+ Closing costs	= $ 5,177
equals	Total cash-to-close	= **$ 37,534**

Now, working through this same affordability methodology, you can figure out how much you would actually have to have in income and cash to buy a home in any price range using the standard 30-year fixed-rate mortgage. To illustrate: Let's say interest rates are at 8.5 percent. To buy a home at a price of $75,000 would require a monthly income of $1,846 and a total cash-to-close of $17,400.

	Purchase price	= $ 75,000
less	Down payment @.20	= 15,000
equals	Amount borrowed	= $ 60,000
	Closing costs @.04	= $ 2,400
	Monthly payment on $60,000 @ 8.5%	= $7.69 per $1,000
	Total mortgage payment (P&I)	= 60 × $7.69
		= **$461.40**

TABLE 2.2
How Much Can You Borrow At Various Interest Rates and Monthly Payment Amounts? (in thousands)*

Monthly Payment (P&I)	4%	6%	8%	10%	12%
$ 400	$ 83.8	$ 66.8	$ 54.5	$ 45.6	$ 38.9
600	125.8	100.2	81.7	68.4	58.3
750	157.2	125.2	102.2	85.5	72.9
900	188.7	150.3	122.6	102.6	87.5
1,000	209.6	166.9	136.2	114.0	97.2
1,250	262.1	208.6	170.3	142.5	121.5
1,500	319.1	250.4	204.4	171.0	148.8

*To calculate similar amounts for any other monthly payment and interest rate, simply divide the monthly payment by the applicable payment-per-$1,000 figure as shown in Table 2.1.

Using a qualifying housing cost ratio of .25, we can compute your required monthly income:

Required monthly income × .25	= $461.40 (mortgage payment)
Required monthly income	= $1,846

Down payment + closing costs	= Total cash-to-close
$15,000 + $2,400	= **$17,400**

To buy a $200,000 house (at 8.5 percent and a .25 qualifying ratio), the numbers look like this:

	Purchase price	= $200,000
less	Down payment @.20	= 40,000
equals	Amount borrowed	= $160,000
	Closing costs @.04	= $ 6,400
	Monthly payment on $160,000	
	@ 8.5%	= $7.69 per $1,000
	Total mortgage payment (P&I)	= 160 × $7.69
		= **$1,230.40**

Using a qualifying ratio of .25, we can compute your required monthly income:

Required monthly income × .25	= $1,230.40 (mortgage payment)
Required monthly income	= $4,922

Down payment + closing costs	= Total cash-to-close
$40,000 + $6,400	= **$46,400**

So, if interest rates are at 8.5 percent, to purchase a $200,000 home using a standard 30-year fixed-rate mortgage with a 20 percent down payment and 4.0 percent in closing costs, you would need a monthly income of just under $5,000, and up-front cash-to-close of $46,400.

How Much House Can You Afford?

By applying the affordability methodology we've just gone through, you can get a pretty good idea of how much house you can afford. Just plug in the relevant numbers (interest rate, income, housing price, cash-to-close) that fit your personal situation. Now, does it look like you can afford the home you want?

If your answer is yes, great!

On the other hand, if you're like the vast majority of renters, your answer is probably no—or at best, maybe. For most first-time home buyers, the conventional 30-year fixed-rate mortgage with the so-called standard down payment of 20 percent just won't work. But that doesn't mean you can't afford to become a homeowner. It just means you've got one or more affordability problems to solve. And that's what the remainder of this book is all about—solutions!

There's a Solution for Every Problem!

Do you need a lower down payment (perhaps even no down payment), lower monthly payments, reduced closing costs, or higher qualifying ratios? Does your credit record need to be improved? Would you like to own a more expensive home than your current finances seem to permit? Do you want to simply stop flushing rent money down the toilet and start building wealth?

Regardless of your specific affordability problem, I'm confident that you can overcome it. You may have to make some trade-offs and compromises along the way. But experience with thousands of students who have enrolled in my real estate classes and seminars tells me that when you plan to become a homeowner, you will become a homeowner. (Remember: Attitude + Education = Homeowner.) And the best time to start toward that goal is now. Let's begin your education with some of the basic ways you can buy with little (or no) down payment.

MORTGAGE INSURANCE AND GUARANTEES

Mortgage insurance works something like *mortgage life* insurance. When you buy mortgage life insurance, should you die, the life insurance company pays off the outstanding balance of your mortgage loan. When you purchase mortgage (default) insurance, the insurer protects the lender against loss if you stop making your mortgage payments and your lender *forecloses*.

Because a mortgage insurer agrees to cover a lender's foreclosure losses, you can buy mortgage insurance (or guarantees) to help you finance a low- or no-down-payment mortgage for nearly any type of home (single-family house; townhouse; condominium; co-op; mobile home; or duplex, triplex, or fourplex). There are three primary sources of mortgage insurance (guarantees): (1) private mortgage insurance companies, (2) the Federal Housing Administration (FHA), and (3) the Department of Veterans Affairs (VA).

Private Mortgage Insurance (PMI)

With private mortgage insurance (offered through most banks, thrifts, credit unions, and other mortgage lenders in association with companies such as General Electric Credit and Mortgage Guarantee Insurance Corporation), you can buy a home with as little as 3 to 5 percent down. In other words, the lender will grant you a loan with a 95 to 97 percent loan-to-value ratio. Usually part of the premium you pay for this insurance is spread out over a number of years and added to your monthly mortgage payments. Part (or all) of the mortgage insurance premiums also may be charged at your mortgage closing. The amount of premium you pay varies according to type of home, location, amount of your initial cash investment, and the specific insurer your lender (not you) selects.

As a first-year premium, for example, one large mortgage insurer often charges 0.4 percent of the amount borrowed. So, if you're borrowing $100,000, you would pay a first-year premium of $400. For each following year, this insurer cuts the premium to 0.25 percent of the loan's outstanding balance. When you shop mortgage lenders, find out the actual mortgage insurance premiums you will be charged. Don't just compare lenders on the basis of their interest rates. You want to compare total costs (closing expenses, loan fees, interest rates, and mortgage insurance premiums).

Also, when you're comparing lenders, ask whether you can drop your mortgage insurance at a later date. Some lenders let you cancel this insurance because over time, your mortgage balance goes down and your home's value goes up. When your outstanding loan balance falls to less than 80 percent of your home's appreciated market value, your lender should let you stop paying mortgage insurance premiums—as long as you haven't had any late mortgage payments during the most recent 24 months.

Check a lender's practices on this issue *before* you formally apply for your mortgage. Then get it in writing. Through savvy buying or value-creating home improvements, you might be able to build your home *equity* and stop paying mortgage insurance premiums within just two or three years after you have bought your home.

Federal Housing Administration (FHA)

The FHA was created in 1934. Since that time, it has been one of the best ways to buy a home with a low down payment. The FHA 203(b) program alone has more than 15 million home mortgages insured. As long as you are a legal resident of the United States, you are eligible for an FHA-insured mortgage. Contrary to what many renters believe, FHA doesn't restrict its most popular loan insurance programs to people with low to moderate incomes. No matter how large your wealth or your income, you can use FHA to help you buy when you are short of cash. As another advantage, FHA generally applies liberal qualifying criteria. For low-priced homes, FHA permits down payments as low as 3 percent of the home's purchase price. In higher-priced areas, though, you will need a down payment of around 5 percent.

Another benefit of FHA 203(b) is often overlooked. If you get behind on your mortgage payments due to job loss, poor health, or an accident, you can apply to the U.S. Department of Housing and Urban Development (HUD) as a *hardship case*. If HUD finds that you deserve hardship status, it will lower your monthly payments until you get back on your feet. HUD/FHA also funds credit counseling for home buyers. Counselors (usually from not-for-profit housing groups) can help you plan your finances to get them in shape for loan approval.

Although FHA loans provide a good way to finance a home, they sometimes fall short in several ways. If you live in a high-cost city, an FHA loan may not work well for you. At present, FHA sets its maximum for loans in the high-priced cities of the continental United States at $151,725. In lower-priced cities, FHA loan limits are at or near the median home price for the area. In Honolulu, however, the FHA maximum does reach almost $200,000. But with median single-family home prices in Honolulu of over $300,000, even first-time buyers will face substantial difficulty finding a house suitable (or affordable) for FHA financing. On a positive note, many members of Congress favor another increase in FHA limits, so ask a Realtor or mortgage lender in your area to keep you informed should Congress raise FHA's loan limits again.

As another affordability strategy, you might consider investing in a duplex, triplex, or fourplex. Both FHA and private mortgage insurers set higher loan limits for these multiple-family buildings. Also, the rental income from these units can count toward the qualifying income you need to get your loan approved. A townhouse, condominium, or manufactured home is another option. Even in (or near) high-priced cities, many of these types of homes are listed for sale below the FHA maximums. And in lower-priced areas, these homes can be purchased for as little as $30,000 to $50,000—often with down payments of less than $2,000.

Perhaps the biggest disadvantage of the FHA 203(b) program is cost. FHA mortgage insurance premiums now generally cost more than private mortgage insurance premiums. During the mid- to late 1980s, the FHA insurance fund went belly-up. FHA's easy-qualifying and liberal mortgage assumption practices attracted too many deadbeats and con artists. Fraud ran rampant. On top of this, hard economic times in the oil patch states dramatically increased foreclosures among average working people.

Congress and HUD/FHA policymakers have been working to solve this cost problem. They realize that FHA is not currently assisting as many home buyers as it could. Since both Congress and HUD/FHA want to encourage home ownership, and since FHA programs enjoy a great deal of political and public support, we could easily see some positive changes in both FHA's loan limits and its costs. A strong housing market means jobs and economic growth. As a result, we are almost certain to get new or improved home ownership programs from Congress. Again, ask a Realtor to keep you informed.

One last remark about FHA: Like all government bureaucracies, the FHA drowns its loan applicants in paperwork. If you decide to use a low-down-payment FHA loan, prepare for an endless stream of forms, documents, rules, and regulations. (But nowadays, even nongovernment loans require documents piled higher and deeper. If you're dealing with a bank or savings institution, you can't escape it.) Nevertheless, here's what Dixie Lee Butler, an experienced FHA mortgage lender, says in praise of the FHA:

> The FHA programs and guidelines are misunderstood because of their complicated procedures and forms. Even so, I like this program best. . . . It fits well for most first-time home buyers. These loans offer the most flexibility. Unfortunately, they cause the most headaches for borrowers because of the time involved and the paperwork needed. [But] don't let this deter you from selecting this loan—any lender worth its salt should know how to process this type of loan promptly!

To help simply the FHA borrowing process, FHA has encouraged lenders to obtain Direct Endorsement (D.E.) status. D.E. lenders can process your loan internally without sending paperwork to FHA for its approval. Generally, if you plan to use (or need information about) the FHA, locate a lender who has met the FHA Direct Endorsement qualifications. With computerized application processing, many D.E. lenders can close an FHA loan in three to four weeks.

Other FHA Programs. Up to this point, we've been focusing on the FHA 203(b) mortgage insurance program. This is FHA's most popular program for helping Americans buy homes with little cash investment. But 203(b) is actually just one of dozens of programs available from FHA. Here are several other lesser-known programs that can help home buyers and homeowners:

- *Rehabilitation Loans (Section 312).* Especially designed to help low-to-moderate-income households rehabilitate single-family and multiple-family homes in designated neighborhoods.
- *Urban Homesteading.* Intended to help revitalize neighborhoods. Federally owned homes are given to local governments or nonprofit housing organizations. These homes are then sold for a token sum to someone who agrees to rehabilitate and live in the home.
- *Homeownership Assistance (Section 221(d)(2)).* Helps any individual or family buy, construct, or rehabilitate low-cost one-to-four-family housing. This program has approximately one million homes in it.

- *Housing in Turnaround Neighborhoods (Section 223(e))*. Another program to buy or rehabilitate homes in areas that will not qualify for other mortgage insurance.

- *Special Credit Risks (Section 237)*. Helps low- and moderate-income individuals and families who have had credit problems obtain mortgage insurance. As in many FHA programs, the limits in this program are quite low. Check local lenders to learn the requirements in your area.

- *Manufactured (Mobile) Homes (Title 1)*. Program to help finance manufactured homes with or without lots. Since mobile home lots can appreciate significantly, this can be a good program for entry into home ownership at a modest cost.

- *Property Improvement Loan Insurance (Title 1)*. Of all the FHA loan insurance programs, this one is the most popular. FHA has insured approximately 35 million Title 1 property improvement loans. You can use this loan to improve either single-family homes or apartment buildings. This program offers one of the most liberal sources of home improvement financing available.

- *Rehabilitation Mortgage Insurance (Section 203(k))*. In contrast to Title 1 home improvement loans, the 203(k) program can help you purchase and rehabilitate a home all in one loan. To date, this program has been little used, even though Congress first authorized it in 1978. During the past year, though, I have seen efforts to better publicize it and gain wider lender participation. Also, FHA has streamlined the application and loan process to make this program much more attractive. If you buy a "fixer," look into a 203(k) loan. These can work very well to give you a no-down-payment mortgage. Secretary Henry Cisneros of HUD has instructed all FHA offices throughout the United States to do all they can to increase the number of FHA 203(k) mortgages.

- *Sweat Equity*. Under this FHA insurance program, FHA and selected new-home builders agree to let home buyers contribute their labor (sweat equity) in lieu of part or all of their down payment. Unfortunately, like many other good ideas, sweat equity is not used as much as it could be. Still, if it appeals to you, phone FHA and see if any builders in your area plan to participate in this program.

- *Alternative Mortgage Instruments (AMIs).* In addition to the standard fixed-rate insured mortgage, FHA also insures a variety of *graduated-payment mortgages* and *adjustable-rate mortgages.* These kinds of mortgages are designed to lower your monthly payments. AMIs are discussed later in this chapter.

- *Demonstration Projects.* As part of its continuing efforts to improve home ownership opportunities and mortgage affordability, HUD/FHA frequently initiates trial runs of new programs. These are called demonstration projects. When checking with HUD/FHA, ask if any demonstration projects are active or planned for your area. In a recent demonstration project (400 developments nationwide), HUD/FHA joined with builders and local governments to slash costly and bureaucratic building and land-use regulations. By cutting red tape, builders were able to reduce new-home prices by 10 to 25 percent.

- *Homes for Members of the Military.* Members of the military on active duty may be able to use an FHA program without paying the loan insurance premium. The Department of Defense may pay it for you.

Overall, HUD/FHA is trying to help middle- and lower-income Americans into affordable home ownership and property revitalization. So learn all you can about HUD/FHA. To better educate yourself about the wide variety of loan programs HUD/FHA offers, write or call your nearest HUD office. Request a copy of the 119-page booklet, *Programs of HUD*: HUD-214-PA(17). If you are like millions of other Americans who are short of cash, HUD/FHA may very well offer you an immediate opportunity to stop renting now.

Department of Veterans Affairs

Perhaps the best low-cash home finance plan available is the VA mortgage. If you are an eligible veteran, the VA will help you finance up to $203,000 with no down payment. In the past, veterans were not even asked to pay an insurance premium. But, alas, good things always seem to end. As in the FHA, losses in the VA mortgage loan program have added billions of dollars to our nation's budget deficits. So, the VA now charges veterans a funding fee around 2 percent of the amount borrowed.

In addition to veterans of the regular armed forces, veterans of the military reserves and the Army and Air Force National Guard are now eligible for VA loan guarantees. If you have six years of reserve service—even if you've never seen active duty— you may participate. Nationwide, this change in eligibility brings 500,000 more Americans into the VA program. If you have served in the active military or reserves, make sure you explore the possibility of a VA loan. It's one of the easiest ways to finance your home.

Summing Up

Don't be misled. You don't need a 20 percent down payment to buy a home. You don't even need 10 percent. And quite often, even little- or nothing-down home purchases are possible. Through the use of private mortgage insurance (PMI), a program of HUD/FHA, or a VA loan, you've got three basic ways to get over the down payment hurdle. Yet PMI, FHA, and VA aren't the end of the story. In later chapters, you'll learn about first-time buyer programs, community reinvestment financing, seller financing, shared equity, sweat equity, lease options, builder's incentives, loan assumptions, and numerous other ways to own a home with little initial cash investment.

Regrettably, in national surveys renters typically report that they can't buy a home because they don't have enough for a down payment. If that's your problem, remember: Solutions do exist. Throughout the United States, a majority of first-time buyers get into home ownership with less than $10,000 of their own cash. Even in high-priced cities, last year many first-time buyers initially invested between $5,000 and $15,000 in their first home. And this amount often included money (gifts, loans from family or friends, or escrow allowances) that didn't actually come from the buyer's own pocket.

Realtor Christina Summers reinforces this point. She says,

My focus has to be on helping first-time buyers secure affordable housing and gain access to programs that give them the financing power to make their dream come true. Many first-time buyers are locked into thinking they need a 20 percent down payment. This falsehood discourages a lot of them from trying to get into the market. I spend a lot of time educating these prospective buyers, showing them how they can buy without 20 percent down, and how little they need each month to pay their mortgage.

Now, let's take a look at graduated-payment mortgages and adjustable-rate mortgages. You can use either (or a combination) of these finance plans to reduce your monthly payments.

GRADUATED-PAYMENT MORTGAGES (GPMs)

Let's say that after you get over, under, or around the cash investment hurdle, you find you can't afford the monthly mortgage payments that will be necessary to get you into the home you want. You can solve this problem through many different approaches. One basic possibility is the graduated-payment mortgage.

In several important ways, the graduated-payment mortgage is like the standard 30-year fixed-rate mortgage. You can use mortgage insurance to reduce the amount of your initial cash investment; your interest rate is fixed for the full 30-year term of your loan; and you know from day one the exact amount of your monthly payments throughout those 30 years. However, the graduated-payment mortgage has a major advantage over the standard fixed-rate mortgage: the monthly payments during your beginning years of home ownership can be 20 to 30 percent lower.

Assume your Realtor tells you it will take a payment of around $1,000 a month to finance the home you want with a standard fixed-rate mortgage of $130,000. You tell your Realtor you would feel more comfortable with a monthly payment of $750 to $800. But if the going rate of interest is, say, 8.5 percent, $750 per month will finance less than $98,000 with a standard fixed-rate mortgage. In this situation, your Realtor might suggest that you consider instead a graduated-payment mortgage.

Here's how the monthly payment schedules for these two basic types of home finance plans might look:

TABLE 2.3
Monthly Payment Schedules for Two Types of Home Finance Plans*

Year	Graduated-Payment Mortgage	Fixed-Rate Mortgage
1	$ 750	$1,000
2	806	1,000
3	866	1,000
4	931	1,000
5	1,001	1,000
6–30	1,076	1,000

*Assumes a 30-year loan of approximately $130,000 at 8.5%.

As you can see from this table, during the early years of home ownership, the graduated-payment mortgage can really boost affordability. To comfortably afford the payments of $1,000 per month, you might need an annual income of $40,000 to $45,000. To afford payments of $750 per month, your household income could drop to $30,000 to $35,000. Over time, of course, graduated mortgage payments increase, whereas monthly payments for the standard fixed-rate mortgage remain the same. That's why the graduated-payment mortgage will work best if you expect increases in your income, definite reductions in your monthly expenses, or a payoff of other debts.

The graduated-payment mortgage can present a drawback. During those early years when your monthly payments are relatively low, your outstanding mortgage balance can actually grow larger. This increase results because your beginning payments aren't large enough to cover your total interest charges. The shortfall in your principal repayment is added to the original amount you borrowed. This process is called *negative amortization* (as opposed to the usual positive amortization where your mortgage balance decreases after each payment).

If you plan to stay in your home for a period of 5 to 10 years, negative amortization shouldn't present a problem because your home can be expected to appreciate. Its increased value should more than offset a temporary increase in your mortgage balance. Similarly, if you plan to create value for your home through improvements, negative amortization shouldn't create a difficulty for you.

On the other hand, a potential problem may arise should you need to sell your home within just a few years after you've bought it. If, during these early years of ownership, your home has not increased in value, you could end up owing the lender more than the cash you would receive from a sale. Instead of getting a check at closing, you would have to write a check.

As a general rule, use a graduated-payment mortgage with negative amortization only when you feel secure in your earning potential and you are ready to settle down in your own home—or, alternatively, use it when you plan to fix up your home and increase its value. In these situations, you might safely use a graduated-payment mortgage to help you reduce your monthly payments and qualify for a larger loan. To decide for sure whether a GPM could work for you, ask a Realtor or mortgage loan officer to go through some actual numbers that would apply to your specific situation. You might find that the increased affordability of the GPM more than offsets the drawbacks of negative amortization.

ADJUSTABLE-RATE MORTGAGES (ARMs)

When Rick and Joyce Lawson decided to stop renting and start looking for their own home, they first decided to consider only fixed-rate mortgages. Joyce says, "We didn't like the idea that if interest rates head back up, our mortgage payments could head up right along with them. We like certainty. We don't like risk."

Rick adds, "But once we really started pricing homes and working out what we could afford to pay, it was a real letdown. It seemed like monthly payments always ran $200 to $300 more than we could afford. In the end, we changed our minds. We came to feel the ARM was best for us after all."

Joyce and Rick Lawson are like most first-time home buyers. They wanted the certainty of the standard fixed-rate mortgage. Yet they also wanted more house than they could presently afford. When faced with this dilemma, Rick and Joyce chose the adjustable-rate mortgage. It gave them far more buying power. At the same time, the adjustable plan they selected minimized their uncertainty.

At the time they bought, here's how an ARM worked for the Lawsons. To get the home they wanted, Rick and Joyce learned they would need to borrow around $160,000. If they had selected a standard 30-year fixed-rate mortgage at 8.25 percent, they would have faced monthly mortgage payments (not including property taxes and homeowner's insurance) of $1,202. However, with the help of their Realtor they found a lender who would give them an ARM with a starting rate of 5.5 percent. Their beginning payment would be $908 per month. Since they were currently paying $950 per month to rent a two-bedroom condo, that $908 monthly payment (before tax deductions) looked too good to pass up.

As for risk, this ARM limited interest rate increases by one percent per year, and places a lifetime cap on the interest rate at 10.5 percent. This means that for the first three years of their ARM, the Lawsons are certain to save money over a fixed-rate mortgage. And if interest rates stay about the same or drop further, the Lawsons will save tens of thousands of dollars over the life of the loan.

Even under a worst-case situation, the Lawsons' interest rate will move up to only 8.5 percent by the fourth year; it will be year five before the Lawsons' monthly payments actually exceed the payments they would have been making had they originally signed up for a fixed-rate mortgage. Even with maximum annual increases in interest rates, for the first six years of their loan the Lawsons' payments with the ARM would average around $1,160 per month—still less than the $1,202 monthly payments of the fixed-rate plan.

Just as important, in looking to the future, the Lawsons believed this worst-case scenario was unlikely. With inflation at less than 3 percent a year, double-digit interest rates didn't seem

TABLE 2.4
Worst Case Scenario (Original Loan $160,000)*

Year	ARM Rate	Monthly Payment	Fixed Rate	Monthly Payment
1	5.5	$ 908	8.25	$1,202
2	6.5	1,010	8.25	1,202
3	7.5	1,112	8.25	1,202
4	8.5	1,201	8.25	1,202
5	9.5	1,315	8.25	1,202
6	10.5	1,425	8.25	1,202

*All figures are approximate. Principal and interest only.

to be on the horizon. And, if inflation does flare up again, they believe their incomes will rise accordingly. So, higher monthly payments will be offset by their higher monthly incomes. In another light, the Lawsons looked at their first house as a starter home. If they move along in their careers as expected, they plan to sell within five or six years and trade up to their first-choice neighborhood. As Rick says,

> Within our time frame of four to six years, once we really thought about it, we didn't see much risk. Besides, the ARM we got gave us several other advantages. Most fixed-rate loans we looked at were going to cost us 2.5 to 3.0 points for origination fees. Our ARM cost one point. That alone saved us around $3,000 in closing costs. And, if we later change our mind about the ARM, we can convert it to a fixed-rate loan anytime within the first five years. Then there's another advantage. Not only did the ARM's lower interest rate help us qualify for a larger mortgage, but to encourage home buyers to use an ARM, our lender qualified us with higher debt-to-income ratios.

The ARM worked well for the Lawsons. But no one would claim that adjustable-rate-mortgages are for everybody. For some home buyers, the peace of mind provided by a fixed-rate mortgage justifies its higher initial monthly payments. And, depending on market conditions, you may or may not be able to find an ARM with terms as (relatively) favorable as the one the Lawsons found. Still, when you begin discussing how much house you can afford, don't toss out the idea of using an ARM without first giving it your considered judgment. Like the Lawsons, with the help of your Realtor or mortgage advisor, you may be able to discover a lender who will give you an adjustable-rate mortgage that just fits your needs. Besides the type of ARM the Lawsons used, here are some other ARM possibilities that can get you a lower interest rate—but also fix your payments for a longer period of years.

The Two-Step

The first step for this ARM may last five or seven years. During this initial period, your interest rate won't change. Then at the end of those five or seven years, your interest rate moves to the current market rate (subject to any applicable minimums or caps). The two-step won't give you the big initial savings of an ARM that adjusts annually or semi-annually. But it might save you between one-half and one percentage point as compared to a standard 30-year fixed-rate mortgage.

For instance, on a $100,000 loan for 30 years at 8.0 percent, your payments of principal and interest would be $733 per month. If the two-step started out at 7.0 percent, your monthly payments would come out to $665—a savings of $73 per month. Or, there's another way to look at the comparison in this example. If you decided you could actually afford a monthly payment of $733, the lower interest rate of the two-step would help you qualify for a loan of around $110,000, instead of the $100,000 you could borrow with a 30-year fixed-rate loan.

Other Combinations

If you look at enough lenders, you'll probably find a near-infinite variety of ARMs. Some adjustables hold steady for their first 3, 5, 7, or 10 years, and then adjust annually for the remaining life of the loan. Others adjust every 3 years. Some adjust every 10 years. There are even ARMs that combine scheduled graduated payments with adjustable interest rates. These are called GPARMs. These GPARMs will probably give you the lowest possible monthly payments during their early years. (In the past, FHA has offered a low-down-payment GPARM.)

Each type of ARM fits home buyers with different needs. And each one may be priced differently as to interest rates and mortgage origination fees. ARMs may also differ in their qualifying standards. With such a menu of ARMs (as well as other home finance plans), you can see why Rick and Joyce Lawson started their journey into home ownership feeling somewhat bewildered. Most home buyers do. This is why you should locate a real estate professional or mortgage loan advisor who will help you match your housing wants to the home finance plans that look best for you at the time you decide to own.

3 STRETCH YOUR POSSIBILITIES

Carl Morgan had just about given up on owning a home. During the past month, he had tried to get preapproved for a mortgage at four different financial institutions. All four gave Carl the same bad news. "We can't help you," they said. "Your employment history is too scattered and you haven't established a solid credit record." Carl didn't know what to do.

Like Carl Morgan, Judy and Paul Davis also felt shut out by typical financial institutions. Several years ago, Judy and Paul began to borrow and spend money faster than they were earning it. For a while they kept their credit squeaky-clean by borrowing from one line of credit to make payments on others. Then Judy was laid off from her job. The Davises' house of credit cards came tumbling down. Today, Judy is working again. The couple is getting their credit record re-established. They would like to buy a home while the market is soft and before home prices or interest rates in their area take off again. Yet they know that for the next year or two, no financial institution is likely to approve them for a mortgage. Must the Davises wait for several years and miss today's market opportunities?

The answer is NO! Carl Morgan and the Davises do have possibilities. Going down to a financial institution and applying for a new loan is one basic choice that's available to all potential home buyers. But it's not the only choice. Not by a long shot. Carl Morgan, Judy and Paul Davis, and all others who find themselves shut out of the mortgage market today or in some future year enjoy a great variety of other possibilities for home financing. In fact, even if you can qualify for a new loan with a mortgage lender, you still might consider other possibilities for financing your home.

MORTGAGE ASSUMPTIONS

Instead of applying for a new loan, you might try to find sellers who will let you take over (assume) their mortgage payments. If successful, you might gain in at least four ways.

Little or No Down Payment

When you assume a mortgage, you pay the sellers the difference between what they owe on their home and your purchase price. If they owe $78,000 and you agree to pay $82,000, your initial cash investment amounts to only $4,000 plus your share of the closing costs. In some rare instances, home buyers have even arranged *cash-back* mortgage assumptions. The sellers pay the buyers. For example, say your purchase price on this home is $74,000. To encourage you to assume the sellers' mortgage of $78,000, the sellers pay you $4,000. Naturally, opportunities for cash-back mortgage assumptions generally arise only in very depressed housing markets. In either case, though, after you take over the sellers' mortgage, you agree to make the scheduled monthly payments just as the sellers would have done had they not sold their home to you.

You stand your best chance to get a little- or no-down-payment mortgage assumption when the sellers have built up little or no equity in their home. On occasion, though, sellers with substantial equity will let buyers assume their mortgage. Then to make the purchase work as a little- or nothing-down transaction, the sellers will carry back a note for much of the remaining difference between the purchase price and the balance owed on the sellers' mortgage. Say that in the above example, you agree to pay a price of $82,000 but the sellers owe only $62,000 on their mortgage. To help you buy with a low cash investment, the sellers might let you pay them a large part of their equity (say $15,000 or more) in installments over a period of 5 to 15 years. As another option, you might also arrange for a lender to grant you a *second mortgage* to help pay the sellers the amount of their equity.

We will look at ways you can handle large-equity mortgage assumptions later in this chapter. For now, let's focus on the most common types of situations that produce low-equity assumptions.

- If the sellers bought with a high loan-to-value ratio, their home may not have appreciated. One technique is to look for sellers who have bought within the past two or three years. Plus, as an added benefit, most of these assumables carry interest rates of 6.5 to 8.0 percent.

- The sellers may have recently refinanced their home with a large mortgage. (Following the refinance boom of 1993–1994, millions of homeowners now fit into this category.

- A home may have declined in value due to a slowdown in the local economy where it's located.

- A home may have declined in value because the sellers did not keep it in good condition.

- The sellers may have spent money on home "improvements" that actually decreased their home's value. Odd color schemes, mismatched styles of renovation or additions, and illogical floor plans represent typical owner mistakes. (I once looked at a home that had been a four-bedroom, two-bath home. The owners had "improved" the house by converting one of the bathrooms into a large closet. That home's value suffered accordingly.)

- A home may have declined in value because optimistic builders created a temporary oversupply of new homes in the area.

- As a result of negative amortization, the sellers' outstanding mortgage balance may have increased after they bought their home.

Although you might be able to find low-equity mortgage assumptions in nearly every price range and geographic area of the country, they are especially common in neighborhoods or condo/townhouse complexes where homes have been financed with FHA or VA loans. Dallas, Texas; Portland, Oregon; Denver, Colorado; Cleveland, Ohio; Salt Lake City, Utah; Memphis, Tennessee; and even San Diego, California are just six examples of cities that have had a good selection of sellers who offer low-equity mortgage assumptions. If you are renting in a city where many homes are moderately priced and the real estate market has been soft, you are fortunate. The chances are very good that you can use a mortgage assumption to move into home ownership with only a small cash investment.

Easy Qualifying

Thanks to an *easy-qualifying* mortgage assumption, Carl Morgan now owns his own home. Here is Carl's story: Although Carl graduated from college with a master of fine arts degree, during the past 15 years he never held a steady job. Sometimes he worked as a temp in legal offices, at other times he operated his own word-processing business, and from time to time he designed and sold jewelry.

"I was never employed steadily," says Carl. "But I always supported myself and earned a steady income. I am ticked many banks won't give new mortgages to people who don't fit their mold. As to credit, I always pay my bills on time. But I don't like to borrow. I've never had a Visa card or even a car loan."

As a stroke of luck, Carl described his home buying problem to a neighbor who happened to be a real estate agent. This Realtor opened the "Homes for Sale" advertising section of the *Austin American-Statesman*, their local newspaper; took a yellow highlighting marker; and started marking every ad that included the phrase *nonqualifying assumption, nonqual assumption,* or *NQ assumption.* Within less than 10 minutes, the Realtor neighbor had highlighted more than two dozen advertised listings. "This is just the tip of the iceberg," he said.

The Realtor went on to tell Carl that nationwide, there are millions of outstanding FHA and VA mortgages that home buyers can assume with little or no qualifying. All FHA loans originated before December 15, 1989, and all VA loans originated before March 1, 1988, may be assumed without lender approval. FHA and VA loans originated after those respective dates also are assumable, but the FHA and the VA will apply some qualifying criteria to the new buyers. Still, these qualifying criteria often are easier than the criteria financial institutions apply to new loan applications.

Once Carl learned about this easy-qualifying possibility, he and his Realtor neighbor set out to look at homes. Forty-seven days later, Carl moved into his own three-bedroom, two-and-a-half bath townhouse that he bought for $119,000. Carl assumed a VA mortgage in the amount of $113,000. His total cash investment, including his share of the closing costs, was just $7,400.

Carl's Realtor suggested one other assumption plan that also might have worked for Carl. The Realtor told Carl that as a general rule, nongovernment fixed-rate mortgages aren't assumable. But most adjustable-rate mortgages may be assumed regardless of whether they are FHA, VA or conventional (i.e., no government mortgage insurance or guarantees). The Realtor said he knew at least one mortgage lender who would approve an assumption for nearly anyone who could "fog a mirror." Although the agent exaggerated for effect, the fact is that some cities do have mortgage lenders who apply liberal qualifying standards for assumptions of their adjustable-rate mortgages. If it turns out that you can't meet the standards necessary to obtain a new mortgage, don't give up on the idea of home ownership. Look for a nonqualifying or easy-qualifying mortgage assumption.

Lower Closing Costs

As another advantage, many mortgage assumptions save you money on closing costs. Depending on the lender and the specific type of loan being assumed, you might save on origination fees, appraisal fees, title insurance, application fees, and other incidental expenses. On Carl's assumption, for example, his share of closing costs amounted to just $1,400. If Carl had originated a new mortgage of $113,000, he might have been looking at closing costs of $2,500 to $5,000.

Lower Interest Rates

Typically, when you assume a mortgage you get the same interest rate the sellers are currently paying. Right now, with interest rates relatively low, most assumptions of older fixed-rate mortgages probably won't give you a particularly advantageous interest rate. On the other hand, should interest rates again hit double digits, don't jump to the conclusion that high market interest rates have priced you out of home ownership. Instead, find one of those lower-interest-rate assumable loans that was originated in the rock-bottom interest rate climate of 1993–1994. (Better yet, buy now and don't risk rates going higher.)

However, even if you do assume an FHA or VA loan with a relatively high interest rate, you are not stuck with that rate forever. Higher-interest-rate FHA and VA loans can be refinanced *without qualifying*. This special FHA/VA refinance program is called *streamlining*. Just make your payments when they are due for at least six months and you can get your interest rates reduced. You may have to pay some refinancing fees, but refinancing an FHA or VA loan is far easier and less costly than going out and getting a completely new loan. FHA/VA streamlining is a great way to reduce your interest rate and monthly mortgage payments.

As another possibility, say you have the chance to assume one of those 9- to 13-percent FHA or VA mortgages originated in the mid- to late 1980s. On occasion, you might be able to get the sellers to refinance their loan at today's lower rates before you buy their home. Then you could arrange to assume their loan, but at the new lower interest rate. (With this approach, though, you would have to meet FHA or VA qualifying criteria even if the sellers' old loan had been a nonqual assumable.)

REFINANCE BLENDS

Some years back, Patrick O'Brien had his home up for sale. His asking price was $110,000. He owed around $72,300 on his old mortgage, which carried an interest rate of 7 percent. Mortgage interest rates at that time were 12.5 percent. Because of these high market rates, many buyers who would have liked to buy Patrick's home couldn't qualify for new financing. To solve this problem, Patrick talked to the branch manager of his mortgage lender. He persuaded her to refinance his home with an assumable fixed-rate mortgage of $88,000 at an interest rate of 10 percent. In effect, this 10 percent rate blended Patrick's old interest rate of 7 percent with the then-current market rate of 12.5 percent.

The mortgage lender profited because it got the old money-losing 7 percent mortgage off its books. Patrick gained because he could now offer his home to prospective buyers with very attractive (relatively speaking) financing. At 12.5 percent, an $88,000 mortgage requires a payment of $939 per month. At a rate of 10 percent, an $88,000 mortgage requires a payment of $772 per month. Three weeks after his blended refinance, Patrick sold his home for $112,000. With an income of $35,000 a year, the buyers easily qualified to assume Patrick's mortgage. At the then-current rate of 12.5 percent, the buyers probably would have needed an income of more than $40,000.

In some future climate of high interest rates, should you find a seller like Patrick O'Brien who has a low-interest mortgage that's nonassumable, approach the lender and try to negotiate a refinance blend. It's another way to beat the affordability problem in times when mortgage interest rates have risen. (Of course, as mentioned earlier, if you buy now you won't have to worry about increases in interest rates. And if rates fall, you can refinance to take advantage of them.)

SECOND MORTGAGES

Using the preceding example, let's say that Patrick O'Brien's $72,300 mortgage could be assumed. Buyers could take advantage of that low 7 percent interest rate. But, with a price of around $110,000, the buyers would have needed close to $40,000 cash to pay Patrick enough to cover his high amount of equity. Naturally, most first-time buyers would find it tough to raise $40,000.

As another possibility, though, Patrick (or a mortgage lender) could have financed some or all of that $40,000 as a second mortgage. For instance, if the buyers had $20,000 in cash, they could offer Patrick a price of $110,000 to be paid as follows: (1) $72,300 mortgage assumption; (2) $20,000 in cash; and (3) a seller second mortgage of $17,700.

Now the question becomes, "What will be the interest rate and repayment schedule for this $17,700 second mortgage?" The answer: Whatever terms can be negotiated to make both parties comfortable with the transaction. No hard and fast rules apply. I have seen second mortgages with interest rates as low as 6 percent and others as high as 16 percent. Sometimes a second mortgage is paid back in monthly payments over a period of 3 years or less. Sometimes it is structured over a term of 15 to 20 years. In the final analysis, the terms of a second mortgage typically evolve according to what you can afford, what the sellers can be persuaded to accept, and what terms are necessary to make the transaction work.

For now, just remember that a second mortgage can move you closer to affordability. Use it when you need to cover the gap between the available first-mortgage financing (assumed or newly originated) and your home's purchase price. (Sometimes, in fact, it pays to use a second mortgage along with new financing, so you can keep the loan-to-value ratio of your first mortgage at or below 80 percent. With a less-than-80-percent loan-to-value ratio, you may not have to buy mortgage insurance and may get a reduced interest rate.)

BALLOON MORTGAGES

It frequently happens that sellers who agree to carry back a second mortgage insist on a term of seven years or less. These sellers want their money, and the sooner the better. From your viewpoint, though, a short-term second mortgage usually won't make much sense. The short term sends the monthly payments too high. But there is a solution to this problem. It's called a *balloon mortgage.*

When you use a balloon mortgage, you typically pay smaller monthly payments, and then pay the full outstanding balance owed after perhaps five or seven years. For example, say your sellers have agreed to carry back a five-year second mortgage for $25,000 at 10 percent interest. You want your monthly payments to be as low as you can get them. The sellers want to receive as much money as they can as fast as they can. Here are five possible payback schedules:

1. *Fully Amortizing.* Under this schedule you would amortize (pay off completely) the $25,000 second mortgage with 60 equal installments (principal and interest) of $531 per month. The sellers might like this schedule. But you might have a tough time paying $531 a month on top of the payments for your first mortgage. Some kind of balloon might be the solution.

2. *Partially Amortizing (15-Year Term/5-Year Balloon).* Under this schedule, you would make monthly payments of $268 per month. After five years, you would pay the outstanding balance of $20,280.

3. *Partially Amortizing (30-Year Term/5-Year Balloon).* Under this schedule, you would make 60 monthly payments of

$219. Then you would make a final balloon payment of $24,100.

4. *Interest Only*. Under this schedule, you would not make any payments on principal. You would simply pay interest of $208 for 60 months. Then you would pay the $25,000.

5. *No Monthly Payments*. Under this type of balloon, you would make no monthly payments. Instead, interest would build and be added to the original balance of $25,000. At the end of five years, the total accumulated interest and principal due would equal $41,133. Although no monthly payments for the second mortgage can really increase affordability, as you might expect, few sellers are willing to accept this type of payment plan.

The great advantage of negotiating second mortgages with balloon payments is flexibility. With the counsel of your Realtor or mortgage advisor, you can tailor a payment schedule to reasonably fit the needs of both you and the sellers. Just one important caveat: BE CAREFUL! Most buyers do satisfactorily pay their balloon balances through either a refinance or the sale of their home as part of a move-up strategy. And balloons do help bring home ownership within reach. But if not structured with a realistic view of the future, balloons can create more problems than they solve. To be safe, allow yourself plenty of time (at least five years) and plenty of breathing room. Don't base your balloon repayment plan on wildly optimistic rates of home appreciation or speculative salary increases. Overinflated expectations can cause a balloon to burst.

CONTRACTS-FOR-DEED

Among the most famous lines in American film history is Oil Can Harry's warning to Pauline, "If you don't give me the deed to your ranch, I'm going to tie you to the railroad tracks." Oil Can Harry knew that if Pauline signed over the *deed* to her ranch, that deed would transfer the property's title to Harry. Although Oil Can Harry's no-money-down approach to home ownership was somewhat unorthodox (not to mention illegal), in general, whenever someone acquires any type of real estate they receive a deed at the time of purchase. With the deed comes ownership.

In some transactions, however, buyers don't receive a deed at the time of purchase. Instead, they buy a home (or other property) on the installment plan. In this type of transaction, buyers usually pay the sellers a small down payment and promise to continue paying monthly installments. In return, the sellers give the buyers possession of the property and promise to deliver a deed to the buyers after they have completed their scheduled payments. This type of home purchase agreement is known by various names such as *contract-for-deed, installment sale,* or *land contract.* For buyers who don't meet the qualifying criteria of a lending institution, a land contract can be an excellent way to buy property. I know from experience.

When I turned age 21, I wanted to start acquiring real estate as quickly as possible. At the time I was an undergraduate college student. I had little cash, no full-time job, and no significant credit record. My immediate chances for getting a bank to grant me a mortgage were zero. But this fact didn't deter me. I simply began to search for properties that could be purchased on an installment contract. By the time I had completed my Ph.D., I had bought around 30 houses and small apartment units. The cash flow from these properties paid many of my college living expenses.

Now you might wonder why some property owners are willing to sell on an installment contract. Shouldn't they just deal with buyers who have the cash and credit necessary to get a loan from a bank? In my experience, I found sellers willing to sell on a contract for some combination of seven different reasons:

1. *No Bank Financing Available.* A home may not qualify for bank financing. The property might be in poor condition, in a less-desirable neighborhood, or functionally out-of-date (rooming house, apartment units with shared bathrooms, irregular floor plan). Also, many lending institutions won't lend in condominium or townhouse developments where more than 30 or 40 percent of the units are occupied by renters instead of owners.

2. *Quick Sale.* One of the best ways for an owner to sell a property quickly is to offer easy terms of financing. The

contract-for-deed is the easiest and quickest type of home finance plan available.

3. *Higher Price.* Property owners who offer easy financing can often sell at a higher price than they otherwise could expect to receive.

4. *High Interest on Savings.* Sellers who plan to deposit the cash they receive from a sale in certificates of deposit or money market accounts can get a higher return on their money by financing a buyer's purchase of their property. A 7-to-10-percent return from a real estate installment sale certainly beats a 5 percent return from a certificate of deposit.

5. *Low Closing Costs.* With a contract-for-deed, sellers and buyers pay far less in closing costs. You avoid nearly all the expenses that a mortgage lender would charge.

6. *Tax Savings.* In many instances, an installment sale of a property produces a smaller income tax bite for the sellers than does a cash sale.

7. *Repossession.* Should the buyers default on making their monthly payments, the installment contract typically gives sellers a relatively quick and inexpensive right to repossess the property.

As a rule, if you and the home you want to buy meet the qualifying standards of a lending institution, you should favor that alternative. On the other hand, if that alternative is not available, or if you can buy on particularly advantageous contract terms, by all means consider using a contract-for-deed. Buying from a seller on the installment plan beats renting, and buying a run-down property on contract and then creating value through improvements can be a good strategy for cash-short buyers. Nevertheless, if you do consider the possibility of using a contract-for-deed purchase, here are a few things to keep in mind:

1. *Buy the Home, Not the Financing.* Don't let easy credit draw you into the purchase of an overpriced property. When circumstances warrant, you might, in good judgement, pay a price slightly higher than market value. But you would not want to pay $5,000 for a 1982 Ford Escort

from Easy Ed's "buy here, pay here" used car lot just because Easy Ed will sell it to you with nothing down and low monthly payments. This same principle applies to home buying. Verify value through an appraisal or other professional opinion.

2. *Beware of Hidden Defects.* A property that seems to be priced right might suffer hidden defects. Take care to obtain experienced and knowledgeable estimates for any repairs or renovations that you plan. Never "ballpark" or casually figure the costs necessary to bring a property up to the condition you want it. Get professional property inspections and cost estimates before you buy.

3. *Contract Terms Are Governed by Law.* A contract-for-deed places you and the seller in a relationship that is governed not only by the contract language, but also by state laws and court decisions. Under an installment sale, your rights and responsibilities differ from those you acquire when you finance a home with a mortgage or trust deed.

Before you sign an installment sale agreement, make sure you consult a real estate attorney who is *experienced* in reviewing these contracts. Lacking knowledge of this specialty, too many lawyers warn against buying a home on the installment plan. (Using similar logic, such lawyers would advise against marriage because divorce can be so painful.) This type of lawyer looks at risks without considering benefits and opportunities. Get a lawyer who understands both. Then negotiate a contract that can work for you and the sellers. Over the years, millions of Americans (especially low-to-moderate-income Americans) have successfully bought homes and small rental properties on the installment plan.

LEASE OPTIONS

Lease options combine a lease agreement for a home, townhouse, or apartment with an *option* (the right) to buy that home at a later date. In the early 1980s, Robert Bruss, the nationally syndicated real estate columnist and investor, called lease options "the most overlooked and underused" home finance possibility. At that time, most home buyers, home sellers, and real estate agents were unfamiliar with its advantages.

Times have really changed. Awareness of this technique has mushroomed. Wherever I travel throughout the United States, I always check through the local real estate classifieds. Seldom do I fail to turn up at least a dozen lease-option ads. In most cities, there are now real estate agents who specialize in lease options and other low-down-payment home finance plans. I have also seen lease options promoted by home builders and developers of new condominiums and townhouses. In San Francisco, one recent ad from Bay Crest Condominiums boldly announced, "If You Can Afford to Rent, You Can Now Afford to Own: Exciting New Lease/Purchase Option." There's simply no question that lease options can bring home ownership closer to reality for many renters in several different ways:

1. *Easier Qualifying.* Qualifying for a lease option may be no more difficult than qualifying for a lease (sometimes easier). Generally, your credit and employment record need meet only minimum standards. Most property owners (sellers or lessors) will not place your financial life under a magnifying glass as would a mortgage lender.

2. *Low Initial Investment.* Your initial investment to get into a lease-option agreement can be as little as one month's rent and a security deposit of a similar amount. At the outside, move-in cash rarely exceeds $5,000 to $10,000, although I did see a home lease-optioned at a price of $1.5 million which asked for $50,000 up front.

3. *Forced Savings.* The lease-option contract typically forces you to save for the down payment required when you exercise your option to buy. Often, lease options charge above-market rental rates and then credit perhaps 50 percent of your rent towards the down payment. The exact amount is negotiable. And once you have committed yourself to buying, you should find it easier to cut other spending and place more money toward your "house account."

4. *Firm Selling Price.* Your option should set a firm selling price for the home, or it should include a formula (perhaps a slight inflation-adjustment factor) that can be used to

calculate a firm price. Shop carefully, negotiate wisely, and when you exercise your option in one to three years (or whenever), your home's market value could exceed its option price. If your home has appreciated (or you've created value through improvements—see below), you may be able to borrow nearly all the money you need to close the sale.

5. *100 Percent Financing Possible.* You also can reduce the amount of cash investment you will need to close your purchase in another way: Lease-option a property that can be profitably improved through repairs, renovation, or cosmetics. By increasing the home's value, you may be able to borrow nearly all the money you need to exercise your option to buy. For example, assume your lease-option purchase price is $75,000. Say by the end of one year, your rent credits equal $2,500. You now owe the sellers $72,500. Through repairs, fix-up work, and redecorating, you have increased the home's value by $10,000. Your home should now be worth around $85,000. If you have paid your bills on time during the previous year, you should be able to locate a lender who will finance your purchase with the full $72,500 you need to pay off the sellers. Or, as another possibility, you could sell the home, pay the sellers $72,500 and use your remaining cash from the sale to buy another home.

6. *Re-establish Credit.* A lease option also can help renters buy who need time to build or re-establish a solid credit record. Recall Judy and Paul Davis who were mentioned earlier in this chapter. They wanted to buy a home before prices or interest rates in their area once again rose above their reach. But the Davises needed time to clear up credit problems created by too much borrowing and Judy's layoff. The lease option could be the possibility that helps the Davises achieve their goal of home ownership.

LEASE-PURCHASE AGREEMENTS

Penny and Jake Olson were out looking at homes. They weren't quite financially ready to buy. But they wanted to explore different neighborhoods and try to figure out what types of homes they liked best. Then it happened. The Olsons saw a house they loved. It was convenient to both their jobs. It was beautifully decorated and landscaped. The floor plan and room layout really appealed to them. The home was nearly everything the Olsons could realistically hope for. Best of all, the home was priced right and the sellers didn't need to get their money out of the home right away. Jake and Penny also learned from their real estate agent that the sellers (the Blakes) had received a job transfer to another state and needed to relocate within the next four to six weeks. The Blakes were open to offers.

Jake and Penny decided to offer the Blakes a lease option for one year. The Olsons believed one year was enough time for them to get their finances in shape (pay off their car loans, reduce their charge card balances, establish a stronger employment history). Their Realtor was reluctant to present this offer. She didn't think the sellers would accept it. Her instincts were right. A lease option seemed too uncertain to the Blakes. The Blakes were afraid tenants might damage the property, later decide not to exercise their option to buy, and move out of the home, leaving it vacant. The Blakes didn't want to be stuck with an unsold vacant home. If necessary, the sellers decided, Mrs. Blake would remain in the home until it was sold. Mr. Blake would move to his new job without her.

Reflecting on the Blakes' objections and comments, the Olsons and their Realtor decided to create another possibility. They offered the Blakes a lease-purchase agreement. Along with this offer, the Olsons provided a $4,000 purchase deposit, references from their current landlord, and a copy of their A-1 credit record from the local branch of TRW, a large credit-reporting agency.

After some negotiation concerning the rent level during the one-year lease period, responsibilities for repairs, maintenance, eventual closing costs, and date of occupancy, the Blakes accepted Jake and Penny's lease-purchase offer. For the Blakes, a lease-purchase agreement seemed more secure than a lease option. The Olsons didn't just say they might buy the Blakes' home. The lease-purchase agreement obligated them to buy it—which is exactly what the Olsons and the Blakes wanted.

4 MAKE BORROWING EASIER

When Sammi Frazer picked up the ringing telephone, it was her loan officer with the much-awaited news concerning her mortgage loan application. "Almost everything looks great, Sammi," the loan officer reported. "You're very close to becoming a homeowner. There are only a couple of things that might raise some concerns at the loan committee meeting. Your ratios are borderline and you've been in your present job only nine months. Because of your excellent credit, though, I still think we'll be able to push your application through. But if you can get your dad or mom to cosign the note, I see no difficulty in getting you approved. You can probably qualify on your own, but a cosigner will make borrowing much easier."

Sammi Frazer was like most first-time home buyers. She didn't precisely fit the ideal of the "perfect borrower." She was stretching a bit to bring the scheduled monthly mortgage payments within her budget. In addition, because she had been employed for less than two years at her present company, the loan committee could question the issue of job security.

Yet if lenders loaned money only to perfect borrowers, they would miss an enormous number of good loan opportunities. Among first-time home buyers, various problems relating to insufficient income, down payments, high monthly debts, credit history, or employment record are standard fare. In fact, last year the Federal Reserve Bank of Boston released a study that showed "only 10 percent of renters unquestionably qualify for the financing they need to buy their first home." On the other hand, the study also showed that only 10 percent were "out-of-the-question credit risks"—when measured by typical qualifying standards. This Federal Reserve Bank study proves that with the right attitude, education, and financial planning, 80 to 90 percent of renters can become homeowners. But they need help. That's why financial institutions, as well as Realtors, home builders, government agencies, and some employers, have developed many different techniques to help make borrowing easier.

COSIGNERS

The technique that helped Sammi Frazer was cosigning. Because Sammi only marginally qualified for the loan she wanted, she helped get her loan approved by bringing in her dad's signature to back up her promise to repay the amount borrowed. If Sammi defaulted, the lender could look to her father for the money. With the additional guarantee of Sammi's dad, Sammi's lender felt secure.

Here are the types of situations where a cosigner might give a lender the reassurance it needs to make the loan you want:

- You are relatively new on your job.
- You are pushing the upper limit of the lender's qualifying ratios.
- Your credit record has some past blemishes.
- Your income sources may be irregular (you work for sales commissions; you are self-employed; you work in an industry with frequent layoffs).
- In moving up from an apartment to a house, you plan to pay substantially more for mortgage payments than you've been paying in rent.

In any situation where you're on the borderline, you probably can make borrowing easier if you bring in a parent, other relative, or possibly a friend as a cosigner.

COBORROWERS

Jesse and Sue Willis had saved diligently for three years. Through careful budgeting, they had accumulated enough to put 20 percent down on the home they wanted. Unfortunately, based on their current income, they fell short of qualifying by $300 a month. Cosigning wouldn't work because their shortfall in income was too great. It wasn't just borderline.

Their Realtor suggested a coborrower. Some lenders differentiate between a cosigner and a coborrower. A cosigner merely serves to back up a borderline borrower. In contrast, coborrowers can help home buyers extend their borrowing limits beyond the amount their own income would seem to support. On their own, the Willises could qualify for a loan of $150,000. With a coborrower, they could qualify for the $180,000 loan they wanted.

Coborrowing can give you greater borrowing power because some lenders will include the coborrower's income directly into the lenders' qualifying ratios. Whereas a cosigner promises to pay if you default, a coborrower may promise to help you make each month's mortgage payments. Whether in fact your coborrower (parent, relative, friend, investor) does regularly pay part of your monthly payments is up to you and your coborrower. As long as someone acceptable to the lender promises to help make the payments, a lender won't actually care where the money comes from.

INTEREST RATE BUYDOWNS

If you don't want to use a coborrower, there are a variety of other ways you can extend your borrowing power. One way commonly provided by home builders or cooperative sellers is the interest rate buydown. An interest rate buydown can cut your monthly payments by 15 to 25 percent during the early years of your mortgage. With a lower payment, you can afford (and qualify for) a larger mortgage. An interest rate buydown works like this:

At an interest rate of, say, 9 percent, your payment for a 30-year fixed-rate mortgage of $125,000 would equal $1,006 per month. If this payment is too much for you to handle, you or someone else could pay the lender a sum of cash at the time you get your loan. In exchange, the lender would reduce your mortgage interest rate. By how much and for how long varies with each individual transaction. One of the most common buydowns is called the *3-2-1 buydown*. During the first year of your loan, your interest rate would be cut three percentage points; during the second year, two percentage points; and in the third year, your rate would be cut by one point. A 3-2-1 buydown would reduce a 9 percent mortgage to 6 percent, 7 percent, and 8 percent for years one, two, and three, respectively. For example, instead of paying $1,006 per month for a $125,000 loan, your monthly payments for the first three years of this mortgage would equal $794, $831, and $917, respectively. The payment difference would be supplied by the *buydown* cash that was deposited in escrow (or paid directly to the lender) when the loan was made.

In the preceding example, the buydown could cost over $5,000. So buydowns aren't cheap. But, if the money is coming from someone else's pocket (home builder, seller, parents' gift, employer), a buydown can clearly make your borrowing easier. Even when you pay the buydown yourself, it can help you afford a mortgage that otherwise might fall outside your ability to qualify. In my *Stop Renting Now!*™ seminars, I sometimes meet older renters who have accumulated substantial cash for a down payment. But they lack the current income necessary to meet the typical lender's qualifying ratios. In those instances, putting less money down and using some of the available cash to buy down the interest rate and monthly payments might get the loan approved.

Realtor Jeff Elias encourages home buyers and sellers to give greater emphasis to buydowns in lieu of negotiating a lower selling price for a home. Elias says, "I believe knee-jerk price reductions are a mistake. Instead, why not try to bring more buyers into the market with seller-paid buydowns. A $5,000 3-2-1 buydown will add more to affordability than will a $5,000 price reduction."

The use of an interest rate buydown is not limited to the standard fixed-rate mortgage. You can also use it to reduce monthly payments for ARMs, GPMs, GPARMs, or any other home finance plan. Home buyers who can count on increasing incomes (or lower debts or expenses) can use buydowns to add tens of thousands of dollars to their borrowing power. As Dave Hershman of American Residential Mortgage Corporation tells Realtors, "There's nothing complicated about a temporary interest rate buydown. . . . You can use buydowns to put you on the upswing, even in a down market."

BUY-UPS (NO-COST LOANS)

For many home buyers, the initial cash-to-close presents a bigger obstacle than monthly payments. If this is your problem, you might use a *buy-up*. Often, mortgage lenders charge 1 to 3 percent of the amount you want to borrow as loan origination fees. These fees are paid at closing. But, if you're short of cash, some lenders will reduce these fees in exchange for a slightly higher mortgage interest rate. (Many mortgage lenders are now referring to buy-ups as "no-cost" loans. Some government regulators, though, think the term "no cost" is misleading.)

The exact amounts of trade-off depend upon the particulars of a given loan and financial institution. In the past, I have seen lenders reduce origination fees by two percentage points in exchange for a mortgage rate that is .25 percent higher. In other words, a 30-year fixed-rate mortgage priced at 7.75 percent and three points could be bought up to an 8.0 percent interest rate. In exchange, the lender would charge just a one point origination fee. You save at closing, but you pay a slightly higher payment each month. (You're actually "buying down" the closing costs by agreeing to a higher mortgage interest rate.) If you're planning to stay in your first home for just a few years, paying fewer points in exchange for a slightly higher interest rate usually makes good economic sense.

REDUCE YOUR CLOSING COSTS

Some lenders will cut back on closing costs and fees even without raising your interest rate. Executive Michael Stutz, of Commonwealth Mortgage, says, "Nobody has cash anymore. And even if they do, they're reluctant to use it. As a result, we've been promoting a special 'no points, no fees' mortgage for first-time buyers. Unlike some other lenders, we're not charging a higher interest rate, either. We think it's good business to make borrowing easier—especially for low-to-moderate income borrowers."

Paul Havenman, a vice-president of HSH Associates, a mortgage advisory firm, points out, "Some lenders will make similar concessions—but only if the borrowers actually request it." When competition among lenders runs strong, interest rates, closing costs, and fees sit as fair game for negotiation—even when lenders don't advertise that fact.

Of course, if you can't get your lender to cut down the amount of the cash you need to close, there's always the seller. Especially in soft markets, or in instances where you are willing to pay a slightly higher price for your house, don't forget that you can ask the sellers to pay part or all of your closing costs and fees.

LOW-DOCUMENTATION LOANS

Several years back, Citicorp Mortgage, one of the nation's largest mortgage lenders, pioneered "Fast Track" lending. Citicorp wanted to make loans much easier to process than the "files piled higher and deeper" approach of most mortgage lenders. Where other lenders would often take 6 to 10 weeks to close a loan, Citicorp promised to get the job done within 15 days. Thus was born the low-documentation loan.

With a *low-doc* mortgage, Citicorp (and other lenders who followed suit) limited their mortgage investigation to a loan application, property appraisal, credit report, and perhaps a copy of the borrower's income tax returns for the past two years. Little else was documented. For home buyers who needed to skip the paperwork and close in a hurry (and who needed to borrow no more than 80 percent of the home's value), the low-doc loan became a hot item.

Unfortunately, low documentation also promoted fraud. More than a few low-doc home buyers falsified the tax returns they gave their lenders, doctored their credit histories, and found appraisers quite willing to give M.A.I. (made as instructed) appraisals. By taking advantage of lenders' efforts to make borrowing easier, unscrupulous borrowers have made low-doc-umentation mortgages more difficult to find and obtain.

Nevertheless, in some cities around the country, there are still lenders who will try to limit the paperwork and speed up the loan process. If you're self-employed, own your own business, work as an independent contractor, or otherwise earn your income in ways that may be difficult to verify, a variation of a low-documentation loan may be just what you need. Also, if you find sellers who, in exchange for a quick closing, may be willing to give you a break on price or terms, a speedy low-documentation loan may help you take advantage of that opportunity.

EASY-QUALIFIER LOANS

Some people confuse low-documentation loans with *easy-qualifier* mortgages. Technically, a low-documentation loan is intended only to reduce paperwork and get you to closing a lot faster. Most lenders don't intend to use low-documentation loans to relax their credit standards. On the other hand, a special small breed of low-documentation lenders may not really mind that you are out of work, have filed bankruptcy, or have suffered a foreclosure. These lenders won't object to your plans to spend 50 percent of your monthly income for mortgage payments. These lenders are called *asset-based* lenders. They are the pawn shops of the mortgage business. These so-called hard-money lenders care primarily about collateral.

A true asset-based lender will concern itself with two questions: (1) What's the property worth? and (2) How much cash are you investing? If the amount you want to borrow falls below a 70 to 75 percent loan-to-value ratio, you will probably get your mortgage.

But it may cost you. Because asset-based lenders naturally attract borrowers who are less creditworthy, they typically experience higher default rates. As a result, their loan fees and mortgage interest rates are usually (but not always) higher than credit-based lenders. Nevertheless, if you can't (or don't want to) pass the scrutiny of a traditional lender, look for an easy-qualifying or no-qualifying asset-based lender. If you're willing to pay the price, these "pawn shop" or "hard-money" lenders will make borrowing for your home as easy as possible. (Remember, too, you don't have to keep this loan forever. Once your credit or finances improve, you can refinance on better terms. You can simply use an asset-based lender as a short-term solution to your home-buying problem.)

ENERGY CONSERVATION MORTGAGES

"The whole idea of energy conservation mortgages," explains John Hemschoot, director of mortgage policy for the Federal

Home Loan Mortgage Corporation, "is to give borrowers credit for doing what makes a lot of sense—buying a house that wastes as little energy as possible." In effect, FHLMC (Freddie Mac), through its energy conservation program, is offering you an opportunity for easier qualifying and larger mortgages. "Show us your future home's monthly savings on electricity, gas, or other energy consumption, and we'll cut you a more generous mortgage deal when you apply for your loan. We'll stretch your buying power, qualify you for a bigger loan, and help push energy conservation to boot," says Freddie Mac.

The Federal National Mortgage Corporation (Fannie Mae) also offers an energy-efficient program to reward people who buy homes that use less energy. Together, Freddie Mac and Fannie Mae make their programs available through thousands of participating local lenders around the country. Unfortunately, according to Richard Burns, an executive with Southern California Edison, "The number one problem with energy-efficient mortgage programs has been that nobody seems to know about them because most participating lenders don't really publicize them very much."

As with many of the mortgage programs we discuss, you may have to do some research to find an energy-efficient mortgage. In the fast-changing world of home finance plans, energy conservation mortgages can get overlooked. So ask your Realtor, local lenders, or telephone Freddie Mac (1-800-424-5401) or Fannie Mae (1-800-732-6643). If you're buying a home that qualifies, an energy-efficient mortgage will make borrowing easier.

GIFTS (GIFT LETTERS)

Think. Who could give you part (or all) of the cash you need to close a home purchase? You never really know until you ask. Many first-time home buyers obtain gifts (sometimes informal loans) from parents or relatives. The practice has become so common that lenders have established *gift letter* procedures.

Most lenders won't object to your raising part of the down payment for your home by gift, but they do want to know about it. They want to guard against the possibility that a gift is actually a loan, which may add to your financial responsibilities and later take away from your ability to make your mortgage payments.

Whether gift or loan, however, if you put the "gift" money in your bank account at least three or four months before you apply for your mortgage loan, the lender may not ask where it came from.

ADDITIONAL COLLATERAL

If you don't have a lot of cash (and you don't want to use one of the no-cash or low-cash home finance plans we've discussed), you can pledge collateral besides the home you're buying. With additional collateral, some lenders will let you finance 100 percent of your purchase price. It doesn't matter who pledges what, as long as the lender feels protected in the event you stop making your monthly payments. Sellers could deposit part of their sales proceeds in a pledged interest-bearing account. Your parents, other relatives, friends, or employer could pledge cash savings, stocks, bonds, autos, or any other assets that can be easily valued. Should you default, a lender can look to the pledged assets to help it collect the amounts you owe.

Merrill Lynch, the big stock brokerage and financial services firm, for example, has developed a *pledged collateral* program called Parent Power. According to Merrill Lynch, Parent Power is a "revolutionary 100% home financing program that makes the cash down payment obsolete." Through this Merrill Lynch plan, your parents or other relatives can pledge either stocks, bonds, or their primary residence in an amount equal to 30 percent of the value of the home you are buying. A cooperating mortgage lender would then lend you all the money you need to pay for the home (excluding transaction fees and closing costs). In effect, you have a 100 percent loan. As long as you make your payments as scheduled, the collateral your parents (or other relatives) have pledged isn't drawn upon by Merrill Lynch or your mortgage lender.

BLANKET MORTGAGES

Another way you might achieve 100 percent financing involves the use of a blanket mortgage. A blanket mortgage gets its name from the fact that it covers more than one property. Here's how a blanket mortgage can work: Say your parents own a $150,000 home with a $45,000 balance on their present mortgage at a 9 percent rate of interest. You would like to buy a $90,000 home. Together, your parents' home and the home you want to buy would have a combined value of $240,000. All you have is a good job and no cash savings. Without much difficulty, you and your parents could borrow as much as $180,000 at the lowest interest rate available by placing a blanket mortgage on both properties. Of course, if you wanted only to refinance your parents' mortgage of $45,000 and raise the $90,000 purchase price you need, you and your parents could borrow as little as $135,000. At an interest rate of 7.25 percent for 30 years, the monthly mortgage payments for both homes would amount to just $921 a month.

Like all home finance arrangements, the particulars for a blanket mortgage will vary according to your needs, market conditions, and the lenders you're negotiating with. But regardless of any specific situation, the basic idea should still work. If your parents (or other relatives you're close to) own a home with substantial equity, consider using a blanket mortgage to help you buy a home even though you haven't yet accumulated any cash savings.

PARENTS' REFINANCE

Your parents also could help you get started in home ownership simply by doing a *cash-out* refinance of their home. The money generated from this refinance could be used to assist with a down payment for your home. Or if the cash-out amount is large enough, your parents could pay for your home in full. Then they could turn around and sell it to you using a *seller mortgage* or contract-for-deed.

The parents of many of today's hopeful home buyers have benefited greatly from the appreciation of their homes. Yet their children can face substantial difficulty just stepping up on the first rung of the home-ownership ladder. Just recently, I met Jane Aspen, a 34-year-old woman who was still renting because she didn't think she could afford to buy. On the other hand, her parents were living in a home that was fully paid for. Her parents had paid $32,000 for their home 28 years ago. Its current market value was around $375,000. Through either a blanket mortgage or some other type of refinancing, it would certainly make economic sense for Jane's parents to convert some of their home equity into cash to help Jane become a homeowner. Some housing specialists have argued that it's not fair for one generation to live house-rich, while another generation remains house-poor. House-rich parents can balance the scale by helping their house-poor children become homeowners.

REVERSE ANNUITY MORTGAGES (RAMs)

Nikki Wendt, a retired widow, is a member of the house-rich generation. "I wanted to travel more, and I wanted to help my kids," says Mrs. Wendt. "But I couldn't do it. I had all this equity tied up in my house but I couldn't do anything with it. It was like having a pile of money in the bank, but not being able to touch it."

Then Mrs. Wendt learned about a new type of home refinancing called the reverse annuity mortgage (RAM). The reverse annuity mortgage differs from other types of refinancings, because it doesn't need to be repaid until the borrowers die or eventually sell their homes.

Like Mrs. Wendt, many homeowning parents may be reluctant to borrow against their paid-off homes because they don't want the burden of making monthly payments again. The reverse annuity mortgage can solve that problem. Under the RAM refinancing plan selected by Mrs. Wendt, her lender agreed to pay her $900 per month for as long as she lives. From this $900 Mrs. Wendt gives $400 a month to her son, and she uses the other $500 a month to enjoy her life more. The extra $400 a month has helped Mrs. Wendt's son, his wife and their two children own their first home. With the extra $500 a month Mrs. Wendt spends on herself, she has taken a trip to Hawaii, paid for some surgery to improve her hearing, and remodeled her kitchen. "Everything is just wonderful now," reports Mrs. Wendt. "I'm not just getting by anymore—my reverse mortgage is providing me a new life. And it's given my son and grandchildren a new home."

A good source of information on reverse annuity mortgages is the booklet *Home-Made Money*, put out by the American Association of Retired Persons (AARP). Also, the FHA has begun to sponsor a variety of reverse annuity mortgage plans. Many older parents believe a RAM provides the best of two worlds: (1) It permits parents to remain in their long-term home and improve their living standards, and (2) It allows parents the opportunity to help their children buy a home now rather than waiting for money they would otherwise inherit later.

MORTGAGE PAYMENT GUARANTEES

During our most recent recession, Volkswagen learned through its market research that many Americans weren't buying new cars because they felt uneasy about their job security. To remedy this situation and get buyers into its showrooms, Volkswagen began offering *payment guarantee* insurance. If a buyer of a new Volkswagen became unemployed, the insurance plan would make the buyer's monthly car payments for up to 12 months.

Taking a cue from Volkswagen, some mortgage lenders, home builders, and Realtors have begun to offer similar plans. Realtor Ron Davies says, "Our program is not a total answer by any means, though it is a step in the right direction. We want to ease people's minds a bit so more renters can take advantage of today's buyer's market."

Kenneth Worden, a recent home buyer who decided to use a layoff insurance plan, says, "I wanted to buy, but at the same time I was apprehensive. When you are in the construction business, you have the psyche where you see a lot of people come and go. To me, the layoff insurance provides a security blanket."

As Realtor Ron Davies admits, mortgage guarantee insurance isn't a total answer. But if, like Kenneth Worden, you're basically confident about your long-term job prospects, yet slightly uneasy about the short-term prospects, perhaps a mortgage guarantee plan can provide that extra confidence you might need to stop renting now.

SPECIAL-ASSISTANCE PROGRAMS— FIRST-TIME BUYERS

Throughout the country, banks, savings institutions, Realtors, government agencies, and not-for-profit organizations are offering many types of special-assistance home finance programs to help make borrowing easier, especially for first-time buyers. Check with local lenders, Realtors, and housing groups to find out what's going on in your area. Old programs are sometimes dropped or changed. New programs are being created. Like other affordable home finance plans, special-assistance programs come and go. Once you find a program that might work for you, act as soon as you can. Don't wait until funding runs out. If you can't find what you need, don't give up. Stay alert for new programs that are being planned.

Here's a sampling of the types of programs that have been generally available.

- Education and counseling
- First-time buyer programs
- Down payment assistance
- Mortgage credit certificates
- Community reinvestment programs
- Fannie Mae and Freddie Mac programs
- Employer assistance plans
- State VA mortgages
- Farmers Home Administration

Education and Counseling

More and more, real estate professionals who work to help renters become owners realize that education and counseling are a must. Home buying and home financing have become far more complex. Hundreds of home finance plans, thousands of potential lenders, a diverse assortment of qualifying standards, lengthy contracts of purchase, seller disclosure statements, environmental concerns, property inspections, neighborhood analysis, value analysis, and other home buying essentials demand educated consumers.

Yet a recent survey revealed hopeful home buyers (those renters who said they planned to purchase within two years) lacked good knowledge of down payment requirements. Sixty percent still believed that 20 percent was the minimum. Few knew about special-assistance programs, and even fewer knew how they might use shared equity, lease option, contract-for-deed, or other widely available alternative home finance plans. In just about all areas of importance, these renters lacked the education they needed.

These survey results are actually even more distressing than they appear. This study omitted renters who said they did not plan to buy or could not afford to buy within the coming two years. It's a safe bet these renters were even less informed than those who considered themselves soon-to-be home buyers.

Fortunately, many concerned people are trying to change this situation. A growing number of Realtors, financial institutions, and not-for-profit housing groups now provide home ownership counseling. Often, counselors work with lower-middle- and lower-income members of the community. "We figured," says Paul Wolgin, executive director of the Southwestern Ohio Savings and Loan League, "that if we could educate renters before they got to the mortgage application process, we could improve our loan acceptance rate. We really did want to make more loans."

In Los Angeles, the Home Loan Counseling Center has helped thousands of potential home buyers clear up credit problems, select affordable homes, and prepare mortgage applications. In Philadelphia, Camile Robinson, president of the predominantly black Associated Real Estate Brokers of Philadelphia, sees her job as educating minority potential home buyers about home ownership. "We spend a lot of time counseling our buyers," says Ms. Robinson.

The Cincinnati NAACP selected Greater Cincinnati Mortgage Counseling Services as that city's best home buyer counseling group. Lisa Carter, managing counselor of the service, reports, "Half of our job is to convince people who thought they could never own a home that they can—if they plan for it." Ms. Carter emphasizes to her clients, "Your attitude is what's going to get you your house. With the right attitude, we're going to damn well get your application past the mortgage underwriter."

Another type of help is provided by the National Foundation for Consumer Credit (1-800-338-2227). Through 617 local offices around the country, this not-for-profit organization works with people to help them get their finances shipshape.

Many local Realtor firms are also increasing their education efforts. Thousands of Realtors (sometimes in association with home builders) run home buying seminars and education programs. During the month of April each year, local Boards of Realtors throughout the United States sponsor American Home Week. Realtors use home tours, educational seminars, and a variety of publications to make American Home Week a celebration of private property rights, home buying, and home ownership.

In commenting on his real estate board's educational seminars, Realtor John Halser reports, "The success of our efforts indicates a very strong interest in home buying. While some of our participants display a great deal of knowledge about real estate, others hope to learn as much as possible about the market and the home buying process. This coincides with our goals for these educational sessions. We experience a two-way learning process made possible by the question-and-answer period included in each session.

"Overall, we are delighted with the results of the seminars," Mr. Halser continues. "In fact, one of the keys to their success is that our seminars maintain a non-selling approach. Quite often, we're helping renters plan to buy who may still be two or three years away from the market."

Newspapers also have joined the efforts to educate renters who would like to buy homes. Often in cooperation with Realtors, mortgage lenders, title insurers, and home builders, many newspapers sponsor home buyer fairs. Call your local newspapers or Board of Realtors to learn of their plans for these activities. Steve Yancey, of Long Beach, California, is certainly glad he did. By participating in the "Time to Buy" sweepstakes sponsored by the *Los Angeles Times* and Coast Federal Bank, Steve won a $50,000 down payment to help him buy his first home.

Remember, becoming a homeowner requires the right attitude and education. Read this book for an introduction. But it's just a beginning. You also need to learn what's happening in your local area. Take advantage of home buyer counseling and home buying seminars that are available. The more you learn, the better you can gain the personal and financial benefits that home ownership offers.

I also encourage you to visit your local libraries. Many libraries now have computerized bibliographies and periodical indexes. Computer searches can guide you to dozens (actually thousands, if you're really motivated) of books and articles that provide more detail about the topics we go over in this book.

In my writings, I often draw on library searches and always find library staffs friendly, courteous, and willing to answer questions about their library materials. Among all the things for which we pay taxes, libraries must rank at the top for money well spent. If after reading this introductory survey on home buying you need more examples and more ideas, you can find them in the books, magazines, newspapers, and videos at your library. Here's a good chance for you to get something in return for those taxes you pay. (Keep in mind too: The next time a ballot measure for increased library funding comes up in your area, support it. Next to home ownership, a good public library is the best investment you can make.)

First-Time Buyer Programs

At last count, more than 180 federal, state, and local government agencies throughout the country offer some type of home finance plan for first-time buyers—typically defined as renters who have never owned, have not owned for at least three years, or are recently divorced singles or single parents. These programs come under a variety of names such as Community Homebuyers Program, Mortgage Revenue Bonds, Home Mortgage Purchase Program, or Home Affordability Program. These home finance plans are aimed at singles, couples, and families who are middle-income or below. In high-cost areas of the country, though, I've seen special-assistance programs for home buyers who earn as much as $90,000 per year. Outside of high-cost areas, the maximum income allowed for participation normally falls within the $35,000 to $60,000 range.

First-time buyer programs usually include one or more of the following benefits:

- Three to five percent down payment (sometimes sweat equity can be substituted for cash).
- Below-market interest rate (generally one-half to one-and-one-half points below market). For lower-income households, though, the savings can sometimes be tremendous. Kentucky, as one example, was offering low-income home buyers mortgage rates as low as 1 percent.
- Relaxed qualifying criteria

- Counseling and education

First-time buyer programs generally are promoted by various lenders, Realtors, or home builders. To qualify in some cities, you must buy a home in specified neighborhoods or new-home developments. In other areas, you are free to choose nearly any home (as long as its price doesn't exceed any program maximums).

There are so many first-time buyer programs being offered in so many different cities and states that it's impossible to list them all. A recent feature article in the *Baltimore Sun* listed 25 different special-assistance programs that first-time buyers in the Baltimore area could use to overcome obstacles to affordability. Besides local newspaper articles, your best sources of information are Realtors as well as participating home builders and mortgage lenders. In addition, all state governments and many cities have set up housing agencies and housing authorities to administer their special-assistance programs. These agencies have names like:

- Alabama Housing Finance Authority
- Arizona Department of Commerce
- Florida Housing Finance Agency
- Maryland Community Development Agency
- Missouri Housing Development Commission
- Washington State Housing Finance Commission

Also, within the past year, the National Association of Realtors and the U.S. Conference of Mayors have set up pilot home buyer programs in 23 cities. Mayor Charles Box of Rockford, Illinois, says, "Basically, we have everybody working together, pulling in new participants, tapping new resources, tapping the experiences of the boards of Realtors to try to provide affordable housing."

Always keep in mind, though, that these first-time buyer programs appear and disappear. Funding is limited. Do your research. Talk to Realtors and lenders. Read closely the real estate sections and real estate advertisements of the major newspapers in your city or state. Telephone your city and state government housing finance/community development agencies. And, don't give up early on trying to locate a first-time buyer program. Many are not well publicized. Keep digging and you're nearly certain to find some type of assistance. The reward will be worth it. First-time buyer programs present a great opportunity to make borrowing easier. "Without the assistance program," says recent home buyer Dilip Kothary, "I don't think we would have been able to buy a house for a number of years. Now we've got our own home in a nice quiet neighborhood and our boys can walk to school."

Down Payment Assistance

To work in tandem with first-time buyer home financing, some cities (both large and small) are pitching in with down payment assistance. Although these programs are not as widespread, they are just as diverse in their features and benefits. Here's a sampling of the types of down payment assistance that your city might be sponsoring:

- *Second mortgage.* Some cities offer low-interest-rate, long-term (15 to 30 years) second mortgages.
- *Equity sharing.* Garden Grove, California, for example, has been willing to advance $25,000 for a down payment on a $150,000 home in exchange for a one-sixth equity share in the home.
- *"Silent" seconds.* These are low-interest-rate second mortgages that require no payment (hence, silent) until the home is sold, transferred, or rented out.
- *Shared-appreciation second mortgage.* These mortgages require no interest payments, but at the time of sale or refinance, the city receives a share of your home's appreciation. (This program operates similarly in effect to shared equity plans.)
- *Matching down payment.* The community will match your cash up to 10 percent of the home's purchase price.

In Portland, Oregon, for example, Realtors, mortgage lenders, and many not-for-profit groups have combined forces to create a $1 million down payment assistance fund called Project Down Payment. In Chicago, one program called New Homes for Chicago has helped more than 300 first-time homebuyers. This

program combines below-market home prices, low down payments, and easy-qualifying financing. Yvonne Hill-Harris, prior
to becoming a homeowner through this program, had lived in
subsidized apartments for 11 years. Now she says, "It's still
hitting me that this is mine. I'm investing in myself and my
family's future."

Mortgage Credit Certificates (MCCs)

Mortgage credit certificates were first authorized by Congress
in 1984 and have been reauthorized off and on several times
since then. Under this program, state and local governments
can issue MCCs to eligible first-time home buyers. If your
state or city offers a mortgage credit certificate program, you
can use your certificate to take thousands of dollars off your
federal income taxes. After receiving an MCC, you can deduct
20 percent of your annual interest payments right off your
federal income taxes. This is not the same thing as the mortgage
interest tax deduction. You're still entitled to that tax advantage.
The MCC produces a *tax credit.*

Here's the way it has worked: Say your home mortgage interest
for your first year of ownership totals $9,000. Also, after allowing
for all your income tax deductions (including mortgage interest),
you calculate your federal income taxes for the year at $6,000.
Your MCC would give you an $1,800 tax credit (.20 × $9,000).
Instead of paying $6,000 in federal income taxes, you would
actually pay $4,200. Even better, you can use the MCC tax credit
every year for as long as you own and occupy your home. In
addition, lenders will treat your tax credit benefit as additional
income. You will qualify for a larger loan.

Community Reinvestment Programs

"We have just felt for a long time that it's a good idea to
make loans in the central city. We've proven you can do it,
and do it profitably," says James Montgomery, chairman and
CEO of Great Western Bank. Putting this philosophy into
practice, Great Western Bank has encouraged loan officers to
get out into the community. "The only way to make money
is to find loans to write," says another Great Western executive.
"And we've found good loans need not be big loans. In fact,
people buying homes for shelter and home ownership give us

much lower delinquency rates than buyers who get into million-dollar homes for speculation."

Just recently, Bank of America, one of the nation's largest mortgage lenders, has created a community-rebuilding low-down-payment home loan program called Neighborhood Advantage. Through Neighborhood Advantage, Bank of America hopes to attract minority and low- to moderate-income renters who need financing to buy their first homes.

In the past many financial institutions have avoided lending to lesser-qualified mortgage borrowers, especially in neighborhoods where homes are most affordable. But mortgage lenders today are developing mortgage plans similar to those of Great Western and Bank of America. Lenders realize that all types of Americans want home ownership, and that once they have achieved it, these Americans will do everything possible to keep it. When lenders make the effort, experience shows they need not restrict their lending to the suburbs to find solid borrowers for home loans.

In response, many lenders are setting aside hundreds of millions of dollars that will be loaned primarily to minorities or to people buying homes located in central cities or low- to moderate-income neighborhoods. In addition, lenders are developing more home buyer counseling programs and revising their lending criteria to better reflect the job histories and credit records of low- and moderate-income borrowers.

On a smaller scale, Hunnington Bank, of Columbus, Ohio, for example, has launched a Community Centered Banking program which it publicizes and promotes with the help of local churches. Hunnington offers seminars on "Why I should buy a house" and "How expensive of a home can I buy?" To cut down on cash-to-close, Hunnington offers low- or no-cash-down mortgages, zero points for loan origination fees, and no premiums for private mortgage insurance. More than 80 other banks throughout the United States have expressed interest in setting up programs similar to Hunnington's.

Realtor Fred Broper says, "I've got a file drawer full of contracts that fell through because our buyers didn't really understand or couldn't dance to the lender's paper shuffle. We're trying not to let this happen in the future. We're lining up lenders who are committed to the spirit of community reinvestment. We've got good people who want to own homes. It's our responsibility and the banks' responsibility to see that they get them." Fortunately, today increasing numbers of Realtors and lenders are exercising this responsibility. When you're considering a home finance plan, make sure you discover the community reinvestment lending programs available in your area.

Fannie Mae and Freddie Mac Programs

"First-time home buyers," writes Kenneth Harney in his nationally syndicated real estate column, "as well as modest-income purchasers short of cash for down payments and closing costs—are almost certain to reap the benefits of a legislative brouhaha on Capitol Hill. The political heat is on for Fannie Mae and Freddie Mac to fund greater quantities and varieties of affordable housing."

Although neither Fannie Mae nor Freddie Mac makes mortgage loans directly, these two quasi-government corporations buy more than one-half of the mortgages made by U.S. banks and savings and loans. As a result, these two giants of mortgage finance dictate the standards and qualifying criteria that many banks and S&Ls rely on for their lending decisions. When Fannie or Freddie decides borrowers "shouldn't" spend more than 28 percent of their income for mortgage payments, the controlling power of that decision echoes throughout the lending industry. This same power to set standards applies to virtually all important factors (property characteristics, neighborhoods, down payments, credit history, employment history, debt-to-income ratios) that influence who gets mortgages—and who doesn't.

The good news for home buyers, Harney writes, is that Fannie and Freddie are going to be "pulling out the stops to produce record volumes of low-down-payment, relaxed credit mortgages." In fact, Fannie Mae has just pledged $1 trillion to fund mortgages for low-to-moderate-income individuals and families during the remainder of the 1990s. That's enough money to finance more than 10 million homes.

You can find out about new Fannie Mae and Freddie Mac affordable mortgage finance programs by visiting local lenders who do business with Fannie and Freddie. Or you can telephone their 800-numbers at 732-6643 and 424-5401, respectively. As with all special-assistance programs, the programs of Fannie and Freddie change frequently. So until you actually buy your home, telephone periodically to see what's currently available.

Employer Assistance Plans

The passage below from John Grisham's recent bestselling novel, *The Firm*, accurately reflects an emerging trend. Increasing numbers of employers are pitching in to help their employees buy their first homes. Here's employer Royce McKnight talking to recruit Mitch McDeere:

> "As you know, it is very important to us that you buy a home. It adds stability and prestige and we're very concerned about these things, especially with our associates. The firm provides a low-interest rate mortgage loan, thirty years, fixed rate, non-assumable should you decide to sell in a few years. It's a one-shot deal, available for your first home. After that, you're on your own."
>
> "What kind of interest rate?"
>
> "As low as possible without running afoul with the IRS. Current market rate is around ten, ten and a half. We should be able to get you a rate of seven to eight percent. We represent some banks and they assist us. With the salary we're paying, you should have no trouble qualifying. In fact, the firm will sign on as a guarantor [cosigner] if necessary."
>
> "That's very generous, Mr. McKnight."
>
> "It's important to us. Once you find a house . . . all you have to do is move in."

In the future, this type of employer-employee exchange is going to become more common. The American Affordable Housing Institute at Rutgers University has just completed a nationwide study of employer-assisted housing benefits. Though, at present, only about 3 percent of U.S. companies help their employees finance or buy their homes, this figure is expected to rise dramatically. Approximately 30 percent of top-level corporate managers report that they plan to get involved in this new benefit area.

Through Colgate-Palmolive's employer mortgage assistance plan, for example, John and Donna Butler were able to get a below-market interest rate and very low closing expenses. "We figure we saved at least $2,500 in immediate costs," says John. "Since we were cash-short and just getting started in home ownership, Colgate's assistance made the difference between buying the house we really wanted and a house that was smaller, older and located in a less desirable neighborhood."

Robert Berg, a vice-president of Colgate, says, "We came up with an assistance plan that used the financial muscle of the company to help our employees get the best possible terms. Our program is a very cost-effective fringe benefit for the company, it's tax-effective to employees, and something that is relevant— much more relevant than just giving people a salary increase."

To encourage more employer-assisted plans, Fannie Mae recently pledged $1 billion to fund employer-assisted mortgages. Fannie Mae calls its program Magnet. Through Magnet, employers can design innovative approaches to attack affordability. To date, the employer-assisted benefits offered run a full gamut:

- Direct grants for down payments.
- Employer mortgages at reduced interest rates.
- Sleeping (silent, soft) seconds.
- Forgivable loans to assist with down payments. (In fact, Fannie Mae offers this benefit to its own employees.)
- Shared ownership and appreciation.
- Monthly payment subsidies.
- Loan guarantees through cosigning or coborrowing.
- Subsidized home prices.
- Payment of closing costs.
- Interest rate buydowns.
- Three percent home buyer down payment loans plus two percent gift or grant.

If your employer doesn't yet have a plan, join with fellow employees to lobby for the benefit. Or try to negotiate housing assistance as part of your own compensation package. Employer housing assistance is a win–win benefit for both employees and employers.

State VA Mortgages

Most veterans know they are entitled to nothing-down mortgages that are backed by the U.S. Department of Veterans Affairs.

However, some states also give veterans favorable home finance options. These plans may call for a 5 or 10 percent down payment, but they are typically funded at below-market interest rates. During the 1980s, for example, market interest rates for mortgages typically ranged between 10 and 12 percent. In California, the CAL-VET mortgage plan kept its rates at 8 percent or less. Recently, the Texas Veterans Land Board was offering Texas veterans mortgage rates of 7.25 percent and home improvement loans at a rate of 9.25 percent.

If you are an eligible veteran, compare your state's mortgage plan (if available) to the federal VA mortgage. The state plan, in some instances, may prove better for your needs.

Farmers Home Administration (FmHA)

If you can live in a rural town of 25,000 or fewer people (in some areas 10,000 or fewer), the Farmers Home Administration, or FmHA (not to be confused with FHA, the Federal Housing Administration), might have a good home finance plan for you. Although FmHA originally offered financing only to farmers, in addition to that mission, it now helps low- to moderate-income renters become homeowners. Unlike FHA, which is part of the U.S. Department of Housing and Urban Development, FmHA is a division of the U.S. Department of Agriculture.

Under one home mortgage program of FmHA, home buyers can buy with nothing down. In addition, FmHA sets liberal qualifying standards. You don't need a spotless credit record to participate in an FmHA loan program, and FmHA will let you devote up to 41 percent of your income toward your monthly housing costs. In some instances, if you are a low-income home buyer, the FmHA will even subsidize the interest rate on your mortgage.

Like all government special-assistance mortgage programs, FmHA programs are subject to change. Plans may be modified, existing programs may be dropped, and new programs may be created. As part of the National Affordable Housing Act, for example, Congress added a very affordable nothing-down loan guarantee housing program for rural home buyers who earn less than $30,400 per year. As an added benefit, this type of FmHA loan (called the 502 Guaranteed Rural Housing Loan Program) limits the cash needed for closing costs. The maximum loan amounts for this program are the same as those that apply to the FHA 203(b) program.

Because FmHA programs are not well publicized, you'll need to periodically contact FmHA or Realtors and lenders who keep their knowledge about FmHA current. Just remember, if you are a low- to moderate-income renter who can live in a small town or rural area, FmHA may have a program that can make it easier for you to become a homeowner. Don't overlook this possibility.

5 MAKE BUYING EASIER

To Margie and Bill Wren, the home of their dreams was a three-story English tudor with tennis courts and a three-car garage. "But that house was priced way out of our league," says Margie. "Instead, we bought an older two-story tract home where we were able to bargain the price down from $150,000 to $120,000. Because the house needed work and was part of an estate, the heirs were anxious to sell. Then, during the next year, we remodeled the kitchen, added a master bedroom suite with sauna and private bath, and installed a large picture window that framed us a beautifully serene view of the Cascade Mountains and Lake Washington."

"As far as we're concerned," says Bill Wren, "It's now a new house, and we love it—not to mention the fact that, even allowing for expenses, our improvements have given us a profit of $30,000."

Like Margie and Bill Wren, Kevin and Christine Baglivi decided to buy a home that didn't match their dreams. In describing the condition of their new home, Christine says, "The hardwood floors were encrusted with chewing gum firmly sealed in place by the previous owners' children. To make matters worse, the little darlings had smashed the bathroom tiles and practiced their artwork on the walls. The home had other problems, too: Every window sash was broken, kitchen drawers were missing, and the bathtub looked as if it had been used to store auto parts. A gnarled mass of weeds covered the entire yard.

"Why would two sane adults purchase such a nightmare?" Christine asks rhetorically. "Because like many Southern Californians priced out of the housing market, investing in a fixer-upper helped us break into Southland real estate. Our 3-bedroom Craftsman bungalow cost $20,000 less than homes in good condition of similar size in the same neighborhood. For Kevin and me, this savings gave us our chance to own a home."

BUY A FIXER-UPPER

Want to own your own home, but need ways to make buying easier? Follow the examples set by the Wrens, the Baglivis, and hundreds of thousands of other first-time buyers. Find yourself a fixer-upper. As Margie Wren puts it, "Since we couldn't afford the home we liked the most, we did the next best thing. We bought a home we could afford, and then made it into the home we wanted." Here are three ways a fixer can make buying easier.

Lower Price

As you might expect, homes with chewing gum stuck to the hardwood floors or avocado-colored kitchen counters punctuated with cigarette burns are not going to command top dollar. (In fact, as one buying strategy, you might even ask your Realtor to show you the homes other buyers want to leave within the first 30 seconds of entering the front door—if they even get that far.) In many housing markets today, buyers are choosy. They are busy with two careers, children, church, clubs, PTA, and volunteer groups. These buyers want a home that is in "move-in" condition. When it's not, it gets rejected fast. If this is the type of market that exists in your area, you can probably buy a fixer at a substantial discount.

Favorable Financing

In addition to (or in lieu of) a substantial price discount, some sellers of fixers might be willing to give you favorable owner financing. On the one hand, sellers may agree to finance a home as an incentive to attract buyers. On the other hand, sellers may offer financing because lenders are wary of the property's condition. Whatever the case may be, in my experience I have found that sellers of properties needing work are frequently good candidates for *owner-will-carry* (OWC) financing.

Here's how Suzanne Brangham, one of the country's most successful home renovators, tells how she arranged seller financing to buy her first home:

While searching for the ideal career, I was also looking for a place to live. I located a lovely but dilapidated apartment house. The building was making a painful transition from rentals to condominiums. Units were for sale or rent. But sales were practically nonexistent.

With my head held high, preliminary plans and a budget tucked under my arm, I decided to make the manager an offer he couldn't refuse.

I told him that in lieu of paying the $800-a-month rent that was being asked for a 2-bedroom, 2-bath unit, I would renovate the entire apartment. I would agree to spend $9,600 for labor and materials, the equivalent of a full year of rent payments. Along with a 12-month lease, I also requested an option to buy the unit at its $45,000 asking price.

Three months later, Suzanne was on her way. She bought her renovated condo unit at her lease-option price of $45,000. Then she simultaneously sold the unit to her buyer for $85,000. After accounting for renovation expenses, closing costs, and Realtor's commission, she netted $23,000. Suzanne no longer had a home, but she had found a career.

Twenty years, 23 homes, and 71 properties later, Suzanne had become not just independently wealthy, but a nationally recognized author, speaker, and entrepreneur. In her excellent book, *Housewise*, she tells about her renovation experiences and the career she found by chance. It's a great book for anyone who would like to learn hundreds of profit-making ideas that can be applied to buying and renovating fixers.

"Instant" Equity and Low Monthly Payments

When you buy at a discount and create value through improvements, you gain "instant" equity in your home. You don't have to wait for the market to appreciate. Like Suzanne Brangham, you can sell your home, cash out your equity, and use the money to trade up to something bigger, better and perhaps more challenging.

Or, like Terry Hughes, and Jerri Fowler, you might consider holding on to your property as a long-term investment and low-cost place to live. Several years ago, Terry and Jerri were hoping to buy their own home, but they lacked enough cash to buy the home they wanted. Through a diligent search with their Realtor, though, they were able to find an owner who was willing to sell them an uncared-for triplex. The seller financed the sale with a three-year contract-for-deed at a below-market interest rate. Instead of making a big down payment, Terry and Jerri agreed to put their available cash and talents into renovation.

To start their fix-up work, the couple remodeled the top floor of the triplex. Working side by side evenings and weekends, Terry and Jerri took the unit through a metamorphosis. "By opening up the floor plan; painting walls; putting in several skylights; and refinishing the kitchen cabinets, counters and floors, we totally changed the personality of the apartment," says Terry. "Once we completed our work, we had potential tenants lining up for the unit. The rent we began collecting covered 60 percent of our own monthly installment payments." With the additional cash from the rental coming in, Terry and Jerri next converted the lower level of the triplex into a home office for Terry's bookkeeping business. "This saved us the $300 a month I had been paying to rent space in an office building, as well as my previous commuting expenses," reports Terry.

With their ability to create value for their property now proven, Terry and Jerri approached a bank for new financing. The bank appraised the triplex at 35 percent more than the couple had paid. The couple then borrowed 80 percent of the property's new increased value and used part of the loan proceeds to pay off the balance of their contract-for-deed still held by the seller. They used the rest of the money to pay for extensive remodeling of the apartment unit they were living in. Once all their work was finished, they owed only $127,000 on a property that had a new increased market value of $175,000.

In less than two years, Terry and Jerri had turned a $15,000 original investment (small down payment plus remodeling expenses for the third-floor apartment) into an "instant" owners' equity of $48,000. As a real bonus, the couple's net costs for the triplex—after allowing for operating expenses, property taxes, rent collections, and the cash savings for Terry's home office—are just $378 per month.

HOW TO FINANCE YOUR IMPROVEMENTS

There are many ways to finance the improvements you plan to make to your home. Credit card advances might be one source of cash. Or you might be able to get a lender to lend you enough money to buy a home and then give you additional draws of loan proceeds as you progressively increase the property's value. The FHA 203(k) program is one type of loan where you can borrow money to buy and improve a property all in one loan. In fact, some financial institutions offer their own particular versions of these *acquisition and improvement* loans. A second mortgage or even a third mortgage also can generate cash to make home improvements.

Shop carefully and you might be able to find lenders who will make improvement loans on very favorable terms as part of their obligation under the Community Reinvestment Act. Some cities and states, too, have made loans or outright grants available to homeowners to improve their homes.

In Virginia, for example, the Virginia Housing Partnership Fund has made direct grants to homeowners for energy-saving improvements. (Utility companies sometimes run similar programs.) This same Virginia fund has financed loans for other types of home improvements at interest rates as low as 4 percent. Check out the redevelopment authorities or housing finance agencies in your city or state. Call your electric and gas company. Talk to Realtors and lenders. Political interests in all parties support home improvement and community revitalization. Investigate carefully. You're sure to find good sources of loans that contribute to these social goals—and contribute to your own efforts to make home ownership affordable and profitable.

FHA TITLE 1 IMPROVEMENT LOANS

I have saved the best for last. In my experience, FHA Title 1 property improvement loans can be an excellent source of money for fix-up work. These property improvement loans are made by banks and savings institutions, but as with FHA home mortgages, the FHA insures the repayment of the loans.

Under FHA Title 1, you don't need to have any equity in your property. No appraisal is necessary. You can even use a Title 1 loan when you have bought your home with little or nothing down using a contract-for-deed home finance plan. To borrow up to $15,000, all you must do is present an acceptable (not perfect) credit record and sign your name. If $15,000 isn't enough, with sufficient equity in your home, you can borrow up to $25,000. Should you want to improve a small apartment building, you can borrow $12,000 per unit up to a maximum of $60,000.

When I first started buying rental houses and small apartment buildings, I relied extensively on Title 1 improvement loans. My technique was to buy a property with a small down payment, renovate and redecorate with cash from a Title 1 loan, then sell or refinance based on the property's increased value. Evidently, many other property owners have found that this technique works. Since 1934, lenders have given more than 35 million Title 1 property improvement loans. For more information, call the FHA at (800) 733-4663.

RESEARCH MONEY-MAKING IMPROVEMENTS

Through cleaning, painting, and general fix-up work, you can nearly always add value to a home. But even here, your "improvements" can on occasion work against you. Should you decide to ignore the market and march to your own drum, your fix-up efforts could actually decrease your home's market value. So don't take a chance. Before you spend any time, money, or effort, find out the kinds of improvements buyers value most highly. During the past 20 years, I have looked at 500, maybe 1,000, houses where owners had painted, paneled, added rooms, converted garages, changed floor plans, remodeled kitchens, or enclosed patios or porches. I would guess that as many as one-third of these owners would be lucky to get back 50 cents for each dollar they had spent.

In fact, some of the most difficult (and disappointed) sellers to deal with are those who think they can pile onto their asking price all the amounts they put into fix-up work or remodeling. "But we spent $15,000 to add on that room" is a familiar lament heard by real estate agents who must tell the sellers the bad news. "It's hard to convince sellers who have put their heart and soul into their house that they can't simply put a dollar figure on their work and add it to the price they're asking," says Realtor Sally Hulbert. Indeed, to tactfully deflate the expectations of sellers who have misspent their improvement monies can be quite important to the art of negotiating. Informing sellers that their bad taste has ruined the property isn't likely to set negotiations on a successful path. If your goal is to add value, then, beware of overimproving, mis-improving, or simply decorating and remodeling to fit your unique tastes or needs. There can be a big difference between fix-up work and creating value.

Fixing up Versus Creating Value

The most important reason to research, research, research homes and buyers is to enable you to create as much value as possible for the time and money you invest. Your goal is not really to fix up your home. You want your efforts to generate a profit. As a first-time home buyer who would like to build instant equity in your home, test every improvement idea with two questions: (1) How much value will the improvement create? and (2) What are the most cost-effective ways we can achieve our improvement goals?

It's not uncommon for well-thought-out improvements to add $3, $5, or even $10 for each dollar invested. Research and planning make the difference. Get the advice of Realtors. Attend open houses. Tour model homes in new home developments. Look through the many home improvement magazines you can find in large supermarkets, bookstores, or your local library. Ask friends and acquaintances for suggestions. Keep your mind open. It is ideas, not just work itself, that create value. Before you begin your improvements, try to find the ideas that will give you the most return for your time and money.

Sweat Equity, Creative Intelligence, Emotional Involvement

In one sense, Christine Baglivi talks about her and Kevin's efforts to create value for their home in terms of simple hard work. "After scraping crusted bubble gum off hardwood floors for nearly two hours, I came to a painful realization," Christine says. "Whoever coined the phrase 'sweat equity' knew what they were talking about. The term refers to repairs you make yourself when you buy a house needing work—a money-saving but exhausting ordeal. I have the perspiration to prove it."

Yet Christine also brings out the need for creative intelligence and emotional involvement. "There was fun in the remodeling, too," she says. "The house was like a lump of clay waiting for strong, imaginative hands to shape it back into a Craftsman show-piece. It was exciting. Friends were supportive, complimenting our hard work. Even through all the dust and clutter, I wouldn't change these months of work for anything. There's a real sense of accomplishment. Kevin and I are rewarded each morning as we stand in the yard and smile at the progress we're making."

What Is a Fixer-Upper?

Once you realize it's really research, creative intelligence, and emotional involvement that create value, you can also see that nearly any home—even the most meticulously maintained home—can offer opportunities for improvement. If the idea of scraping encrusted chewing gum off hardwood floors or fighting the jungles of an overgrown, out-of-control backyard doesn't appeal to you, don't push aside the idea of buying a fixer-upper. Just change the definition of the term. Redefine "fixer-upper" to include any home that can be redecorated, redesigned, remodeled, expanded, or romanced.

The name of the home improvement game is profitable creativity. You can make nearly any home live better, look better, and feel better. Focus on increasing its emotional appeal. When shopping for a home, don't necessarily concentrate on whether you like or don't like a particular house or its features. Ask yourself: Based on what we have learned about the market, how can we improve this house? What problems does it present: traffic noise, floor plan, lack of natural light, house too small (or large), rooms too small (or large), no garage, no backyard, unsightly view, repulsive decorating schemes, no excitement, no personality, no character, no romance? How can the problems be solved? Your best opportunities to locate a bargain and create value lie with ideas and solutions that most people would never think of. Profits result from spotting opportunity. As renovator Suzanne Brangham advises, "Get started in home improving so you can eventually get the home you want but can't afford right now. By starting small and continually trading up into one house after another, you will soon own the home of your dreams."

Pointers, Guidelines, Questions, and Generalities

To create value through renovation, remodeling, or redecorating, no absolute rules apply. The value-creating ideas that work best will depend upon your local market, the specific features and possibilities of the homes you are looking at, and your own creative intelligence. With this said, though, you still might find the following pointers, guidelines, and questions helpful:

1. Never depend on any specific cost/return figures that you read in magazine and newspaper remodeling articles. I have seen $15,000 kitchen remodeling jobs pay back less than $7,500. I have seen $1,500 kitchen renovations pay back $10,000. Use remodeling articles to help you generate ideas. But rely on the advice of local real estate professionals and the past sale prices of comparably improved homes in the neighborhood to help you figure out how much value you can create.

2. Set a minimum payback figure for any work you are considering. I suggest at least $2 of return for every dollar spent.

3. When calculating improvement costs, build into your costs a fair hourly rate for whatever labor you intend to contribute. Your sweat should not go unpaid.

4. Never rely on simple ballpark cost estimates. Base your cost figures on firm estimates of experienced architects, home inspectors, contractors, or designers. Even then, it's often smart to add another 20 or 25 percent for the unexpected.

5. Don't overlook used materials. An old building that's about to be torn down can sometimes be a great source for bricks, lighting, plumbing fixtures, wood beams, cabinetry, windows, and even flooring.

6. Don't overimprove. Try to keep the price of your renovated home at least 20 percent below the top-priced homes in the neighborhood.

7. Never settle on a solution to a problem until you have considered as many alternatives as your research can turn up. Often you can solve 80 percent of a problem for 20 percent of what it would cost for a total solution. For example, a complete kitchen update can cost $10,000 to $30,000. But for $3,500 or less, you can (1) replace cabinet exteriors and countertops, (2) paint awful-colored tile and

appliances to give them a new look, (3) add a skylight and greenhouse window, (4) replace the sink and faucets, and (5) replace lighting fixtures.

8. Try to create ways to inexpensively increase a home's living area or storage area. Can you finish off a basement, attic, or garage? Can you install dormers? Can the house be extended to the side, front, or rear? Can you make better use of cabinets or closets? Does the home have dead spaces you can bring to life? Caution: Additional living space or storage space should be integrated smoothly into the present living space. Add-on space that looks like add-on space seldom creates as much value as does smoothly integrated space. Make sure your renovations work functionally and aesthetically. Anything that prospective buyers perceive as weird or strange will take away from your home's value.

9. Look for ways to enhance the home's natural light. As a rule, the more natural light you can bring into the house, the higher its value.

10. You can often solve the problem of unpleasant views with landscaping, fencing, an enclosed courtyard, a change in the placement of windows, or even substituting glass block or frosted windows for clear pane windows.

11. Traffic noise problems can be significantly reduced with landscaping, supersoundproof windows, or earth berms (mounds of soil piled next to the side of the home that's bringing in the noise). If your soundproofing improvements cause you to lose window light, add a skylight or a row of superinsulated windows (a clerestory) that run just below the ceiling.

12. Flower beds, window boxes, and shutters can pay back 5 to 10 times their cost.

13. When redecorating for profit, always temper your personal preferences with the question, Will most prospective buyers like it? Will they be willing to pay extra for it?

14. Energy-saving improvements offer higher paybacks. Check with your local and state government agencies as well as your utility companies. You may be able to get a grant or

low-interest-rate loan for energy-saving improvements, especially if your family is low or moderate income.

15. Above all, blend together your improvements to make a favorable emotional impact on potential future buyers. Distinguish your home from others. Go for the creative touches to make it a home that is remembered for its better looks, livability, storage areas, comfort, warmth, and romance. When friends and neighbors voluntarily remark, "We love what you're doing to your home," you can pretty well bet you are on the right track.

GENERATE INCOME WITH YOUR HOME

Creating value through improvements provides just one good way you can make buying easier. You might also consider using your home to generate income. Many homeowners help make their mortgage payments by taking in housemates, operating a bed-and-breakfast, renting space for a studio or office, or creating an accessory apartment.

Share with Housemates

"At the time I bought my first house," writes Doreen Bierbrier, "I was working in government and earning a modest salary (by Washington, D.C., standards). I decided the only way I could afford a house in a good neighborhood was to buy one large enough to accommodate a couple of housemates who paid rent. If everything worked out, the rental income would cover more than one-half of my monthly house payments and two-thirds of the utilities."

From the tenant's side of the picture, Mike Kafa tells why he is searching for a house-sharing arrangement. "I'm in a state of flux right now," Mike says. "Until I pass the bar exam, I'd rather not be saddled with a long-term lease. Besides, I spent all my money (plus some) paying for school. Maybe I could rent a place of my own, but I don't want the financial burden. Besides, I'm trying to save on expenses so I can buy my own home."

All across the country, the problem of affordable housing is bringing together home buyers and renters. For people in transition, renting via house sharing can mean a comfortable home at an economical price. For home buyers, house sharing can generate enough extra income to bring home ownership within reach. With a home mortgage interest rate of 7.5 percent, two housemates who each pay $275 per month can stretch your buying power by around $80,000. In higher-priced areas such as Washington, D.C., San Francisco, Boston, and New York, two housemates paying market room rents of say, $350 to $600 a month can lift your buying power by as much as $100,000 to $150,000.

If you highly value your privacy, or if you're somewhat reluctant to take a stranger into your home, house sharing might not instantly appeal to you. But before you reject the idea, think also about the nonfinancial payoffs. Here's what Doreen Bierbrier says about her experience:

> For me, the advantages of sharing my house with tenants have overwhelmingly outweighed the disadvantages. Having housemates made it possible for me to buy and maintain a house at a time when most people told me my salary was too low to buy a home. In addition, tenants have provided countless hours of companionship, laughter, and insights into everything from Republican fund-raising to Vietnamese cuisine—topics I never would have discovered had I lived alone.

Laura Huff, who rents out a bedroom in her home, feels about the same as Doreen. "Every time somebody moves out," Laura says, "I feel like I'm losing a friend." For Pat Riley, age 33, house sharing earns her enough money to hold on to her home after her divorce. She also welcomes the added security a housemate provides. "I like the feeling," Pat says, "that if I needed help in the middle of the night, someone would be there."

Admittedly, house sharing can have some drawbacks. To a great extent, though, you can minimize whatever inconveniences house sharing might create. If you plan for house sharing before you buy, select a home where the floor plan, entrances, and room count and sizes (bedrooms and bathrooms) are well suited for house sharing. A properly designed house, good procedures for selecting compatible tenants, and a good management system for taking care of household operations (bill paying, cleaning, cooking, overnight guests) can go far to make house sharing profitable and personally rewarding.

Tim Parks and his wife, Cheryl, have been sharing their home with two housemates for five years. Tim sums up his attitude toward house sharing:

> *Is it worth it? All I can is that after five years, we have gained a larger network of friends than we ever could have met on our own. As to money, we've got $40,000 of equity built up in our home. That's $40,000 we wouldn't have if we had continued to rent the apartment where we were living. And since we recently refinanced at lower interest rates, after tax deductions for interest, our net mortgage payments are a lot less today than the rent we paid five years ago. The way I look at it, our housemates are buying us a home. Rather nice of them, don't you think?*

Bed-and-Breakfasts, Offices, Studios

Besides house sharing, you can use your home in other ways to generate income. You might operate a bed-and-breakfast, rent out a room as a (nonpublic) office, or convert a garage or backroom into a studio for an artist or writer.

Bed-and-Breakfast (B&B). Nearly any city or rural area that attracts tourists can support a bed-and-breakfast operation. *The New York Times* reports:

> *Increasingly, New York homes, from hi-tech lofts in Soho to Victorian brownstones in Brooklyn to prewar apartments in Queens, are being opened to travelers. Visitors are offered comfortable surroundings, continental breakfasts, and a whole new way to see New York: as paying house guests of real New Yorkers, rather than simply as tourists.*

Barbara Notarius, president of Bed & Breakfast U.S.A., Ltd., has revealed that New Yorkers sometimes earn as much as $1,500 to $2,000 per month with their B&Bs. Valerie Griffith, a freelance writer and consultant, runs a B&B from her brownstone and enthusiastically endorses this opportunity to bring in extra money. "It's been really wonderful," she says. "It's almost never empty. . . . We were a little cautious in the beginning, but in more than three years, we've never once had a problem."

Workspace or Studio. The following ad recently appeared in a Berkeley, California, alternative newspaper under "Offices for Rent":

Beautifully converted garage. Very quiet. Large skylights. Windows
looking out to a Japanese garden. Excellent workspace for writer or
artist. $450 per month. Call 440-4100.

I telephoned the number listed in this ad. The unit had rented
the first day.

Accessory Apartments

Can you create an accessory apartment? In some areas of the
country, these types of apartments may be called *granny flats*,
in-law suites, *studios*, or if detached from the home, a *carriage
house*. But whatever name they go by, the rents they provide can
likewise extend your buying power by tens of thousands of
dollars.

Some homes are laid out so you can create an accessory
apartment from already existing living space within the home.
Homes that are built into hills, for example, often have a
lower-level den or recreation room with an outside door. You
could probably convert such a room to an accessory apartment
for less than $5,000. Or, instead of converting existing living
space, you might also convert a garage, attic, or basement into an
accessory apartment. Some homeowners even build a unit over
their garage. Absent existing space you can convert to an accessory apartment, you might also build from scratch.

As with all improvements, before you buy, do some research.
Determine how much you will have to spend for renovation or
construction to create the accessory apartment. As a rule of
thumb, take the amount of monthly rent you can charge and
multiply it by 25. For instance, it would certainly make economic
sense to spend $10,000 (possibly more) to create an extra, say,
$400 a month in income.

One last point: Make sure your research includes a look at
zoning ordinances and enforcement practices. Unless you want
to risk a fine or other penalty (although millions of homeowners
do take these risks), find a home located in a neighborhood where
accessory apartments are permitted. Sometimes you simply need
to learn the governing regulations—and then find a way around
them if they present an obstacle.

Outside of exclusive, privately controlled housing developments, accessory apartments seem to be gaining popularity and acceptance. They help make housing more affordable for tenants and homeowners. That's a combination of benefits that politicians are finding it tougher to turn against.

To find out whether you could generate income from housemates, a B&B, an office, an artist's studio, or an accessory apartment, you would have to do some market research in your own area. You can review local newspaper ads (especially alternative newspapers) and public bulletin boards. Ask around. Learn what people's needs are. With some investigation, you can probably figure out ways to generate extra income with your home. The key is to plan ahead. If you need extra money to help you move up to home ownership, shop for the type of home that can easily accommodate the income-generating uses you have in mind. At today's interest rates, monthly rental income of $200 to $400 can add $25,000 to $50,000 or more to your buying power.

BUY WITH SOMEONE ELSE (EQUITY SHARE)

When Paul and Beverly Grubb began their search for a home, they had trouble coming up with a down payment. Says Beverly,

> When we finally got the cash, we couldn't get a loan. The condo complex we first wanted had too many units occupied by renters, so the bank wanted a 20 percent down payment and we just had 10 percent. Next, we decided we would rather own a house. But we never could quite get together as much money as we needed. Then one day we saw a newspaper ad placed by Home Partners of Aurora. The ad told about a realty firm that matched home buyers and investors. We called them up and later attended one of their introductory seminars. We were surprised to learn that somebody else would be willing to make our down payment for us.

Shortly after attending this Realtor's seminar on equity sharing, the Grubbs bought a $220,000, three-bedroom, two-and-a-half bath home. To help the couple make their purchase, Home Partners found an investor who put up $22,000 as an initial investment in the home and paid one-half of the closing costs. The Grubbs paid the other half of the closing costs and split with the investor a payment of a $5,000 matching fee to Home Partners. According to Paul,

Since the investor came in as a coborrower on the mortgage, we had no trouble getting financing. It's true, when we sell the property to move up, we will have to share our gains with our investment partner. But in this case, for us at least, we felt one-half a loaf was better than no loaf at all. Profits, though, really weren't our only concern. In our new home, each of our kids now will have their own separate bedrooms—and a backyard to play in. The school district for the neighborhood is great, too.

Equity Sharing: How It Works

Real estate lawyer, advisor, and investor Robert Bruss writes, "You have a good job with an excellent salary. You have a flawless credit report. You want to buy a home but have only $1,000 in your savings account. Don't give up. Yes, you can own a home. The solution to your problem is equity sharing."

Through organized networks of investors and specially designed shared equity programs, various Realtors are now able to match home buyers who need money with investors who believe in home ownership and the investment returns it produces. Typically, an investor puts up all (or part) of your down payment and closing costs. If you do have money for a down payment, though, but lack enough income to own the home you want, you can arrange a shared equity agreement with an investor who will chip in several hundred dollars (more or less) toward your monthly mortgage payments.

In exchange for the investor's help, you agree to share your profits with the investor when you sell (or refinance) your home—generally within 10 years or less. In addition, the investor receives various income tax benefits. Under some shared equity plans, you also may be asked to pay rent to the investor for the portion of the home that he or she owns.

No set rules fix the split of costs and returns between investor and homeowner. Each shared equity agreement should be negotiated individually. What is fair and acceptable for one agreement may not suit another. Market conditions, expected rates of appreciation, fix-up efforts and costs, negotiating skills, and your personal needs all will influence the exact agreement to be struck. Since shared equity agreements depend on many complex property and tax issues, don't negotiate yours without the advice of someone who is experienced in shared equity agreements—and someone who will weigh the agreement from your perspective.

Most first-time home buyers use shared equity to grab the first rung of the home ownership ladder. You might also rely on it to upgrade your housing ambitions. Without shared equity, you might be able to afford a lower-priced condominium or townhouse. With shared equity, you might instead buy a three-bedroom, two-bath house in the neighborhood of your choice.

To use a shared equity agreement, you don't need to enlist a professional investor. You might instead ask for the help of a friend, your parents, or other relatives. In fact, most advisors would encourage you to try this possibility first. If unsuccessful, then bring in a professional investor. Either way, part ownership of a home will give you higher returns than full ownership of a stack of rent receipts.

Buy with Someone Else

If you can't find or would prefer not to buy a home with an investor (whether friend, family member or professional), buy a home with someone you can live with. This past year in California (which generally sets the trend for the rest of the United States), more than 100,000 people became part of nontraditional homeowning households. To make buying easier, increasing numbers of singles, divorced single parents (especially mothers), and groups of several unrelated individuals are joining together to buy their first homes. It may take two incomes today to afford a home, but the second income doesn't have to come from a spouse.

Lois and Barbara, for example, were divorced mothers. Both were working, both were trying to care for their children, and both were trying to find affordable housing. Lois had some cash from her divorce settlement. Barbara had little cash but earned a substantially higher salary than Lois. Neither Lois nor Barbara could have bought a home (that she wanted) by herself.

Their solution: Join forces, find a large house with a split floor plan for privacy, and buy together. Not only did this approach solve their housing problem, but each woman also gained more free time because she was able to share housekeeping, shopping, cooking, and child care with someone else. Lois told me, "This arrangement is better than when I was married. Now I have someone who helps out equally around the house and with the kids."

A couple in their mid-30s with two children just bought an expensive home near where I live. They solved the affordability problem by getting Grandma to come up with a big chunk of the purchase price. The grandmother plans to live part time with the family and help care for their children.

Christy and Sam had been going together for two years. They spent most nights at one or the other's apartment. Sam wanted to invest in a home, and his employer offered down payment assistance. But Sam didn't earn enough income to cover the monthly payments on the house he wanted. Solution: Sam and Christy bought the home together. To reduce problems later, should Sam and Christy decide to go their separate ways, they consulted an attorney who drew up a shared ownership and living agreement. This agreement also included a mutual buyout provision. Sam and Christy now pay less each month than they were paying for rent, they are getting the income tax benefits of home ownership, and they are building equity.

Co-ownership Investing: Best of All Worlds

Having been raised in the housing projects of New York, Cheryl Harrington knew one of her top priorities in life would be to own her own home. As an aspiring actress, though, Cheryl also knew home ownership would not come easy. Fortuitously, Cheryl mentioned her goal to C. C. Pounder, a friend of six years who at the time was also struggling to find steady work in television or the movies. Together, Cheryl and C. C. decided to pool their resources and buy a home.

Considering the fact that neither woman had established a substantial credit record, nor even a sure source of income, theirs was a bold decision. But it was a decision that paid off handsomely. Cheryl and C. C. found a fourplex with extra large units. The owner of the fourplex agreed to give the young black women owner financing for five years. Cheryl lived in one side; C. C. lived in the other. To help cover mortgage payments, they rented out the top two units. Now, four years later, the rents from the upstairs units pay more than one-half of their monthly mortgage payments. Cheryl and C. C. have successfully refinanced the property and paid off the owner financing. The property has appreciated significantly, and they are still good friends.

By going together to buy a fourplex, Cheryl and C. C. achieved the best of all worlds. The rental units' income helped them make their mortgage payments. They bought more home than they otherwise could have afforded. They were able to maintain their own separate living units. They were able to share management and upkeep of the property. And they successfully combined their goals of home ownership and real estate investing. "It's a great achievement that we couldn't have done without each other," Cheryl Harrington says proudly.

AFFORDABLE NEW HOMES

"An industry-wide introspection is underway that could change the housing landscape. The trend is unmistakable. The first-time home buyer is king and everyone is struggling to offer an affordable house." This statement comes from Gary Hambly, president of a large home builders trade association.

David Coombs, a vice-president of one of the country's largest home building companies, reinforces this view. "We suddenly woke up and realized," says this building executive, "we were building houses our intended buyers couldn't afford to buy."

In face of the rising costs of land, lumber, infrastructure, and government regulations, home builders can't produce miracles. Yet many builders are going all out to build homes for first-time home buyers at lower prices. William Camps, an over-the-road trucker, can testify to this fact from experience. Mr. Camps, his wife, and their three children had been long-term renters—18 years, to be exact. "We looked and looked to buy," William said, "but we found nothing in our price category."

Then the Camps family heard about a new affordable housing development being built by Inco Homes. The builder was offering a four-bedroom, 1,675-square-foot house for $105,000—a real steal by the pricing standards in their area of the country. The Camps jumped at their chance to buy. But they weren't alone. The 55 homes in the Inco Development sold out in three hours.

"We've got a real market for affordably priced homes," says builder Gene Pines. "And this is where the action's going to be throughout the rest of the '90s. I would advise anyone who thinks they can't afford a new home to think again. At our last NAHB convention, I talked to builders from all over—Georgia, Connecticut, Illinois, Kansas, and North Carolina. They were all saying the same thing—We've got to cut costs, profit margins, and prices if we're going to survive."

Many news stories on real estate have focused on unaffordability and slow markets. But despite the headlines, hundreds of builders are creating ways to bring the joy of a new home to a wider market of buyers. Don't forget that many new-home builders as well as condo–co-op sponsors and developers offer very favorable financing to their buyers. Both low- and no-down-payment and below-market interest rates are frequently available.

Sometimes, though, demand outstrips supply. Another development of 124 homes by Inco called American Traditions sold out the first weekend the homes were put up for sale. Naturally, not all affordable home developments sell out in a matter of hours or days. But as a rule, low-priced new homes go fast. To succeed in buying, contact builders, Realtors, lenders, and government planning and building permit offices in communities near you. Find out what affordable home developments are available or are on the drawing boards. In many instances, these developments are not advertised widely. Some are even small in-city developments ranging between 8 and 30 homes.

In the past, the trade-up market for bigger and better homes dominated builders' ambitions. For the remainder of the 1990s, increasing numbers of builders will be trying to produce affordable homes with affordable financing for first-time buyers like Jim and Amy Chen of Cincinnati. "We were about to continue renting," says Amy. "But a Realtor friend tipped us off about an American Heritage development. We got a new three-bedroom, two-bath ranch for $65,350."

"It's not our dream house," Jim Chen adds. "But it is our dream home."

Private–Public Partnerships

Sometimes, in their efforts to build affordable homes, builders have been able to strike deals with the government to make buying easier for first-time buyers. By getting government authorities to approve higher densities and grant property tax abatements, the Parr Development Company was able to dramatically enhance the affordability of its Park Row homes located on Long Island, New York.

At Park Row, home buyers were offered two-family, Victorian-style, brick-faced homes with garage, balcony, and basement for $199,990. Buyers needed a down payment of only 5 percent. Counting allowances for property tax savings and rental unit income of $750 per month, families could qualify to purchase these $200,000 homes with earnings of just $35,000 a year.

In Orlando, Florida, developer Tim Leadbetter built his planned unit development called Timberleaf with homes ranging in price from $52,500 to $79,000. "The city agreed to cut the red tape and cut development specs to allow us to be really innovative," said Mr. Leadbetter. With low prices and special-assistance financing, home buyers at Timberleaf needed just $3,348 cash-to-close and the ability to make payments of $520 per month. Families qualified with incomes as low as $21,517 per year.

"The reason I'm so excited about these affordable new-home projects," says government planning official Leo Johnson, "is that they can serve as models for other communities. It proves the private sector can build affordable housing with sensitivity. When you look at design, you can see their attractiveness. This hopefully will encourage other communities to move in the same direction."

Take a look around your nearby communities. Talk to people in the know. Private–public home development partnerships are growing in number. Maybe such a development could be your ticket to home ownership.

Not-for-Profits

In association with banks, builders, and government agencies, hundreds of not-for-profit housing groups are working throughout the United States to bring home ownership to low- and moderate-income families. Sometimes, these organizations recycle homes through urban homesteading. In other instances, they build new homes. In either case, not-for-profits typically arrange special-assistance financing, subsidies, volunteer labor and materials, and cash donations. The result is affordable homes for people who previously believed they could never afford to own.

On New York City's Lower East Side, for example, the Housing Development Institute of the Archdiocese of New York is acquiring two abandoned buildings for the token sum of $3,000 per unit. Using low-cost mortgages, the Institute will see the project through until it becomes 27 units of co-op (owner-occupied) homes for families who otherwise could not buy (and could hardly afford rent). "Home ownership builds hope and a sense of dignity and self-worth, which contributes to breaking the cycle of poverty," says Julia Janecki, a director of not-for-profit housing.

Virginia Ghazarian was able to secure her own home through a not-for-profit organization called RAIN (Rehabilitation in Action to Improve Neighborhoods). Ms. Ghazarian described her condition before taking advantage of the rehab work and home ownership opportunities offered by RAIN: "I wasn't able to find decent affordable housing anywhere. Buying? That was out of the question." Now Virginia owns her own two-bedroom home and she says, "It was a huge and positive change for me. I feel great!"

In Orange County, California, Habitat for Humanity is finishing up a 53-home project at Rancho Santa Margarita called Carino Vista (Caring View). This internationally respected Christian organization put together a team of volunteers, obtained donated land from private builders (The Fieldstone Company and The Santa Margarita Company), and received low-cost and discounted building materials and skilled labor from dozens of suppliers and contractors. The result of this work: low-cost homes—homes that are sold for $50,000 instead of their market value of $125,000.

Hector Ramirez, one of the owners-to-be, says of Carino Vista, "Every Sunday, my children, they are eager to come and see the house." To buy his family's home, Hector will pay $500 down and around $500 a month. Elias Rosales, another lucky buyer, is moving into Carino Vista from a rented garage and attached small trailer where he had been living with his wife and five-year-old daughter for the past five years. "For us," beams Mr. Rosales, "it's just like a dream come true."

Home ownership can be an achievable dream for all Americans. Through the work of hundreds of not-for-profit housing groups with generous volunteers and donors, many Americans are helping to make home buying easier for low- and moderate-income families. "When it comes to the housing work of the not-for-profits," reports *Shelter Force* magazine, "bricks and mortar don't tell the full story. These groups are restoring hope and prosperity in poor neighborhoods and rural areas across the United States."

Why not look into the not-for-profit home building and

renovation activities in your area? If not as a home for yourself, then perhaps you can help others by donating some time, work, money or materials. As Habitat volunteer Sam Walker says, "Our home buyers have no chance of coming up with a substantial down payment. They're not people of means, but they're good people. I like the satisfaction I see in other people's faces. . . . You get a warm fuzzy feeling when you come home tired, but you feel good about having done something for someone else."

6 SELECT YOUR REALTOR

"Tell us how you bought your first house," the *Los Angeles Times* asked its readers. "We'd like to know if you used a specific method or can offer advice other first-time homebuyers might find useful." Answering the *Times'* request, here's what Valerie J. de Pourtales recommended:

> *Get a good agent. Mine was tops. Her name is Karen O'Connell. I would recommend her to anyone looking for a single-family home in the Glendale/La Crescenta area. I think good agents rely on referrals and will do their best to have long-term happy clients. Tell your agent everything you can about what you can afford, what you want, and what your priorities are. The agents also can help educate you on what the market is doing and what price range is realistic.*

"Get a good agent." That really is the best advice any first-time buyer can receive. More than most renters realize, getting the right agent will be one of the most important decisions you make. A good agent can help you evaluate neighborhoods, get your finances in order, negotiate your purchase offer, develop a home finance plan, locate a lender, and handle a dozen other problems that can throw a monkey wrench into the works if not dealt with quickly, competently, effectively, and quite often, creatively.

Never forget: Good real estate agents don't merely show houses. The agent who is right for you will carefully consider your home-buying needs, wants, priorities, and financial abilities. Based on this analysis, your agent will take you through the total home-buying process—from financial planning to move-in day. So select your agent with care. Once you've met an agent, look for a good match between your needs and the agent's capabilities and willingness to help you. As a start, you might ask these four questions:

1. Is your agent a Realtor?
2. Is your agent a possibility thinker?
3. Is your agent committed to education?
4. Can you pledge undivided loyalty?

IS YOUR AGENT A REALTOR?

Contrary to popular belief, the term *Realtor* does not include all real estate agents. As a matter of law, the only agents who can legally refer to themselves as Realtors are agents who are members or associate members of the National Association of Realtors. The term REALTOR® is a copyrighted trademark. Over the years, only about one of every four agents licensed to help people buy and sell homes actually becomes a Realtor.

Why does being a Realtor matter? Because as former U.S. President Theodore Roosevelt pointed out many years ago, all Americans owe something of themselves to their profession. You've probably heard the cliché, "Anyone can get a real estate license." Although not true, this cliché does underscore the fact that preparing for a real estate license exam doesn't require years of training. This makes it important for you to ask whether the agent you're working with has gone beyond the basics and devoted himself or herself to real estate as a profession. You want an agent who lives by the REALTOR® Code of Ethics—an agent who is:

> Zealous to maintain and improve the standards of his calling and shares with fellow Realtors a common responsibility for integrity and honor. The term Realtor has come to connote competency, fairness, and high integrity resulting from adherence to a lofty ideal of moral conduct in business relations. No inducement of profit and no instruction from clients ever can justify departure from this ideal.

Search for a professional who takes these words seriously. Don't simply get in a car with an agent who offers to drive you around to look at homes. Don't enlist the help of Uncle Harry or Cousin Carol just because he or she has managed to pass a real estate license exam. Qualify your agent according to his or her commitment to real estate as a profession.

IS YOUR AGENT A POSSIBILITY THINKER?

It's not enough for you alone to carry a positive, can-do attitude into your home buying efforts. Just as important, your Realtor must be willing to adopt the attitude, "We will make it happen."

Recently, a divorced 35-year-old woman I will call Sue enrolled in my *Stop Renting Now!*™ seminar. When married, Sue had been a homeowner, but now she was reluctantly renting. Sue had $30,000 in cash from her divorce settlement and no outstanding debts. Her credit record was unblemished. Her income was $3,000 a month, and she was currently paying $1,000 a month in rent. Sue had called an agent for help because, having once been a homeowner, she really wanted to own—not rent. Without even itemizing Sue's possibilities, the agent casually dismissed her with "You can't qualify." The agent told Sue her monthly earnings were too low and he wouldn't be able help her. Sue had signed up for my class because she wanted a second opinion. "Is it true?" she asked me. "Do I have to continue wasting money on rent?"

Regrettably, Sue's story sounded familiar. Time and time again, I meet renters who want to buy—renters like Sue who are quite capable of buying. Yet they've been discouraged by uncaring agents whose lack of thoughtful consideration blocked them from figuring out possibilities. In this instance, the agent had assumed Sue would need to spend around $200,000 to get the home she wanted. With a $25,000 down payment, Sue would borrow $175,000. At the then-current 8 percent interest rate and a 30-year fixed-rate mortgage, Sue's mortgage payments including property taxes and insurance would run around $1,600 a month.

When Sue's home-buying problem is looked at through this limited perspective, the agent is certainly right. It would be tough for someone earning $3,000 a month to qualify for mortgage payments of $1,600 per month. But a straightforward purchase using a fixed-rate mortgage only gives a starting point for affordability calculations. It's the beginning, not the end.

Here are just a few of the possibilities we've looked at throughout this book that may have worked (either individually or in combination) to make home ownership possible for Sue:

1. Sue could have put less cash down, switched to an ARM, and then bought down the interest rate with her remaining cash.

2. She could have brought in a cosigner, coborrower, or cobuyer.

3. She could have used shared equity, only instead of contributing the down payment, the investor could have paid part of each monthly payment.

4. She could have shared her home with a housemate or housemates, or converted part of the home into an accessory apartment.

5. She could have limited her mortgage amount to, say, $125,000, and then found a seller to carry back a balloon second mortgage with interest-only payments for five to seven years.

6. She could have bought a fixer-upper for substantially less than $200,000, and then enhanced her affordability by improving the home and increasing its value.

7. She could have bought a nice condominium or townhouse for far less than $200,000.

8. She could have found a low-down-payment, low-interest-rate first-time buyer program (for which she would have been eligible because of her recent divorce).

9. She could have bought a triplex or fourplex. The income from the tenant-occupied units would have counted toward the income she needed to make her monthly payments.

10. She could have worked out a total package of seller financing. With seller financing, a buyer and seller can set price, interest rate, and terms in any way that makes sense to both parties.

11. She could have continued to rent her own living quarters, but also have bought a rental house. This solution would have at least protected her against future price increases in the housing market and allowed her to build home equity (wealth).

12. To protect herself against future inflation of home prices, Sue also could have lease-optioned a property for a two- to three-year period.

13. Sue could have switched her search to lower-priced neighborhoods or communities farther out (see chapter 7).

14. As an absolute minimum, the agent should have en-
courged Sue to review her earnings and spending. If her
current finances really didn't permit home ownership, he
could have helped her develop a financial plan that would
steer her get to where she wanted to go. (See later
discussions in this chapter and chapter 9.)

As Sue's example illustrates, many renters who can and should
become homeowners never learn of their possibilities because
they fail to select the right real estate agent. Realtor Dennis Hatkin
agrees. In the following passage, Dennis reports how he has seen
renters get the brush-off by unmotivated agents. But more important, Dennis shows how agents should turn rental inquiries
into home-buying possibilities:

*Into the real estate office strolls a smiling young couple. Up jumps a
salesperson. "Good afternoon. How may I help you?" the floor agent
asks. "Well, we're looking for a rental," replies the young man. "Oh,
uh, let me see if someone can help you," says the salesperson as he
heads into the next room. "Does anyone want to handle a couple of
renters?" The fellow salespeople quickly answer: "No, they're all yours.
Good luck."*

*How often have I witnessed this scenario? All too often. It's amazing
how many home buyers are lost because of this negative attitude
toward renters. But I've learned the average couple looking to rent are
often qualified buyers who just don't realize it.*

*They don't know that in most areas, they can buy a home with as
little as three percent down, or that with an adjustable-rate mortgage
their monthly payments might be only slightly higher (or maybe even
less) than they would be paying in rent. They might not realize the tax
advantages of owning a home instead of renting, or appreciate the fact
they are building equity, in most cases, faster than they could save
their money in a bank.*

*Usually, they are delighted to discover they should be looking to
buy, not rent. Now, who would be the most logical person to help them
find an affordable home? The person who enlightened them to the joy
of home ownership.*

*I find it a great personal challenge to take would-be renters and turn
them into buyers. Of course, there are times when all they actually can
afford to do is rent. However, eventually, they will buy. And the real
estate salesperson who helped them find a rental, will probably be the
person they will call when they're ready to buy a home.*

As a Realtor, Dennis goes on to give this advice to his fellow agents:

> Remember, we're still in a people business. The more people we meet, help, and become friends with, the more chances we have of getting future referrals. The next time renters walk into your office, think twice before you refer them to one of the other salespeople. You might be giving up an opportunity to help a buyer, a seller, and yourself.

As Dennis Hatkin emphasizes, true real estate professionals don't dismiss renters as unqualified to buy. Instead, professionals know that buying sometimes presents a challenge, and as professionals they do what they can to meet that challenge.

Carol Sarrosick and her husband, Joe, have certainly learned how the right agent can make a critical difference. The Sarrosicks were living in a roach-infested apartment building in Queens, New York. To say the least, they were eager to move. Yet, with less than $3,000 in savings and an income of less than $30,000 per year, "We got laughed out of several real estate offices," Carol recollected. But then the Sarrosicks located a Realtor who was willing to work with them.

This agent examined their possibilities and found them a real fixer-upper. The couple paid $61,000 for their home in a neighborhood where most homes were valued at more than $100,000. How did they finance it? Here again, the Realtor helped. He found the Sarrosicks a mortgage broker who (for a fee) got them a loan on terms that fit their strict limitations. Once settled in their home, the Sarrosicks set out to completely remake the property. And remake it they did. Within three years, they sold their fixed-up home for $127,500, clearing $50,000 above the total amounts they had invested. With that $50,000 the Sarrosicks moved up to a nicer home in the suburbs.

In their *Reader's Digest* article, "Smart Ways to Afford a Home of Your Own," Sonny Bloch and Grace Lichtenstein tell how a good agent helped the McKees of Montana buy a home:

> Myrrisa and Mark McKee of Billings, Montana longed for a house. But with four young children, a combined income of $25,000 and no savings, the McKees assumed—as so many families do—they would never be able to buy. They were wrong.

Why were they wrong? Because as the article discusses, the McKees fortunately had a creative real estate agent working for them. The agent found the McKees a bank repossession they were able to buy for nothing down. The McKees paid just $1,058 cash-to-close. Their payments were an easily manageable $452 per month. Best of all, the price they paid—$35,500—was nearly $15,000 less than the home's market value (once the McKees moved in and made the house a home).

Now let's return to Valerie J. de Pourtales, the woman whose advice, "Get a good agent," was quoted at the opening of this chapter:

> Although I was looking for a single-family detached home, my price range limited my options. My agent showed me a property way above my price range, but it had two older homes on it (one that I could rent out). This was not what I originally had in mind, but this kind of property enabled me to get the kind of home I wanted (with the income from the rental helping me qualify for the loan). I even got the extras that were last on my list of priorities, like a Jacuzzi, walk-in closet, built-in storage, attached garage and more. If I hadn't kept an open mind, I never would have even looked at this type property.

As Valerie brings out, a good agent will not merely follow a path you suggest. Good agents are always looking for different ways to help you reach your most important goals. A good agent will frequently say something like, "Here are several possibilities I want you to consider." When you open your mind to your Realtor's possibility analysis, the chances are strong that, like Valerie, you can get the home you want.

IS YOUR AGENT COMMITTED TO EDUCATION?

Side-by-side with the idea of possibility thinking stands a commmitment to education. Real estate agents who are committed to real estate as a profession continuously educate themselves. They don't stop with just the minimum knowledge necessary to pass a real estate license exam and meet their license's continuing education requirements. A real estate professional will subscribe to various real estate periodicals, read the latest books in the field, attend seminars, participate in the educational programs of state and national Realtor conventions, and work toward professional designations such as GRI (Graduate Realtor's Institute) and CRS (Certified Residential Specialist). Many sales agents also show their commitment to education by working toward and obtaining a broker's license. All states have two classes of real estate licenses: the sales license and the broker's license. The broker's license requires significantly more experience and real estate coursework.

One of the hottest topics for Realtor education is how to improve service for first-time home buyers. The NAR and state Realtor organizations are emphasizing the need to convert more renters into homeowners. Ira Gribin, a recent past president of the NAR, says, "Unless we solve the affordability problem [for first-time buyers], we won't produce any volume." Mr. Gribin is highlighting the fact that when renters stand on the sidelines, homeowners who want to trade up can't sell. Sales volume falls for both starter homes and move-up homes. Another Realtor tells agents, "To help first-time buyers find affordable housing and financing, Realtors must be persistent and creative." And Mack Powell, former president of the largest state Realtor organization in the country (in California) agrees:

> We have a lot of opportunities to help [renters] learn what they need to know to make informed decisions about their first purchase of a property. . . . We sometimes overlook the fact that there are a lot of people who could purchase a home if only someone would take the time to explain how to go about it. . . . This month's issue of California Real Estate is dedicated to helping [Realtors] learn how to work more effectively with first-timers of all types.

Perhaps Realtor Yvonne King captures the basic idea in a nutshell:

> To be successful with first-time buyers, you need to do more than just call yourself a specialist. You need to be a specialist. Know the market. Understand renter concerns. Explain the advantage of home ownership. Be sincere. Show renters how they can achieve their goal of home ownership. With your help, they'll be home in no time!

After getting a license, some agents drift along with a sale here or a sale there. They learn no more than they have to. Others commit themselves to their profession. They stay on top of new ideas. They open their minds to creative and imaginative possibilities. They persistently strive to educate themselves, their buyers, and their sellers. Ask friends, relatives, and other recent home buyers you know to help you locate this kind of agent.

CAN YOU PLEDGE UNDIVIDED LOYALTY?

Once you select a Realtor to work with, give that Realtor your undivided loyalty. Too many first-time buyers mistakenly flit from agent to agent. Whenever they see a "For Sale" sign or a newspaper ad that piques their interest, they call the listed number and talk to the listing agent, or perhaps anyone else who happens to come to the telephone.

"We drove by 838 Maple yesterday," the caller says. "We like that neighborhood. Can you tell us about the house and how much the sellers are asking?" The agent may try to get more personal information from the caller. But the caller wants to get straight to the point. After some brief conversation back and forth, the agent may set an appointment to show 838 Maple and maybe two or three other homes that are similar. The buyers look, say they will think it over, and thank the agent for showing the properties. A week or so later, these same buyers see another property they like. They call the number listed, and go through the same motions.

And so it goes. Eventually, the buyers may find a home that suits them. But just as likely, they won't. I've seen renters meander for months—sometimes years—using this hit-and-miss aproach. To a large extent, these renters don't realize that investing in a home doesn't mean just "looking at houses." Successful home buying requires financial planning; solving problems; getting over, under or around obstacles; exploring tastes, preferences, and lifestyles; setting priorities, and gaining knowledge of homes, sellers, neighborhoods, and financing alternatives. It's only when all these factors are matched, blended, and formulated that you can discover and create your best possibilities. That's why the great majority of buyers today need a full-service Realtor, not simply a chauffeur.

And how do you get full service? Locate an agent who is right for you. Then give your agent undivided loyalty. Assure your Realtor that in exchange for full service, you will call that agent whenever you have a question or want to see a home—even if that home is not listed for sale with your Realtor's specific brokerage firm.

You should understand that the Realtor you choose to work

with can help you buy nearly any property that's for sale in your area. The great majority of brokerage firms, new-home builders, real estate owned by banks (REOs), auction companies, government agencies with foreclosures (FHA, VA, Resolution Trust Corporation [RTC]), and even most FSBOs ("for sale by owner") will cooperate with the Realtor you select to help you. Most people with properties to sell know that cooperation with Realtors produces quicker sales than "going it alone."

KNOW WHAT SERVICES TO EXPECT

Of course, loyalty needs to run both directions. Once you agree to work with a specific Realtor, you should expect your agent to:

1. Clarify and rank your housing needs, wants, and objectives.

2. Locate various neighborhoods, developments, and communities that can fit your budget and preferred lifestyle.

3. Reveal market information such as past *sale* prices of homes (as opposed to *asking* prices), time-on-market data, neighborhood trends, appreciation rates, and local economic conditions.

4. Alert you to good buys as soon as (sometimes even before) they come onto the market.

5. Disclose the negative characteristics of a home, as well as accent its positive features. In fact, today increasing numbers of Realtors are asking sellers to complete seller disclosure statements. These statements list a property's known defects. You should insist on receiving a disclosure statement.

6. Point out ways you can shape up your finances to make buying, qualifying, and ownership easier.

7. Show you the income tax advantages of ownership as compared to renting.

8. Walk you through the total home buying process from home search to mortgage closing so that you fully understand how to prepare and what to expect.

9. Suggest the home finance options that you might use in your local area.

10. Guide you to sellers or mortgage lenders who are most likely to approve you and a finance plan that will work for you.

11. Suggest other professionals to bring into the home buying process when they are needed. Besides your Realtor, you may want to rely on an attorney, income tax advisor, appraiser, property inspection service, escrow company, title insurer, and home warranty company.

12. Give you advice concerning the price and terms of your offer, as well as help you negotiate that offer. (See box, *The Law of Agency*.)

13. Suggest ways that you can improve the market value of a home, or otherwise improve it to better meet the needs of your family.

14. Explain various compromises and trade-offs that may help you achieve your most timely and important objectives.

15. Identify motivated sellers who may be willing to offer a bargain price or OWC (owner-will-carry) financing in exchange for a quick sale.

16. Tell you about the various rules, regulations, laws, and local practices that bear upon the home buying process.

17. Stay on top of your home buying search from start to finish. Handle details. Try to anticipate and overcome potential problems. And always stand ready to figure out how best to ethically and professionally help you achieve your goal of home ownership.

The days are gone (if they ever existed) when real estate agents simply tried to sell whatever they could to whomever they could. Today's career-oriented real estate professional must put your needs first. Top real estate educator and sales trainer Danielle Kennedy says, "Every active sales agent will frequently encounter situations where people want to buy houses they should not buy, where the agent must advise against the purchase in question, or even against any purchase at all." When you give your Realtor loyalty, he or she should give you full service—even to the point, perhaps, of advising you to postpone buying.

In addition to better service, though, there's another reason you should try to show loyalty to your agent. That reason is

THE LAW OF AGENCY

Until recently, real estate agents who helped home buyers typically worked as agents or subagents of sellers. However, in most states the law of agency has been changed (or clarified) to give home buyers several different choices. In general, you may now work with a Realtor under one of these types of arrangements:

1. You can stay within the historically dominant type of system where you work with an agent (or subagent) of the sellers.

2. You might elect dual agency. Under this arrangement, Realtors help both buyers and sellers, but they also agree not to pass along confidential information that could harm either a buyer or a seller at the expense of the other party.

3. Some agents are now promoting their role as facilitators. Under this type of agency, the Realtor would perform the role of mediator. The Realtor would not legally represent the buyers or the sellers. The goal would be to find a mutually satisfactory agreement—not the "best" price or terms from either the buyers' or sellers' perspective.

4. The fastest-growing type of agency is called "buyer's agency" or "buyer brokerage." This type of agency is frequently compared to the use of lawyers. With buyer's agency, your agent legally represents you. The listing agent represents only the sellers. Each agent fights for the best deal for their respective clients.

Which type of agency should you choose? There's no set answer. Since state laws and local customs differ, the advantages and disadvantages of each type of representation will also differ. Therefore, before you begin to work with a Realtor, you should discuss what alternatives for representation exist in your area. (In fact, to promote this explanatory discussion, a majority of states have now enacted "agency disclosure" laws.)

Regardless of the type of legal relationship you establish with your Realtor, make sure he or she meets the criteria set forth in this chapter. In addition, no matter who they represent, Realtors are required by a variety of laws, rules, and regulations (e.g., civil rights, consumerism, professional ethics, licensing law, torts, misrepresentation) to conduct their real estate activities with competence, integrity, and fairness. Unlike lawyers, who work within an adversarial system, Realtors work within a system of cooperation and mutual gain. In a lawsuit one party loses and one party wins. In home buying, the best transactions are those where everybody wins, and both buyers and sellers feel satisfied with the price and terms of their agreement. (See tips on negotiation in chapter 8.)

fairness. Sometimes, buyers and their agent may have worked productively together for weeks, or even months. Then, out on their own for a Sunday drive, the buyers drop in for an open house at a home that's just been listed. Bingo! The buyers fall in love with the home. Without thinking, they get the agent on duty at the open house to write up and present their offer. Those buyers have treated their own Realtor unfairly.

"Please do not have me spend weeks researching, previewing, and showing you properties," asks Realtor Vicki Boisells, "only then to have your cousin, who manages a fast-food drive-through but still has an active real estate license, write the offer for you." As a matter of courtesy and fairness, Vicki's right. Once you choose an agent, as long as he or she is doing a good job, stick with that agent. Remember, a good agent provides needed services, not just up to the point when the sellers accept your offer—but all the way through from agreement to closing, and sometimes beyond.

REALTORS CAN HELP YOU IMPROVE YOUR FINANCES

In addition to helping you compare homes and set priorities, many Realtors will help you improve your finances. When Janis Haske finally decided to end her trips to the laundromat and become a homeowner, she called an old friend and former college classmate who had established himself with a career in real estate. "Steve," Janis said to her friend, "am I crazy or is it remotely possible that I could buy a home?"

"Janis," Steve replied, "you're going to have to tell me everything about your finances before I can tell you."

"So, painfully, we arrived at the conclusion," says Janis, "it was remotely possible, if just."

"You're about as entry-level as they get," Steve told her. "But it is a buyer's market."

With this encouragement, Janis began to put a financial plan into action. "I saved—Lord, how I saved—although this was very hard," says Janis. "It isn't easy for a born grasshopper to turn into an ant overnight. Luckily, as a small theater producer, I am very good at finagling. For extra income I wrote a couple of freelance stories. I squeezed every paycheck until it squeaked."

To come up with the small down payment required by her FHA financing, Janis pulled together her available cash, borrowed some money against her 401(k) retirement savings, and accepted a "gift" from her retired schoolteacher mother. And when the mortgage company telephoned and said, "You know, you'll probably qualify on your own, but if you want to avoid delays, could you get your mom to cosign?" Janis again enlisted her mother's help.

Once closing was behind her, Janis moved into her home. She affectionately describes it as "tiny, one-bedroom, one-bath, but light and airy. Hardwood parquet floors. And a deck! It overlooked the canyon and I could see myself having coffee on it in the mornings." In fact, one of the movers Janis hired summed up her home best. "This is a cool house, lady," the mover told her. Then, as she sat amid the boxes on her living room floor, Janis knew her decision to buy had been worth her efforts. She really had become a homeowner.

Decide to Buy—Then Find the Money

Hundreds of times I've heard renters say, "Sure, we'd like to buy but we don't have the money." My response is, "All right, you can choose one of two options: (a) You can wait until you somehow miraculously come up with the money—keep buying those lottery tickets—and then decide to buy; or (b) You can first decide to buy; then (like Janis), with the help of your Realtor (or other financial advisor), you can figure out how to get your finances in shape to move towards home ownership."

Experience shows choice (b) works far better than choice (a). Once firmly in place, your decision to own will motivate and encourage you to change from "grasshopper to ant," from living for the present to planning for a better future. To stop renting and start owning, don't defeat yourself with negative self-talk like "We don't have the money," or "We can't afford it." Make the decision to own. Like Janis, once you've committed yourself, you'll find the money.

Finding the Money

As the people mentioned throughout this book have demonstrated, individuals and families at all income levels have found the money they need to become homeowners. Even in high-priced areas of the country, some home buyers earn as little as $15,000 to $20,000 per year. In contrast, I've frequently met renters earning $40,000, $50,000, even $60,000 a year and more, who say they don't have the money to buy.

Perhaps David Schumacher, in his book *The Buy and Hold Real Estate Strategy*, says it best. "You don't get rich by making money," he emphasizes. "You get rich by wisely handling the money you make." In other words, finding the money to buy is not determined chiefly by how much money you earn, but by how well you plan your finances.

Remember when Janis Haske met with her Realtor friend, Steve. He told Janis, "You're going to have to tell me everything about your finances." With that discussion behind them, Steve didn't advise Janis, "Sure, you can buy. No problem." Nor did he tell her, "Nah, you can't qualify. You don't have enough for a down payment." Instead, he pointed out how she could buy if she reorganized her finances. With the decision to buy as a motivating force, Janis then planned ("finagled") her spending, saving, and borrowing so she could find the money she needed to realize her goal of home ownership.

Test yourself with this "find the money" quiz: (1) Do you know, down to the last dollar, where your money goes each month? (2) Does your spending perfectly match your core values? (3) Are you saving as much as you could save? If you're like most Americans, your answer to each of these questions is probably no.

But let's go further. To the extent you can, retrace your spending for the past 60 to 90 days (or longer). Write down everything you can think of, as specifically as possible. (Or, alternatively, keep a detailed record of your spending for the next 30 to 60 days.) Don't just list groceries as a category. Try to piece together the specific items you've purchased. Don't just list restaurant meals. Try to recall the menu items, drinks, and desserts you ordered. What specific clothes have you bought? What about movies? Sporting events? Plays? Books? Magazines? Newspapers? Cassettes or compact discs? Here's a partial list of other items to help jog your memory:

- Rent
- Car maintenance & operating expenses
- Credit card payments and interest
- Utilities

- Car insurance
- Public transportation
- Air fares
- Hotels
- Restaurant meals
  (breakfast, lunch, dinner)
- School tuitions
- Telephone
- Sports equipment
- Computer equipment
  and software
- Car payments
- Health insurance
- Property insurance
- Laundry and dry cleaning
- Cigarettes, alcohol,
  illegal substances
- Prescription drugs

- Doctor bills
- Dental bills
- Furniture
- Appliances
- Life insurance
- Cable TV
- Household services
- Donations
- Pets
- Club memeberships and
  dues
- Child care facilities
- Cosmetics
- Hair stylist
- Savings and investments
- Miscellaneous
  household items

Next try to think of any other things that you've spent money on that aren't listed. Once you've completed a list of your spending, rank your expenses from the highest amounts to the lowest. Now you can see where your money has really been going. With your eyes opened, you'll most likely discover three facts: First, you'll notice you're spending for some things that aren't giving you your money's worth. Do you subscribe to magazines you don't read, buy clothes you seldom wear, pay for a membership in a health club you rarely visit? What else?

Second, even for things you enjoy, you'll probably find you're spending more than you need to. When it comes to nearly all spending—car, rent, groceries, car insurance, life insurance, restaurant meals, entertainment, travel, clothes, furniture, etc.—most of us could spend much less and still get about the same (sometimes greater) satisfaction than we are getting now.

In their book, *Penny Pinching*, Lee and Barbara Simmons tell how quitting their jobs and starting a new business forced them to reevaluate their spending. "We weren't poor by any standards," they report. "But we realized we had to cut back somehow."

After three years of learning, testing, developing, and living with the strategies described in our book, we have good news. The process can be painless. You can easily cut a lot of expenses without lowering your standard of living or toiling hours each week obsessively searching newspapers, department stores, and supermarkets for bargains. We know because we have done it.

For most people, changing just a few habits can lead to very substantial savings. Spending less does require a more organized approach than most people take to managing their money. But in the end, financial planning will actually save you time as well as money.

You can first find money by eliminating unnecessary spending. Second, you can pay less for the items you do buy. And third, you will find your largest amount of money when you reset your spending (and saving) priorities. Every time you start to write a check or hand a clerk a credit card, ask yourself, "Is what I am about to buy more important than owning a home?" If the answer is no, then don't do it. Instead, put the money into your "house account."

For most Americans, home ownership fulfills a core value. Buying a $50 blouse, taking a weekend ski trip, or borrowing $15,000 for a new car does not. Too many renters have remained renters because they forgot this critical question: "What are my core values?" Don't ask, "What do we want?" Don't even ask, "Is this a good buy?" Instead ask yourself, "Among all the things we want, does the item I'm about to buy rank higher or lower than owning a home?" The key to home ownership lies with financial planning.

Of course, if you're like most people you'd rather get your wisdom teeth pulled out than sit down and sort through a pile of checks and receipts. Even worse, financial planning implies cutting back and doing without the things you want. But if you feel this way, change your perspective. Don't look at financial planning as tiresome bookkeeping, with self-denial as the reward.

Think of it in these terms: Through financial planning, you gain the self-discipline and willpower to pass up things you merely want, so you can achieve the goals you value most. Can you honestly say that all your current spending goes for goods or services that rank higher in importance than owning your own home? If not, reorganize your spending to match your priorities. Make the decision to own. You will find the money you need to move up to home ownership.

Increase Your Income

Dr. David Schwartz, author of the million-seller *The Magic of Getting What You Want*, encourages everyone to remember that financial planning doesn't just refer to spending and saving. It also means planning to increase your income. Dr. Schwartz says:

> Recently, I was in a savings bank. This bank was giving away a packet of 12 brochures on how to improve fiscal fitness. I took the brochures home and examined them. Each brochure told how to save money by doing with less . . . not one suggested any ideas about solving a money problem by making more money and creating financial independence!

Ask yourself, "How can we increase our income?" Janis Haske wrote freelance articles. From an earlier chapter, recall the newly engaged couple, Nancy and Jim Lopez, who decided to begin their married life as homeowners. To increase their incomes, they both took on second jobs. When Yolanda Williams tried to buy a home, her Realtor told her she would probably need another $2,000 a year to get the home she wanted. "Two thousand a year?" Yolanda responded. "I don't think that's a problem." She told her employer what she needed. The company gave her a well-deserved raise. Chuck Kejunas didn't ask for a raise to increase his income, but he did manage to earn more by working overtime. Sometimes he even worked double shifts to fill in for other employees who were out sick or on vacation. Says Chuck,

> I admit my wife and I had some difficult times. Often I would get back to the apartment around midnight after Sandy had gone to bed. Then I'd be gone by 6:00 A.M., before she got up. It wasn't easy. But would I do it again? You better believe it. You can't know how bad we wanted to get out of that apartment, buy a house, and start a family.
>
> It even worked out better than we expected. After the plant manager took notice how hard I was working, he recommended me for one of the company's advanced training programs. When I get through it, I'll be in line for promotion into a new department at higher pay. Not bad, eh? A new home, a new promotion, and yes, a new son.

As Dr. David Schwartz advises, don't just reorganize your spending. If you're not making enough to satisfy your core values, develop a plan to increase your income.

Financial Planning and Choosing a Realtor

Realtors know that home ownership means financial planning. Many are willing to help you put your finances in order. "Changing market conditions have created a host of opportunities for first-time buyers to purchase affordable properties," says Realtor executive Tom Russell. "Yet, understanding first-time buyers' motivations and financial resources are paramount to Realtor success. Although helping a renter become an owner can be difficult, it also can be rewarding. First-time buyers can become fiercely loyal customers of the Realtor who helps them through their first home buying experience."

Florida Realtor Cathy Whatley confirms Tom Russell's comments. Cathy says, "I find working with first-timers to be one of the most challenging—and rewarding—parts of our business. . . . If the numbers aren't working, I'll ask my buyers to let me be creative in negotiating terms and finding financing. . . . There are literally dozens of financing possibilities we might consider. . . . [Even] before we find a home, I often say something like, 'Now you're going to need approximately X dollars for the down payment and closing costs. Can you save part of that each month, or will you be getting a bonus, income tax refund, family assistance, or inheritance that might help?'"

In his or her own way, each of these Realtors is emphasizing the same thing: Today, buying a home requires a loyal working partnership between you and your Realtor. Together, you must coordinate your financial planning—matching your capabilities, resources, and priorities with the right property, the right neighborhood, and the right home finance plan. So, look for a Realtor who will sit down with you, review your finances, make suggestions, and with a positive "can do" attitude, explore your present and future possibilities. Even if you can't buy right at this moment, that simply means that you have a problem to solve. With financial planning and the expertise of a Realtor (or other home-buying or home financing advisor), who is well versed in possibility analysis, you can still be home in no time!

7 DISCOVER AN AFFORDABLE NEIGHBORHOOD

You may already be familiar with the following question and answer:

Q: What are the three most important factors to look for in a home?
A: Location, location, location.

Nearly all real estate advisors tell you to choose a neighborhood (location) first. Then choose the best home for your needs located within that neighborhood. No doubt, this advice can work pretty well when: (1) you already know all the features you want in your neighborhood; (2) you know such a neighborhood exists; and (3) you've figured out how you can afford the neighborhood you have chosen.

Given today's market, though, many renters who would like to buy their first home can't answer yes to one or more of these three conditions. Even when they know the features they want in a neighborhood—well-kept single-family homes, manicured lawns, walking distance to shops and restaurants, good schools, location close to work—such a neighborhood may not exist. And if it does exist, homes in the neighborhood may be priced too high. In fact, most experienced real estate agents have seen "sticker shock" turn the joy and excitement of looking for a home into borderline hopelessness. ("We'll never find anything we like that we can afford.") Faced with this attitude, many renters mistakenly give up.

Mary Ortez of the Home Buyers' Counseling Service explains, "There are a lot of people who want to buy their first home in a nice area, but I tell them, 'you have to realize you can make any area nice.' I bought in Fair Oaks. It wasn't the dream area I wanted to move into, but I got much more house for my money.

"In my counseling work," Mary continues, "I've developed a list of six or eight neighborhoods where first-time buyers can find good buys. When I suggest them, some clients respond, 'But we don't want to buy in that area.' In turn I tell them, 'OK, that may be the way you feel. But if that's the case, then you may not buy at all.'

"I feel so sad for those people," Mary adds, "because many don't buy and I feel I've failed them. I recall one couple who came in four years ago. I urged them to buy in Fair Oaks, just as I had done. They told me that neighborhood didn't fit the image they were looking for. I did some follow-up work for our records recently and discovered this couple is still renting. But you know what? During the past four years, prices for average homes in Fair Oaks have gone up around $20,000. Our neighborhood association's Take Pride in Your Home campaign really helped to get things around here fixed up."

Throughout many higher-priced American cities, good people—willing to exercise the virtues of hard work, personal responsibility, pride of ownership, and community participation—who earn between $20,000 and $60,000 per year have been priced out of "middle-class" neighborhoods. If you fit this category, you still might be able to afford the home you want. You can use one or more of the techniques discussed in earlier chapters that make borrowing or buying easier. But as another path to follow, you also can broaden your neighborhood search.

BROADEN YOUR NEIGHBORHOOD SEARCH

If, like many renters, your home-buying problem seems to be, "I can't afford to buy in the neighborhood where I would like to live," try broadening your neighborhood search. Don't miss out on the number one priority of home ownership because you must pass up lower-priority items such as specific neighborhood features. Every neighborhood has pluses and minuses. If you carefully shop and compare, you'll find many possibilities for home ownership opportunities that beat renting. Twenty-seven-year-old graduate student Jill Fredericks gives this advice:

After moving from the Midwest to a high-priced part of the country, I thought I'd never be able to buy anything here. At first, I wanted the College area or Atlantic Park. But after looking for several months, I learned cheap meant $150,000. Just as I was about to give up, a Realtor friend suggested I take a look at Rogers Point.

Rogers Point? All I knew about Rogers Point was crime, vandalism, and school busing. But I was wrong. Sure, there are some problems here. But the neighbors take a lot of pride in their homes, and around here you really feel like you're in the country, with the hills, grassy knolls, and even horses galloping by my living room window. I was able to buy a great 2-bedrooom with a large yard for my three Irish setters to run around in. With income from my roommate and two part-time jobs, I've no problem handling the monthly payments.

From my experience, here's the advice I would give first-time buyers: Don't let certain parts of the city scare you away. Don't be biased because of what you've heard. You can buy. You may not get everything you want, but you've got to start somewhere.

In speaking of his recently purchased home in a neighborhood called Avondale, Richard Winston says,

Many people think this is a 3-G (gangs, gunfire, and graffiti) neighborhood. It's not. Some gang members do hang out over on Lincoln Boulevard, but over in our area, it looks like Beaver Cleaver Street. To tell the truth, my wife wasn't so excited about buying here. She was a little afraid and we had a lot of work to do on the inside of the house before we could move in. But now we can say it's ours. We earned this. So she's coming around. When we're all finished and it's nice and we sell it for more, she'll be happy. I'm sure.

NEIGHBORHOODS CAN GET BETTER

The past 5 to 15 years have seen many previously "marginal" neighborhoods revitalized and gentrified—but now priced beyond the means of many first-time buyers: the Wrigley section of Long Beach, South of Market in San Francisco, South of Houston in Manhattan, Lincoln Park–De Paul in Chicago, and Capitol Hill in Washington, D.C., are just a few examples. "Boy, I wish I had gotten into Rockridge (Oakland, California) ten years ago," someone recently said to me. And on my last trip to Chicago, I talked with a now not-so-young renting couple who complained, "In

the early '80s, we could have bought a house on a decent block
in Hyde Park for $62,000. But we eventually decided against it.
Now we can't find anything like it for less than $150,000."

Ten years ago, every one of the above-mentioned neighborhoods was experiencing its share of the urban problems typical
of larger cities everywhere. And none of these neighborhoods is
free of problems today. But each of these neighborhoods has
enjoyed renewed popularity and price increases of 100 percent
or more.

What's more important for your future, though, is that hundreds of somewhat similar neighborhoods are positioned for
turnaround during the next 10 years. As good people are priced
out of "highly desirable" neighborhoods, they move into "less
desirable" neighborhoods. But that's not where the story ends.
As Mary Ortez points out, "You have to realize you can make
any area nice."

Neighborhoods aren't inherently good or bad. It's the people in
them and the standards and values they enforce that determine a
neighborhood's future. No one would encourage you to buy into a
neighborhood where kids dodge gunfire as they walk to school, or
a neighborhood where residents post signs in their car windows
reading, "Please don't break in. Radio already stolen." But stand-
ing in between our "worst" and "best" neighborhoods are many
areas that are improving because the people living in them are
working to make better lives for themselves and their families.

EXPLORE YOUR NEIGHBORHOOD
POSSIBILITIES

You may believe you can't afford to own. But your problem may
be that you've written off some neighborhoods or communities
that actually could work for you. Or you may simply not have
investigated your total market area thoroughly enough. In my
research for this book, I talked with dozens of Americans and
recent immigrants throughout the country who had been discouraged about their chances to own until they broadened their
search and found additional neighborhood possibilities.

Few neighborhoods in the United States have come to
symbolize urban problems any more than the Los Angeles area
of Watts. The April 1992 riots reinforced that bleak image. Yet

Wilma Haynes, chairman of the Watts Homeowners Association, says, "People who come to Watts are very surprised at what they see. All around me people are fixing up their houses, buying lots that have sat vacant for years, taking pride in their neighborhood again."

Fred Greer, codeveloper of the new Santa Ana Pines subdivision in Watts, says:

> We'd like to bring back to Watts those people who have moved out to rent in Gardenia and Inglewood, people who are tired of driving in from Palmdale and Rialto, people who want to move back to the neighborhood where their mama still lives. We're trying to build nice enough homes to give them a reason to come back to Watts. There's no reason you can't put up nice homes here. Watts deserves decent homes as much as any other place.

After comparing home prices, neighborhoods, and communities throughout the Los Angeles area, legal secretary Tracy Brewer has found the Santa Ana Pines new-home prices of $140,000 to $160,000 tempting. Tracy admits,

> Yes, we're concerned about crime in the area, but we're first-time home buyers and we don't want to buy something way out in Palmdale and then spend two hours a day on the freeway. When I first moved to Los Angeles, I wouldn't have considered Watts. But after living four years in an apartment and seeing what house prices are around town. . . . Well, now I am considering it.

The problems of Watts have been well publicized; the advantages have not. "It's the only affordable area close in," says Realtor board president Leslie Bellamy. Other Realtors point out that the neighborhood sits right next to the University of Southern California. And while home and lot prices have stalled in much of Los Angeles, lot prices in Watts are up 30 percent since 1989 and home sales are outpacing other parts of the city. Between 1987 and 1992, median home prices in Watts and other South-Central neighborhoods rose from $79,000 to $125,000. Although the riots have heightened the wariness of some buyers, prices still seem to be holding steady.

In one of its many articles on home buying, *Money Magazine* tells its readers, "With prices in check and interest rates sinking, it's a great time to shop for your dream house. . . . You'll need to seek out the neighborhoods where property values are rising faster than your community average." Surprising to many home buyers, though, is the fact that the neighborhoods where prices are rising fastest may not be the most prestigious or well-established neighborhoods. Often, the largest price increases can be expected in areas that are poised for turnaround and renewed popularity.

NEIGHBORHOOD VALUE SIGNALS

The concerned residents of Watts and South-Central Los Angeles have demonstrated that even amid disastrous setbacks, the most severely disadvantaged neighborhoods can make significant progress toward neighborhood turnaround. The old idea that neighborhoods can only deteriorate and can never improve has been proven wrong. All across America, neighborhoods previously declining, stigmatized, or overlooked are experiencing renaissance, revitalization, and rediscovery. Throughout the remainder of the 1990s, buying into an affordable turnaround neighborhood will represent one of the best ways to achieve home ownership. If you give it a chance, this ownership strategy might work for you. Watch for these seven signals to help you spot turnaround potential:

1. Good value
2. Strong sales
3. Convenient location
4. Community spirit
5. Community action
6. Renovation and new construction
7. Something special

Good Value

"We bought in Brentwood because we had to buy at the low end of the market," says recent home buyer Peter Shapiro. "It's one of the few neighborhoods in the Washington, D.C., area where single-family homes could still be bought for less than $100,000."

Talking about Dumfries, a small town outside of D.C., Alfredo Calerdon says, "For me and my wife, this was the only affordable place we could find to live. Most of the people who live here are working-class people who moved here to buy an affordable home, the same as we did."

Portland, Oregon, resident Larry Hollibaugh had wanted to buy in a southeastern neighborhood of Portland. But he couldn't find the home he wanted at a price he wanted to pay. So he switched his search to the North Portland neighborhood of St. Johns. There he found an 1,800 square-foot home priced at just $46,000. He bought it.

One of the best signals for turnaround potential is good value. In one sense, good value can mean the lowest price possible for a single-family home in an area (as in the preceding examples). In another sense, though, it can mean well priced relative to similar homes in nearby areas.

In Richmond, California, a somewhat distressed city on San Francisco Bay, the Marina Bay redevelopment project is succeeding because it is offering waterfront homes at prices 30 to 60 percent below other communities around the Bay. With home prices ranging between $150,000 and $300,000, no one would call Marina Bay prices low in any absolute sense. Yet compared to most other San Francisco Bay areas, as well as some outlying suburbs, Marina Bay is offering excellent value for the money. Although the new residents of this formerly abandoned shipyard must work to change the negative image associated with a Richmond address, they are gaining "one of the last opportunities to live on the water at an affordable price this close to San Francisco," says Kenneth Ambrose, an executive of the firm that's redeveloping the area.

Strong Sales

In addition to apparent good value, look to see whether homes in a neighborhood are selling relatively quickly at close to their asking prices. Realtor Larry Bragg says of the Brentwood neighborhood, "The market is extremely strong because it is affordable. A lot of people are so happy to get a house here."

In Candler Park, a turnaround neighborhood in Atlanta, Mike Kind, president of the Candler Park Neighborhood Association, says, "People pass the word when they're ready to sell and the houses are gone." Candler Park resident and Realtor Maya Hahn paid $18,000 for her home in the late 1970s. "The average price of a house here now is $125,000. Things are really moving in that price range. It's the one people are looking for," reports Maya.

Convenient Location

Add convenient location to good value and strong sales and you've really got the makings of neighborhood potential. Candler Park sits within a close commute to downtown Atlanta; walking distance to MARTA (a rapid transit station); shopping; and the pool, golf course and tennis courts at Asa Candler Park. Marina Bay in Richmond is located just 10 minutes from the San Francisco Bay Bridge. St. Johns, the Portland neighborhood, is well served by shops and restaurants and sits just minutes from downtown Portland over the St. Johns bridge. Sepulveda, a Los Angeles turnaround neighborhood, is convenient to downtown Los Angeles, the beach, and Westwood (UCLA).

When Esther and Mike Spinoza told friends they were considering a home in Sepulveda, their friends told them they shouldn't move to "that area." "I was a bit apprehensive at first," says Esther, "but you have to be realistic. Moving to Sepulveda allowed us to buy a nice home without a long commute."

Sepulveda resident and Realtor Kim Van Dyk says, "The neighborhood has everything I need. We have great shopping, banks, and restaurants. I like shopping within walking distance of my home and could even do without a car for a day or two if I had to."

Community Spirit

Another good sign of turnaround potential is community spirit. Speaking of Sepulveda, a police officer and member of the Sepulveda Community Council says, "We all have a stake in the neighborhood and we're committed to making a difference in the area."

To check out a neighborhood for community spirit, talk to residents, merchants, police officers, and community leaders. Listen for positive attitudes, upbeat forecasts, optimism, and neighborly affection and friendliness. A St. Johns resident says, "St. Johns is one of the friendliest neighborhoods with this real small town charm. St. Johns could get swallowed up by the bad perception of being near the Rivergate industrial area and the landfill, but instead I think it will be the next great neighborhood of Portland. St. Johns is really an undiscovered gem."

In Brentwood (near the District of Columbia), Peter Shapiro fondly recalls that the weekend his family moved into their home, 90 percent of their new neighbors dropped by to welcome them into the community, and five or six even brought home-prepared food.

In Richmond Annex, a community being discovered by first-time home buyers, Jerome Potts expresses great satisfaction. "This neighborhood is real nice and friendly," he says. "Everyone looks out for each other. If you leave your house and come back, someone will tell you if a blue car stopped by your house; or, if a package is delivered for you, neighbors will keep it until you come home. And we do the same for them."

"In Richmond Annex," adds Doug Bruce, president of the Richmond Annex Neighborhood Council, "we don't think in racial terms. Everyone lives and works together here. It's definitely a place where you get to know your neighbor."

With awareness of potential, many residents who live in emerging neighborhoods and communities compare their own areas to neighborhoods that have already progressed further toward transition and improvement. John Greene, a school-teacher and recent home buyer in Candler Park says, "Changes could make this neighborhood the next Buckhead." St. Johns merchant Ken Gritzmacher chose that neighborhood because he saw St. Johns as having "the potential of the Hawthorne district." And new homeowners in low-priced Mount Rainer, Maryland, often speak of their community as the next Takoma Park. With so many examples of neighborhoods that have been revitalized, residents of emerging neighborhoods often point to these other successes as goals they themselves are planning to achieve.

Community Action

Of course, residents need more than positive attitudes, optimism, and community spirit to improve their neighborhoods and communities. They also need community action. So to find out whether a neighborhood or community is actually trying to make itself better, see what activities and accomplishments the residents have taken on for themselves. All emerging neighborhoods have some type of image or social problem that needs to be remedied. What positive steps are the residents putting into action?

In Brentwood, residents volunteer for "street corner vigil" to help stop vandalism and thefts, and they are fighting the liquor license renewals of two nightclubs that seem to bring unsavory elements into the community. In St. Johns, according to the Portland *Oregonian*, residents "are looking toward the future, working hard to overcome the stigma of its North Portland address." The active neighborhood association of St. Johns has organized foot patrols to help assure resident safety. "Community response toward the foot patrol has been extremely positive," says a recent home buyer. "If people believe their neighborhood is safe, they are out on the street and using their parks." The neighborhood also sponsors "the largest free jazz festival in the Northwest" featuring "a wealth of world-class jazz talent."

As of the mid 1980s, the SoBe (South Beach) area of Miami Beach, Florida, had deteriorated to the point where crack dealers and prostitutes had created an open-air market for drugs and sex. Derelicts and criminals from the Mariel boatlift filled the neighborhood's cheap hotels and efficiency apartments. Then Tony Goldman, "urban warrior" and New York entrepreneur, discovered SoBe. "I took a ride around the area and it was love at first sight. I was immediately smitten," Tony recalls.

Seeing potential, he then went to work. With friends, Tony began buying properties and fixing them up. He encouraged a police crackdown on the criminal elements. Others had also seen the potential for the area, including a prominent Miami resident who pushed successfully for a section of SoBe to be listed in the National Register of Historic Places. With progress in view, Tony Goldman next organized the Ocean Drive Association and lobbied the city to float $3 million in bonds. The money was used to further improve public areas, widen streets, and beautify Ocean Drive, the main thoroughfare of SoBe. Today, SoBe is well on its way to renewal. As one observer has said, "Tony Goldman put the chic back into SoBe." Madonna must agree. This pop star recently bought a home in a SoBe neighborhood.

Several years ago, in the community of Wheaton, George Baker and his wife, Donna, were surprised when they discovered a crack house operating just several doors down from them. At that point, George Baker knew somethng had to be done. The neighbors got together and formed a community watch group. "The difference now is like night and day," says George. "We think we're well on the way to renewal."

Realtor Frances Jason calls Wheaton "a community that has reclaimed itself." A recent home buyer, engineer and immigrant from the Ivory Coast, Kondombo, agrees. He says the social fabric of Wheaton reminds him of his hometown in Africa. "This was for me, a pleasure to have a community like this," he says.

Referring to the turnaround of Wheaton, homeowner Ann Hauser says, "You can clean it up. There is a way for it to be done. We did it, and it can be done in other places, too."

Renovation and New Construction

It's a sure sign of progress when residents cooperate with each other through community action to improve their neighborhoods. But turnaround also brings out individual efforts. In evaluating a neighborhood, find out whether individuals are making substantial investments in fix-up work, renovation, and even new construction.

Thad Williams, one of the codevelopers of Santa Ana Pines in Watts, says, "People would tell us, 'You're building these homes because the government's offering you lots of money.' We'd tell them, no, it's totally free market. They couldn't believe a bunch of black guys were going into Watts to make a profit without any government assistance."

Recall Wilma Haynes, chairman of the Watts Homeowner's Association, "All around I see people fixing up their houses, buying lots that had been vacant for years, taking pride [making financial investments] in their neighborhood again," she says.

For the past several years, Candler Park residents were worried about a proposed highway that would cut through the neighborhood. Now with the neighborhood battle against the highway won, homeowner Mike King says, "We're really going to kick our renovation plans into high gear."

Tony Powers, manager of a neighborhood hardware store, reports, "We get a lot of people from Candler Park fixing up and adding on." Local real estate agents point out that the neighborhood still has many handyman specials that are affordable for first-time buyers. As the *Atlanta Constitution* puts it, "Anyone willing to roll up their sleeves will find plenty of good buys in that area."

Gail Bluestone and Dianne Montagna recently combined forces to buy a new home in Sepulveda. "We found low prices on brand-new housing," says Gail. "I know the area has been marred by graffiti, and by people who haven't taken care of the area. But there's lots of new construction. As they clean up the area, it's going to bring in a different element of people. It will be like starting over again with a new community."

Something Special

Although not essential to neighborhood improvement and increasing home values, the popularity of an area also can be enhanced if the neighborhood has (or can create) something special about itself. This "something special" can be as simple as the sincere friendliness of St. Johns or Brentwood. It can be sophisticated such as the art deco architecture of South Beach. Or it could be the rural feeling—"It's like an oasis in the big city. We have owls living in our trees and all kinds of animals"—like Montecito Heights or Rogers Point. It can be the waterfront of Marina Bay, the ethnic diversity of Richmond Annex, the American heritage of the historical district in Annapolis, or the Victorians of Hyde Park.

As part of their efforts to create an improved neighborhood, some residents of Sepulveda have formed a new community and renamed it North Hill. In Maryland, Gaithersburg has changed its name to North Potomac, attempting to capitalize on the prestige of its nearby neighbor. Some residents of North Hollywood got the official name of part of their community changed to Valley Village. "With the name change," says Realtor Jerry Burns, "residents take more pride in their neighborhood."

YOU CAN DISCOVER
AN AFFORDABLE NEIGHBORHOOD

Every medium-to-large-sized city in the United States has a good selection of lower-priced "comeback" neighborhoods that first-time buyers can call home. Mike Chen, Navy petty officer, recently bought a home in such a neighborhood. Mike explains his choice: "High housing prices are forcing more younger people and families into the low-cost areas of town. Those new homeowners take pride in their properties. They fix them up and improve the neighborhood. This improvement then attracts more new owners. With more buyers wanting to come back to the neighborhood, prices are pushed up. I'm looking forward to good appreciation. I think my area's a real sleeper."

Real estate advisors used to tell first-time home buyers, "Find the best neighborhood, then achieve affordability by investing in a fixer." That's still good advice. The only problem is that in many high-priced cities, fixers in the "best" neighborhoods may be priced anywhere from $150,000 to $300,000. Without creative financing or special-assistance programs, these homes lie beyond reach for many first-time buyers. So at least for the remainder of the 1990s, increasing numbers of renters will follow this advice: To achieve both affordability and price appreciation, discover a low-to-moderate-priced neighborhood that's a real sleeper—a neighborhood that's primed for revitalization turnaround, and renewed popularity.

OTHER LOCATION POSSIBILITIES

As you've just seen, to achieve affordability and investment gains, locate an emerging, turnaround neighborhood. In addition to that option, though, here are several other locational possibilities you might look into.

New-Home Developments

As mentioned earlier, during the 1980s most developers and home builders went upscale. By 1989, the average size of a new home in many areas of the country exceeded 2,000 square feet. In addition, luxury items such as hot tubs, saunas, gourmet kitchens, multiple fireplaces, tile floors and enormous master bedroom suites with king-size bathrooms became almost standard fare. Of course, all of these extras drove up the cost of housing.

Now many home builders have switched strategies. They are building new homes with a back-to-basics approach. The name of their game is affordability. To increase affordability for first-time buyers, not only have builders found ways to slash building costs, but many are also helping out with financing (see also chapter 5).

If new-home builders are active in your area, you can probably locate developments that offer one or more of the following types of assistance to make borrowing and buying easier: low or no down payments, sweat equity, lease options, buydowns, below-market long-term financing, no closing costs, deferred monthly payments, easy qualifying, below-market pricing, accessory apartments or other income-producing property features (two master bedrooms, garage apartments, finished lower levels), guaranteed buy-backs, mortgage credit certificates, and mortgage bond programs.

In fact, I've seen builder promotions that offer just about every kind of financing assistance that's introduced in this book. And, even if new-home builders in your area don't feature financial assistance in their promotions, given the current (but rapidly disappearing) buyer's market in many cities, your Realtor might be able to negotiate a builder finance plan for you.

Moving to a new-home development may mean a longer commute. But if your choice comes down to renting close in or owning farther out, don't pass up ownership without at least shopping new-home developments.

Ron Egar and his wife, Beverly, were renting in the close-in DePaul area of Chicago. Although the Egars preferred to buy in this neighborhood, they found nothing they liked that they could afford. Ron says, "I tried to convince Bev we should look for a home in the suburbs, but she wanted no part of it. Then one Sunday we were driving around and I took her to see some outlying new-home developments. 'Wow,' she said, 'I didn't know we could get so much home for our money out here.' After that Sunday drive, Bev really got excited and wanted to buy a new home."

"Now that we're here," says Bev, "we love it. It's quiet. We feel like we're in seventh heaven. When we're home, it's like drop-out time."

Edge Cities

Although buying in the suburbs and commuting to downtown (central business district) is still common, millions of Americans have moved both their homes and their jobs to outlying areas. A recent article in *American Demographics* reports, "Edge cities are the new standard of American urban development. Every single American city that is growing is sprouting multiple urban cores. Edge cities have more jobs, more office space, and more people than the central cities they surround."

Anthony Downs, economist and researcher at the prestigious

Brookings Institution, has found that "employers follow the labor force." A move to the suburbs may not mean a long commute for long. Taking a look at this trend, *U.S. News & World Report* advises, "Buyers on the tightest budgets should consider bedroom communities on the outskirts of fast-growing, high cost urban areas. Prices are still relatively low and the potential for appreciation high."

Lower-Cost Cities

Claire Timmons was a registered nurse working and living on Staten Island in New York City. She was earning $38,000 a year. Claire wanted to buy a home for herself and her two daughters. Unfortunately, the homes she looked at on Staten Island were priced upwards of $180,000. No way did Claire think she could afford such a home.

So Claire picked up and moved to Gainesville, Florida. Since her new nursing job in Gainesville paid $27,000, Claire lost $11,000 in salary. But with much lower taxes (income, sales, property), Claire easily qualified to buy a new three-bedroom, two-bath home less than 15 minutes from the hospital where she worked. The price of her new home was $69,000. Because Claire was a first-time buyer, she also was able to get a below-market mortgage interest rate through Florida's mortgage revenue bond program.

Every so often, publications such as *U.S. News & World Report*, *Money Magazine* and *USA Today* review and compare home prices throughout the United States. If you know you can't own the kind of home you want where you're currently living, and you don't want to use one or more of the available techniques to make borrowing or buying easier, then consider relocation. No one should get stuck in a place as a long-term renter.

"Vacation" Homes

Our most recent recession (and some overbuilding) has brought distress to many vacation home markets. According to a poll by one of the nation's largest real estate companies, "Home prices in many up-and-coming vacation areas remain relatively low, while the potential for double-digit price increases will be better than normal over the next three years."

Think about it. Perhaps your first home should be a vacation home. Do you live within one hour or two of a resort or retirement area, or an area where second homes predominate? Carrie and Kevin Kendall work in Charleston, South Carolina. They recently bought a home in the nearby resort area of Seabrook Island. "Due to the large number of homes for sale," says Carrie, "we were able to get a great deal for the money. Besides, the area is so beautiful. It's really an escape for us. We don't even mind the drive in too much. Kevin and I both have flexible work schedules. We've set up a computer, laser printer, fax, photocopier, and business telephone in our home. Some weeks we only go to the office a couple of times."

"The way we figure it," adds Kevin, "with the population getting older, and the older population getting wealthier, homes in retirement-vacation areas like ours are almost sure to appreciate substantially. Even if ours doesn't, we won't have any regrets. We were tired of renting and wanted to become home-owners. And we couldn't dream of a better place to live."

8 CHOOSE YOUR HOME

Phil and Lisa Chandler faced a critical decision. They could continue to rent an apartment in the close-in neighborhood of Hacienda Heights. Or they could move further out and buy their own home. The Chandlers chose to own.

"Where we live now has some inconveniences," says Phil. "But we are confident we made the right decision. The area is very nice and the neighbors are terrific. Even though buying meant we had to sell our ski boat, borrow money from our parents, and ask Lisa's dad to cosign our note, we have no regrets. There's really nothing that compares to the satisfaction we get from owning our own home."

Lori and Todd McMann, too, faced what seemed to be a difficult choice. "We were tired of flushing rent money down the toilet every month," says Lori. "We had a good combined income. But we were having trouble coming up with the down payment. Without ready cash, we didn't think we could get the kind of house we wanted. So in the end we decided to buy a townhome with a low-down-payment VA mortgage assumption. It's not our dream house. But it is a good start. The best feeling, though, is coming home at night, looking around our home and saying, 'Hey, we own this. This is ours.' There's simply nothing like the feeling you get when you own your own home."

As a single mother, Gwen Hale had wanted to own a home in which to raise her six-year-old daughter. Because Gwen worked as a legal secretary, she was operating on a tight budget. "I talked to a number of real estate agents," says Gwen, "but all I got was disappointment. Then one day I passed by an open house. It was a small corner house with bay windows, two bedrooms, one bath with walk-in shower, and the most beautiful fireplace I had ever seen. It was my good fortune," Gwen adds, "the Realtor at the open house turned out to be someone who was really willing to work with me. She knew how much I wanted the house and went beyond the call of duty to get me qualified. Surprisingly, though, it's not the house I like the most. It's ownership," says Gwen. "Owning my own home has given me more confidence. It has made me realize that with determination and some sacrifice, I can reach my goals."

FIRST, CHOOSE OWNERSHIP

In his highly acclaimed book, *Ideas Have Consequences*, Richard Weaver calls property ownership, especially home ownership, "the last metaphysical right." In a sometimes chaotic world, Weaver writes, home ownership provides a sanctuary; it promotes thrift, responsibility, and civic virtue; and it embraces the soul. Home ownership is far larger than itself.

Most often, we speak of our homes as investments, or as comfortable places to live. But as Richard Weaver points out, the most important meaning of home ownership is transcendental. It's wrapped up in the feelings expressed by the Chandlers, the McManns, Gwen Hale, and the more than 150 million other Americans who can say along with Lori McMann, "Hey, we own this place. This is ours."

After you embark on your journey toward home ownership, you may get discouraged along the way. You may not be able to find the exact home you want. Your commute may be long. The neighborhood may not seem to match your ideal. The house may be smaller or older than the home in your dreams. But if your home search (introduction to market realities) does frustrate or disappoint you, keep in mind one critical fact: Ninety percent of the satisfaction of owning your own home comes from ownership itself.

You may be tempted to say, "We can't afford to buy the home we want," or, "Sure we could buy, but not where we'd really like to live." While there's a real possibility that this type of negative self-talk indicates lack of knowledge (hidden neighborhoods, alternative home finance plans, or improved financial planning), most important, it misses the idea that ownership itself produces feelings and satisfactions that transcend the particular home and neighborhood you choose.

Unlike the physical characteristics of a house, you can't see, touch, or experience these feelings before you become a home-owner. But the feelings are real. So if you want to stop renting, first decide to own. Don't concede ownership for the want of a third bedroom, a double-car garage, a chic neighborhood, or any other specific features you might place on your "must have" list. Don't become another Anne Lange or Sam Sloan (from our beginning chapter). Make ownership your first priority. Then mix and match your finance plan, buying tactics, neighborhood, and chosen home in a way that permits you to achieve this goal.

SHOP WITH AN OPEN MIND

After you commit to ownership, you must develop priorities that can guide your search. The difficulty here is that until you have searched the market, looked at different homes and neighbor-hoods, and started to compare specific homes, prices and terms, you won't really know the trade-offs and possibilities you face. That's why so many home buyers eventually buy a home (or into a neighborhood) that differs from their original ideas.

When you begin your search, you may think you prefer a three-bedroom, two-bath ranch in Rolling Meadows. But even if you find such a home, you may decide to pass it up in favor of a fixer-upper Victorian in Rosemont.

Think of Valerie de Pourtales from an earlier chapter. She began her home search hoping she could stretch to buy a home that met her most important priorities. But because Valerie and her Realtor kept an open mind, they worked out a way Valerie could afford two houses—one of which even had the extras that sat far down on her list of priorities, like a Jacuzzi, attached garage, and built-in storage. "If I hadn't kept an open mind," Valerie admitted, "I never would have even looked at this type of property."

When your Realtor asks you what kind of home you're looking for, don't be too eager to paint some idealistic picture. Let the Realtor know you're open to suggestions. As real estate sales agent and author Joan Meyers says, "Experienced agents—those agents who have shown hundreds or even thousands of houses—know that most buyers are searching for something they cannot describe."

So, you've got to walk a fine line. You must develop some good ideas about your priorities. Your agent can't work in the dark. But on the other hand, don't automatically shut out potentially workable options. Shop with an open mind.

EVALUATE POTENTIAL AND POSSIBILITIES

"I wanted to buy a home for all the usual reasons," says Jo Mancusco. "Paying too much for rent. Not enough space for all my stuff. Bumping up against neighbors and parental landlords. Tired of pouring time, effort and money into each rental only to lose it all when I moved on to the next." Jo says that after deciding to buy, she followed the recommendation of a friend and called a Realtor named Wyn. "Feeling totally out of my element, I went to Wyn's Montclair office," Jo continued. "I babbled about tenancy-in-common, lofts, and my top, top price. Wyn did not blink; instead, she smiled delightedly and said, 'I love a challenge.'"

Like Jo Mancuso and her agent, you may find it a challenge to locate a home that immediately ignites your hot spot. But before you turn thumbs down on a home, ask yourself: Are you reacting to the property as a whole? Or, are you reacting to certain negative features (odor, color scheme, furnishings, darkness, poor condition, unkempt yard or exterior, home size too small or too large, rooms too small or too large, irregular floor plan, grease and grime, structural defects)?

If the total home can't work for you, tell your agent why and move on. If you object only to certain defects or drawbacks, explore possibilities. Some problems you can eliminate. Some you can alleviate. Some you can learn to live with. Others you may actually be able to turn to your advantage.

When Lisa and Phil Chandler bought in the suburbs, Lisa traded a three-mile trip to work for a 25-mile commute. "At first," says Lisa, "I dreaded the thought of commuting 35 minutes each way. But then I discovered that our new community's local library has a great selection of audio cassette tapes. Since I don't get to read as much as I would like, during the commute I listen to best-sellers on my car's cassette deck. From the tapes, I'm also learning Spanish, negotiating skills, and sales closing techniques. All of these will help me in my job."

In his book, *Awaken the Giant Within*, Tony Robbins emphasizes that "our self-imposed, arbitrary rules control our responses every day of our lives." Tony goes on to say, "Most of us have created numerous ways to feel bad, and only a few ways to feel good. I never fail to be amazed," says Tony, "at the overwhelming number of people whose rules wire them for pain."

Now ask yourself, "Do my rules empower or disempower me?" To get what you want, Tony encourages you "to develop rules that move you to take action, that cause you to feel joy, that cause you to follow through—not rules that stop you short!"

Think about Tony's advice when you look for a home and neighborhood. Don't impose rigid and arbitrary rules to your search. Stay flexible. Don't "wire yourself for pain" by setting far more ways to reject than accept. Explore how disadvantages (poor condition) can be turned into advantages (opportunity to create value); how costs (commuting) can produce benefits (time for self-improvement); or how problems (out of your price range) can be reformulated as possibilities (potential for room rental, accessory apartment, or co-ownership).

To a large degree, your success in choosing a home will be determined by the rules you set to guide your search. Keep an open mind; don't arbitrarily reject; fully spotlight, list, and compare trade-offs. Never view a problem without also weighing in its offsetting benefits or opportunities.

"If I compare my home to an imaginary dream house," writes Dr. Theodore Rubin in *Overcoming Indecisiveness*, "my house comes off poorly and I destroy any chance of enjoying it. On the other hand, if I compare my home to other choices that actually exist, it will likely come out well in terms of any *real* specifications a home requires to be comfortable. This is a true luxury; one I can appreciate in reality."

MATCH POSSIBILITIES TO PRIORITIES

When you fail to consider your options, you suffer from *option blindness*. Just as fatal, too many possibilities can create *option confusion* or *analysis paralysis*. After looking at different types of homes, neighborhoods, and price ranges, you might be ready to throw your hands up and shout, "We just don't know what to do."

You must guard against this dilemma. How? "The key to success in home buying," advises Realtor Joan Meyers, "is to act on the market. Don't let it act on you." You've got to match the possibilities you've discovered to the priorities you believe important.

OWNERSHIP: THE FIRST PRIORITY

As I have emphasized, to stop wasting money on rent, you must rank ownership as your first priority. Focus on the personal security, the financial security, and the transcendental satisfaction that will come when you're able to say, "I own this—this is mine."

From time to time, I've heard nearly everyone I know who works in real estate sales, home buyer counseling, or mortgage finance remark in one way or another, "Failure to save, plan, and prepare are the major reasons that block people from buying their first home." The block is not simply high prices. Too many renters fail to develop a buying (and financing) strategy. Even in higher-priced areas of the country, the great majority of honest, income-earning Americans can own their own homes. But to achieve this goal, you must position home ownership as your first priority—in terms of both goal setting and financial planning.

Placing ownership itself as your first priority also helps you in another way. Recall how chapter 6 explained why you need to carefully select a Realtor to work with. That chapter, though, slid over the fact that a good agent must also choose you. All top-notch Realtors have to manage their time as productively as possible. Naturally, they must deliver their greatest service to people who really want to buy—not those who are merely "looky lu's."

To receive full service, you need to show your Realtor you're not merely a "tire kicker." The more seriously you plan your finances, gather market information, give your Realtor feedback on the homes you've viewed, and set a time frame for buying, the better the service your agent will be willing and able to provide.

Stated most simply: As your first priority, commit to the goal of home ownership. Then, once you've committed to ownership, you'll need to screen properties according to several other priorities. By comparing homes and neighborhoods, you will discover the trade-offs home buyers in your area face. With this information, you can figure out which priorities you want to emphasize. Are you willing to trade off a home in move-in condition for the opportunity to create value? Home size and condition for convenience to work? Neighborhood for affordability? Here's where your personal preferences will guide your home buying decision.

Always remember, though, home buying requires choice. And choice means excluding as well as including. As Dr. Rubin points out, "The desire to realize all options blocks the decision-making process by making true choice impossible. Wanting it all, in fact, often destroys the possibility of getting any of it. Wanting it all leads to the paralyzing illusion that if you delay, eventually a comprehensive solution will come along that will combine the advantages of all available options so that, in effect, you will compromise nothing."

While only you can identify, define, and rank the priorities that will guide your home buying decision, here are several you might want to talk through with your Realtor:

- Affordability
- Neighborhood
- Appreciation potential
- Bargain price

- Create value
- Emotional appeal
- Comfortable place to live

AFFORDABILITY

Nearly every first-time home buyer must give some attention to affordability. Naturally, the more cash you have to invest in a home, and the larger the amount of monthly payments you can afford, the more you can push this priority closer to the bottom of your list. With fewer constraints on your budget, you can place more emphasis on neighborhood, home size and condition, appreciation potential, or other priorities.

On the other hand, for many renters, achieving ownership will mean giving top priority to the two central questions of affordability: (1) How much cash-to-close is required? and (2) How much are the monthly payments? If affordability ranks high on your list of priorities, you might direct your search toward low-equity mortgage assumptions, new homes with builder incentives, fixer-uppers, homes that are offered with favorable seller financing, or entry-level condominiums and townhouses.

When, as a college student, I first started buying small rental houses and apartment buildings, I ranked affordability just under ownership. As long as a property was priced right and could be purchased on terms I could afford, I didn't insist on tough criteria about property condition or neighborhood. Considering my limited credit and finances, I knew if I were going to own, I couldn't be too picky about other things.

After I completed graduate school and began to move along in my career, affordability became less important. My priorities changed and potential choices grew. The lesson is simply this: How much money you have and how much income you earn are not the most important factors that lead to home ownership. What's most important is that you locate homes and home finance plans that fit your personal situation.

Experience proves that the sooner you get started in home ownership, the more likely you will own the home you want at age 40, 50, or 65.

NEIGHBORHOOD

Most home buyers highly rank neighborhood and community. More than likely you also carry strong feelings about location. And fortunately, if you live in a city with moderate home prices, you can probably find an affordable neighborhood that offers what you most want such as good schools, location close to work, convenience to shopping and recreation, pleasant surroundings, and low crime.

But if you live in a high-cost city, you may have to trade off some neighborhood characteristics for the higher priorities of ownership and affordability. If your choice comes down to owning in a less prestigious location or renting in a more favored location, your longer-term personal and financial interests will most surely be better served by owning.

Admittedly, I'm biased. Through my teaching I have met so many renters in their late 30s and early to mid-40s who could have become homeowners at some point 8 to 15 years ago. Yet they kept putting it off. Why? Because many were unwilling to trade off location for ownership. They didn't want to commute. They didn't want to move into a turnaround neighborhood. Some didn't want to give up the prestige and convenience of neighborhoods like Los Angeles, Westside; Washington, D.C., Georgetown; San Francisco, Marina District; Chicago, Lincoln Park; or New York's Upper East Side.

Regardless of the specific reasons, nearly all now regret not buying when they were younger because they have lost tens of thousands (in some cases, hundreds of thousands) of dollars of equity buildup. They see with admiration (or envy) the homes now owned by their friends who did buy years ago—homes that those who waited now can't afford. Even more disheartening, homeowners who bought years ago are making monthly mortgage payments (especially with refinancing at lower interest rates) that now cost less than the rents paid by those who are still renting. As it always turns out, long-term homeowners enjoy far better housing at far less cost than long-term renters.

For these reasons, become a homeowner today, even if it means accepting a smaller home or a less desirable location. Remember, homes in Candler Park sold for $18,000 to $25,000 in the late 1970s—well within the means of most renters at the time. Today these homes (with fix-up work) sell for $100,000 to $150,000. Ten to 15 years from now, all throughout the United States, similar stories will be told. The only differences will be the names of the neighborhoods—and, of course, their much higher prices.

APPRECIATION POTENTIAL

Let's say you could choose between a home in Rosemont or a home in Pinehaven. The Rosemont home will give you a great location and a comfortable place to live. During the next five years, you expect this neighborhood to appreciate about 4 percent a year.

In contrast, in Pinehaven you'll give up one or more features you might want such as pleasant surroundings, convenience, house size, livability, or condition. But during the coming five years, Pinehaven homes will appreciate at the much higher rate of 10 percent a year. Would you choose Rosemont or Pinehaven?

If you answered Pinehaven, perhaps you should place appreciation potential high on your list of priorities. Ideally, you would like to find good affordability, location, livability, and above-average price gains all in the same home. In some cities, though, you may have to trade off one or more of these priorities. Seldom do all homes and neighborhoods grow in value at the same rate of appreciation. So if strong price gains appeal to you, try to ferret out your town's most promising "hot neighborhoods."

BUY AT A BARGAIN PRICE

You may also be able to achieve good appreciation if you shop for a bargain-priced home. At any given time, maybe 4 to 10 percent of the homes up for sale can be bought for less than their market value. You might look for bargains among motivated sellers, probate sales, auctions, homes owned by lenders (REOs), foreclosures, and builder closeouts.

Don't incorrectly assume, though, that homes available through auctions, builder closeouts, motivated sellers, or other bargain sources necessarily represent a bargain. As in any other real estate purchase, don't buy without the help of a Realtor or other knowledgeable real estate advisor. Bargain properties may have title problems, hidden physical defects, or outstanding liens. They may not even sell at a true bargain price.

For example, 20 to 25 percent of auctioned homes sell for prices equal to or greater than their market value. Sixty to 70 percent sell at prices 3 to 15 percent less than their market value. Only a relatively small portion of auctioned properties actually sell at deeply discounted prices. Often auction sales may look like bargains because the homes sell for far less than their original asking prices. These asking prices in many (not all) cases, though, may have been pure wishful thinking.

Nevertheless, if you do decide to rank bargain price as a top priority, I'm confident you will be able to achieve this goal with a concerted effort. Just shop carefully, get good advice, and be prepared to push other priorities further down your list of requirements.

CREATE VALUE

Recall Suzanne Brangham, the San Francisco home renovator and author of *Housewise* whom you met in an earlier chapter. Suzanne turned her ability to renovate homes and create value into a net worth of several million dollars. Suzanne says she is frequently asked, "Is this a good time to buy a home?" She answers, "There is no wrong time to buy a home. Regardless of the market, regardless of interest rates, I've bought and resold my homes for a profit through good times and bad—every year for the past 15 years." Suzanne goes on to say, "If you're patient and careful in your selection of a home, you can find a good buy and sell at a profit. Of course, you must beautifully improve your house. But if you've got quality, you'll sell. It makes absolutely no difference what day, month, or year it is."

Although many home buyers shop for fixers as part of their affordability strategy, some (like Suzanne) evaluate fixers primarily for their profit potential. When Suzanne began investing in homes, she didn't ask, "Will this home perfectly suit my needs for a comfortable and convenient place to live?" Nor did she forecast long-term rates of appreciation. To Suzanne, the question, "Can I improve this home and turn a quick profit?" became her motivating priority.

Would this same strategy work for you? If you can't now afford the home you want, buy a home you can afford. Then create value. By repeating this process and reinvesting your profits (tax-free, even), there's no reason you can't eventually move up to your ideal home. For some home buyers, creating value ranks as one of their most important reasons for investing in a home. They know that the sacrifices and trade-offs they make today will pay large future rewards.

EMOTIONAL APPEAL

It's sometimes said, "Home buyers buy only what they can see. They have no imagination." It would probably be more accurate to say that people buy only what they can feel. More than for any specific architectural style, size, condition, floor plan, or room count, most home buyers choose homes that generate the most favorable emotional impact.

That's why so many buyers can't fully describe the home they will actually buy, or they buy a home that doesn't match the description they have previously recited. No matter how many times you hear the advice, *act rationally*, the chances are you will *react emotionally*.

There's nothing wrong with this. Becoming a first-time homeowner ranks as one of life's most emotional experiences. Home buying often brings out potentially conflicting emotions such as fear, excitement, romance, pride, frustration, envy, disappointment, opportunity, joy, security, and self-esteem. In many ways, your home projects your ego and self-image. Don't try to ignore your emotions. Try to sort through and understand them.

Don't let fleeting negative emotions (frustration, disappointment, fear) take priority over long-term positive feelings like pride of ownership and financial security. More specifically, when you look at a home, identify the features that give you positive feelings. Then identify features that turn you off. Talk through these feelings with your Realtor. Here's where good real estate agents can really help. By tuning into your feelings (your likes and dislikes), your agent can better select homes that appeal to you. At the same time, by exploring the "whys" of your reactions to homes, your agent can suggest ways to overcome your objections and find satisfying alternatives. In addition, once you've discussed priorities with your Realtor, he or she should keep you focused on those that are most important.

As veteran Realtor Ann Freedman tells other sales agents, "Home buyers don't care what you know until they know you care. You must empathize with buyers. Cater to the buyer's personality, while submerging your own. See the homes and buying situation through their eyes. Focus on what they think and feel." Don't try to sidestep your emotions. Instead, bring them into the open. Talk out your feelings with your Realtor.

COMFORTABLE PLACE TO LIVE

For many home buyers, "a comfortable place to live" ranks as one of their top priorities. In choosing a home, these buyers focus on floor plan, room count, room sizes, color schemes, natural light, internal traffic patterns, storage capacity, emotional appeal, time and expense of maintenance and upkeep, and assorted amenities (fireplace, deck, pool, garage, hot tub, built-in appliances).

By now, though, I hope you can see that "comfortable place to live" stands as just one potential priority among many others. How heavily you weigh this goal depends on the amount of time you plan to spend at home, the number of years (or months) you plan to own the home before you move up, and your present range of affordability. If your goal is to create value, generate income with the home, or achieve high rates of appreciation—or maybe if you rank neighborhood as a top priority—you should be willing to ease up on finding a home that includes all the creature comforts that meet your ideal.

DECIDE WHAT'S IMPORTANT FOR THE FUTURE YOU WANT

Confusion among priorities as well as the unrealistic desire to "have it all" blocks most renters from buying. The old saying, "A confused mind always says no," reflects a great deal of truth. Therefore, after setting ownership as your first priority, think through all the benefits you would like to realize from home ownership, then rank them. Don't just define your priorities in terms of the home features you would like. Maybe you should give more emphasis to affordability, appreciation potential, the chance to create value, or buying at a bargain price.

Remember, your first home won't be your last. Your most important question is, "What is the best decision I can make today that will move me closer to the future I want?"

NEGOTIATE LIKE A PRO

Once you've found a home you'd like to own, you need to negotiate a purchase agreement. Many first-time home buyers approach purchase negotiations with uncertainty and nervousness. They don't quite know what to expect. Others falsely believe that a "skillful" negotiator dips into a bag of tricks and pulls out deceptive techniques like lowballing, weasel clauses, running a bluff, shotgunning, "dressing to impress" (pretending to be something you're not), bad-mouthing (deflating the owners' high opinion of their home), asking for the moon and the stars, and eleventh-hour surprises (at the last minute before closing, insisting on contract changes in your favor). One book on real estate negotiating even advises, "Remember you are in a war and you must use every weapon available to win."

These hardball tactics might seem to make sense to those immoral enough to use them, but experience shows just the opposite. To negotiate like a pro, you don't need sophisticated expertise, theatrics, or deception. In most home-buying negotiations, you succeed by sticking to a few basic principles:

- Develop a cooperative attitude.
- Learn the sellers' objectives.
- Clarify your own goals and priorities.
- Do your homework.
- Make a solid first offer.
- Don't just compromise—conciliate.

Develop a Cooperative Attitude

Bob Woolf, agent, attorney, and past negotiator for many well-known figures such as Larry Bird, Gene Shalit, Larry King, and Joe Montana, says,

> When I enter a negotiation, my attitude is, 'I'm going to make a deal.' I don't start with a negative thought or word. I try to foster a spirit of cooperation. I want the other party to feel that I'm forthright, cheerful, confident, and determined to reach a fair agreement.
>
> When you're upbeat and positive, people will respond to you in kind. And when you are in the right frame of mind, you are more likely to feel you are going to reach your goal. If I'm sufficiently sensitive to the other party, I firmly believe they will be predisposed to make an agreement with me. To a degree, your attitude will become a self-fulfilling prophecy.

Bob Woolf's professional advice applies whether you are negotiating a big-time sports contract or a purchase agreement for a home—especially a purchase agreement for a home. Usually, you're wise to display a cooperative "Let's reach an agreement" attitude. Act in good faith. Play by the rules of courtesy. You want to buy a home. The sellers want to sell a home. Your best chance for success comes when all parties cooperate to help each other.

Learn the Sellers' Objectives

To find common ground for cooperation, find out as much as you can about the sellers' needs. Why are they selling? What time pressures do they face? Have they planned a moving date? Have they agreed to buy another home? Are they in a position to carry back financing? How much equity do they have in their home? Find out the sellers' fears, wants, and "have-to-haves." Are they really motivated to sell?

Everyone knows that buying a home arouses strong emotions. But so does selling a home. The sellers may be leaving friends and neighbors. Their children may be losing friends and classmates. Over the years, the sellers may have invested heart and soul to maintain their home, cultivate a flower garden, or redecorate and remodel. The sellers may have years of fond memories attached to the home. The more you learn about the sellers' financial, personal, and emotional needs, the better you and your Realtor can steer a cooperative path for negotiations.

One last point: Note that people from different cultures approach personal negotiations from different perspectives. If you are buying a home from sellers whose ethnic or religious background differs from yours, stay alert to how these differences may affect their expectations. Celia Young, a consultant in cross-cultural business etiquette and negotiating skills, says, "When doing business cross-culturally, we need to be aware of our own reactions and interactions. . . . That way we will be more sensitive to possible misunderstandings."

Clarify Your Own Goals and Priorities

After you have learned as much as possible about the sellers' needs and selling objectives, make sure you clarify your own goals and priorities. You can't get what you want unless you know what you want.

Try to match the things you want (or are willing to give) with the sellers' objectives. Are you willing to delay closing until the sellers find another home? Are you willing to meet the sellers' price in exchange for terms? How much cash do the sellers really *need*, not merely want? What are your financial abilities and financial limits? The more common ground you find to stand on, the more likely you will be able to reach an agreement.

Do Your Homework

To negotiate effectively, you must understand the home and the current market. Know the features of the home, its relative desirability, recent selling prices of other homes in the neighborhood, recent sales activity (buyer's market or seller's market), normal terms of financing, and typical closing costs and procedures. Why? Because negotiations won't center exclusively on either your needs and wants or the sellers' needs and wants. Negotiations will operate within the context of market conditions.

Sometimes sellers say something like this: "We spent $20,000 to add on a den and remodel the kitchen and bathrooms. We have to get our money back for these improvements." But if you don't think the sellers' improvements add $20,000 of market value to the home, don't pay it. The sellers aren't real sellers. Until they price their home in line with the market, they are wasting everybody's time, including their own.

On other occasions, though, it's buyers who live in a dream world. They may have attended a "get rich quick" real estate seminar. These seminars often mislead buyers into believing they can buy homes for 70 cents on the dollar. Seminar leaders tell the gullible to find "motivated" sellers who will rush to give them this kind of deal. Or they advise buyers to use the shotgun approach—make 100 lowball offers and surely one or two owners will accept. (Think how much time it would take to fully inspect 100 properties, value them, and then submit 100 offers.)

Both approaches are out of touch with the way homes are actually bought and sold. Good negotiators tie their wants to reality. When either buyers or sellers unrealistically inflate their expectations, they usually end up disappointed. Understanding market realities not only helps you shop for a home, it helps you negotiate a fair agreement.

Make a Solid First Offer

What price should you *first* offer for the home you've chosen? In theory, the answer to that question is easy. Don't make your first offer too low or too high. Sellers often have their egos, their emotions, and their self-image wrapped up in their home. They're likely to take an unrealistically low offer as an insult. It destroys good will and shuts down their urge to cooperate with you. "Since it's quite obvious a 'lowballer' is trying to take advantage of the sellers," says Realtor Brenda Flagg, "the sellers don't come back with any counteroffer at all."

Norm Flynn, former president of the National Association of

Realtors, agrees. "An angry seller will take a ballpoint pen and write 'REJECTED!' across the offer forms in big capital letters," says Norm. "Or, the sellers will grab the forms, rip them up, and throw them in the nearest wastebasket."

Just as you don't want to offer too little, neither do you want to offer too much. Ideally, you should aim for an opening price bid that's high enough to pique the sellers' interest, but somewhat less than the price you actually expect the sellers will accept. You want the sellers to see you as a serious buyer. In other words, your first offer should look like a solid, yet conservative, offer.

As a practical matter, though, you can't draw a fine line between a lowball offer and a solid, conservative offer. It depends on local market conditions, local negotiating practices, and the sellers' needs, motivations, and perceptions. You've got to rely on the advice of your Realtor, your own reading of the sellers, and the prices at which other homes in the neighborhood have recently sold. Although many exceptions exist, you might consider offering 3 to 6 percent less than the lowest price at which you might realistically be able to buy the home. Then raise your offer gradually as you move through various offers and counteroffers. Avoid the tendency to immediately "split the difference."

Let's say the sellers are asking $89,500 for their home. Based on your study of comparable sales and the sellers' goals and motivations, you figure a realistic selling price for the home should be $84,000 to $86,000. Since you would like to buy at the low end of that range, you open with an offer of $81,000 or $82,000. To most sellers, this offer would be high enough to get them negotiating. Regardless of the price the sellers counter with, however, increase your offer slowly. Don't automatically agree to split the difference. At this price level, an increase of $500 to $750 would be reasonable. Then as you continue to negotiate, ease upward as necessary toward $84,000.

Don't Just Compromise—Conciliate

Throughout your negotiations, don't forget—you are not negotiating price, you are negotiating an *agreement*. Don't let negotiations focus on price alone. Don't just compromise—conciliate. Look for other parts of the agreement that may be important to you or the sellers. Besides price, here are some other negotiating points you can use to get the sellers to accept your offer:

Relieve the Sellers' Anxiety: Sellers worry that their sale won't close for some reason or another. The more you can assure the sellers that you're solid buyers who are willing and able to close, the more they may be willing to accept a lower price. To relieve seller anxiety, try one or more of these techniques:

1. Increase the amount of your earnest money deposit.

2. Produce a *preapproval* letter from a mortgage lender.

3. If you're making a large down payment, emphasize that fact. Large down payments increase credibility. If you've got it, use it to boost your position.

4. Get your Realtor to emphasize the strength of your character, stability in your job and community, how well you will take care of the home, or other positive personal factors.

5. Avoid weasel clauses in your offer. A weasel clause is any clause that lets you "weasel out" of a contract without obligation. One of the easiest and most obvious weasel clauses states, "This offer is subject to the approval of our attorney." If you need to consult an attorney (or Uncle Harry), it's best to do it before you begin negotiations. (In some states, by custom, attorneys routinely get involved in negotiating home purchase agreements. Nevertheless, the same advice holds. The firmer your offer, the more likely the sellers will treat you as a serious buyer and increase their willingness to make concessions to work toward an agreement.)

6. Avoid indefinite contingency clauses: "Offer subject to borrowing $10,000 from our parents"; or, "Offer subject to our landlord releasing us from our lease"; or, sometimes move-up buyers write into their offer, "Subject to the sale of our current home." Clauses like these raise the sellers' doubts, increase their anxiety, and generate reluctance to accept your offer.

7. When you do write a contingency clause into the contract, make it definite and as short-term as possible. "Buyers will secure a property inspection report within five days." Or, "Buyers agree to submit mortgage loan application within 48 hours." Or, "Sellers are released from obligation

if buyers do not produce a letter of mortgage loan approval within 30 days." These clauses indicate you're not going to drag your feet through the transaction.

8. Make your contingency clauses realistic. Don't condition your purchase on finding mortgage money at 8 percent if market rates are at 9.5 percent. Don't require a 27-year-old house to be free of all defects.

Just remember, the firmer your offer, the more willing the sellers may be to accept less than they originally had in mind. Plan your offer with no more escape hatches than you need (but no fewer, either). Many sellers will trade a lower price for the peace of mind of a near-certain sale.

Possession Date and Closing Date: How soon do the sellers prefer to close? When do the sellers want to give possession? Home buying and selling often calls for a balancing act. Sometimes sellers need to speed things up. On other occasions they may want to close quickly, but delay turning the house over to you until after they have bought another home. Or the sellers may want to keep their children in the same school until the end of the term. It's possible the sellers may even want to give possession before they close. (For example, to obtain favorable tax treatment of their gain from the sale, the sellers may want to schedule closing after their 55th birthday.) Before you begin negotiating, find out whether the sellers strongly prefer any specific dates for closing and possession. If they do, you may have a bargaining chip for a reduced price.

Nominal Price versus Effective Price: Some sellers may be tough to negotiate with on price. They know the lowest price they will accept and won't budge further. Sometimes price stands as a symbol of the sellers' egos. If you run up against sellers like this, you might agree to the price they insist on. At the same time, you can ask the sellers for concessions that reduce the effective price you'll pay. For example:

1. The sales price could include personal property such as the washer and dryer, kitchen appliances, window blinds, an oriental rug, or that antique buffet that's too large for

the sellers' new home. Maybe the sellers will throw in that 1965 Ford Mustang that's sitting in the garage.

2.   The agreement could shift more of the closing costs to the sellers, including some of your mortgage points. Or you could ask the sellers to buy down your interest rate.

3.   The agreement could give you an escrow credit for repairs or decoration. Some lenders may even let you use this money as part of your down payment.

4.   In exchange for the price they want, the sellers could agree to carry back some or all of the financing you need. If seller financing saves you money on points, closing costs, or interest rate, it might make sense for you to trade off a higher price for favorable terms.

Leave Something on the Table: As you conciliate the terms of your agreement, don't push for everything you can possibly get. Negotiating pro Bob Woolf points out, "A successful negotiation isn't one where I get everything. I haven't done a single contract where I couldn't have got more money. I always leave something on the table." Why? "Because," says Woolf, "it's possible to push too hard so you create antagonism. If someone feels you held them up, they're going to try to get back at you later. The idea is to make an agreement that works."

When you get a signed purchase agreement, you step closer toward home ownership. But much more needs to be done. You and the sellers may run into unanticipated snags which concern any number of things: closing date, credit check, mortgage approval, closing costs, property inspections, property condition, seller disclosures, property repairs, appraisal, title search, survey, moving date, personal property, or fixtures. If you and the sellers both feel good about each other and your basic agreements, you should be able to resolve any surprises or setbacks that come up. In other words, leaving something on the table can help you and the sellers pave over any rough spots you may hit on the way to a successful closing.

Win–Win Negotiating: Throughout the entire negotiating process and up to the day you walk through the door of your new home, never stray far from the idea of fairness. Pay close attention to the sellers' needs, wants, and expectations. Similarly, make sure the sellers understand and appreciate your situation.

You and the sellers should see each other "as working side by side to attack the problem, not each other," advise Robert Fisher and William Ury of the Harvard Negotiating Project, authors of *Getting to Yes*. Focus on underlying interests and potential benefits. Try not to get bogged down in ego battles by arguing things like, "Well, our *position* is. . . ." Forget about your *position*. Look for possibilities. "Invent options for mutual gain," say Ury and Fisher.

With good knowledge of the market, cooperative sellers, a "Let's make a deal" attitude, and a Realtor skilled in possibility analysis, you and the sellers can really achieve the goal you need most: a win–win purchase agreement.

9 AFFORDABILITY DEPENDS ON YOU

Have you heard of McMortgage? Or Jiffy Loan? Or the Fifteen-Minute Mortgage Qualification Program? No matter where you live, more than likely, lenders in your area are encouraging home buyers to stop by (or phone in) to find out how much home you can afford. Some lenders call their programs *instant prequalifying* or *preapproval.*

John Silverman, a mortgage loan specialist in St. Louis, says, "By prequalifying, you'll quickly know exactly how much home you can afford. You won't waste time looking at homes outside your price range. It doesn't cost anything and you might as well get the mortgage paperwork rolling before you even think about making an offer. Just tell us about your income and bills and we'll plug the numbers into our computers. We'll get you an answer in less than ten minutes. Plus," says this mortgage specialist, "a preapproval letter will make you a more credible buyer. If you show a seller you're preapproved, you've got an advantage over any other buyers who aren't prequalified, because there's no proof the other guys can actually get the loan they need."

PREQUALIFYING VERSUS POSSIBILITY ANALYSIS

In recent years, mortgage lenders, real estate agents, and financial planners, all have endorsed preapproval or prequalifying. It makes sense to figure out how much home you can afford before you begin to plan your house hunting.

But here lies the danger: Not all prequalifications are created equally. Unless a prequalification is performed as possibility analysis, prequalifying can understate the kind of home and home financing you actually can afford. I know many successful home buyers who have been wrongly informed, "You can't afford to buy," or, "You can only afford to buy a condo."

Respiratory therapist Karen James recently bought her first home. When talking about her achievement, Karen said, "The first lender I talked to led me to believe I couldn't afford anything but a condo. But I found a Realtor who located the perfect home for me in a nice neighborhood. The seller was an 89-year-old woman who wanted to move to a retirement home in Nebraska. She wanted a quick, clean sale (i.e., no unusual or time-consuming contingencies) and accepted a price that was $10,000 under market. For financing, I got a 5-percent-down Neighborhood Advantage loan. "I'm really glad," says Karen, "I didn't give up when that first lender told me I couldn't buy. I'm thinking about calling him and saying, 'Look at me. I am a homeowner.'"

Prequalifying: How It Can Fail

To perform a prequalification analysis, some lenders or sales agents will ask you about your monthly income, debts, available cash, and other assets. They may also look over a copy of your credit report. Then, if your credit looks good and you have enough cash, the lender or sales agent can use several standard affordability ratios to calculate how much home you can afford.

Under this simple type of prequalification, you're evaluated only in light of your existing financial condition, typical mortgage loan products, standard underwriting criteria, and current market interest rates. Unfortunately, if your credit is blemished, if you lack cash, if your monthly income is too low, or if your debts are too high, you may be told you don't qualify. Or you may be told you can only qualify for a price range that puts buying the home you want out of reach.

In the case of Karen James, during her first prequalification she was told she couldn't buy the kind of home she wanted because she didn't have enough cash and because single-family homes were out of her price range. Karen's first lender didn't mention the fact that Karen might be able to find a bargain-priced house and buy it with a low-down-payment, liberal-qualifying loan like Bank of America's Neighborhood Advantage program. Fortunately, Karen didn't give up. She found a lender who understood possibility analysis.

Prequalification as Possibility Analysis

If, like Karen James, you need to get over, under, or around one or more affordability hurdles to become a homeowner, avoid lenders who try to answer the question, "How much home can you afford?" with a 15-minute McJiffy prequalification exercise. Locate a Realtor, home buying counselor, or mortgage loan consultant who will sit down with you to thoroughly discuss your personal finances, a variety of home finance options, affordable neighborhoods, and other potential home buying opportunities.

Your advisor should not only go over your present income, assets, and debts, but should also suggest how you can get your finances in better shape. Should you encounter some credit or financial problems that need to be solved, good financial planning can most likely steer you into a position whereby you can own within the coming 3 to 18 months.

Although many mortgage lenders will help you thoroughly review your finances for purposes of prequalifying, you may get a better *possibility analysis* from your Realtor. Even the most cooperative lenders will generally qualify you according to their own loan programs and underwriting practices. On the other hand, a Realtor who works with first-time buyers will know the loan products and underwriting practices of a variety of mortgage lenders. After a preliminary review of your finances, your Realtor can then direct you to the best lenders for your current situation.

Your Realtor also may know of mortgage brokers who can match you up with a lender who offers what you need. In addition, your Realtor can help with alternative affordability strategies like seller financing, lease options, shared equity, mortgage assumptions, contract-for-deed, creating value, or any other technique we've discussed. A financial institution won't prequalify (or pre-approve) you for these alternative affordability strategies.

A great advantage of America's housing and financing bazaar is that you can turn to many different sources and types of home finance plans. If you can't qualify for a fixed-rate mortgage at First National, you still might be able to get one at Home Savings or Union Bank. Maybe you should forget a fixed-rate and shift to an ARM. If that doesn't fly, maybe seller financing or a nonqualifying assumption will work. Or perhaps you should turn to the FHA, the FmHA, the VA, or a liberal-qualifying first-time buyer program. If these don't offer what you need, there's Mom and Dad, Aunt Roberta, or your employer. Maybe, too, you can bring in a cosigner, coborrower, co-owner, or investor to tip the scales in your favor. Possibility analysis explores any or all of these options. It can't be done in 10 minutes.

STRENGTHEN YOUR BORROWER PROFILE

A past president of the Mortgage Bankers Association gives this advice: "Primarily, buying the home you want depends on two things: (1) get your borrower profile in the best shape you can; and (2) look for the lender, loan product, and underwriting standards that best fit your needs and finances."

When this banker advises you to strengthen your borrower profile, he's referring to the 4 C's of mortgage lending: credit record, cash, collateral, and character. To qualify with confidence, you want to do all you can to make your 4 C's look as good as possible.

CREDIT RECORD

Nothing stands more important to home buying than paying your bills on time—especially your rent. If you regularly make all your monthly payments on or before their due dates, you're 80 percent of the way toward home ownership. On the other hand, if, through casual neglect or inadequate financial planning, you've often been late in paying your bills, you face a problem that needs to be solved.

Conventional mortgage lenders, at most, may be willing to forgive one or two late payments on your car loan or credit cards during the past 12 months, and maybe one (seldom two) late rent payments. Even with just a couple of slip-ups, though, forgiveness won't be easy. You'll have to write the lender a satisfactory explanation. You must alleviate lender concerns by showing unusual, never-to-happen-again circumstances to be at fault. If you've had more than one or two late payments, the lender is going to suspect you're either careless or overextended. With more than a blemish or two, unless you've got an extraordinarily good reason, a conventional lender will probably hold back your loan approval until you improve your credit record.

Nevertheless, don't prejudge your possibilities. Under pressure from government regulators, many mortgage lenders are trying to be more accommodating in their credit evaluations. Plus, special-assistance and first-time buyer programs often incorporate easier qualifying criteria. And should these efforts not progress, you've still got many mortgage lenders who will accept "B," "C," and "D" class borrowers in exchange for lower loan-to-value ratios and higher interest rates.

Improve Your Credit Record

If for the past 12 to 24 months you have paid your bills somewhat carelessly or haphazardly, it doesn't mean you can't qualify for *any* home financing. It does mean you may have to turn to alternatives other than the most popularly known financial institutions. Your choices are reduced.

Given this reality of home financing, do everything possible from this day forward to pay your rent and other bills *before their due date*. Don't think that paying a bill within a grace period gives you as strong a borrower profile as paying on or before your due date. As a former landlord, I know that property owners give stronger credit references for tenants who pay their rent before the first of the month. Owners often tolerate—but they don't appreciate—those tenants whose rent checks regularly come drifting in on the fourth, seventh, or fifteenth of the month.

If your paydays and payment due dates don't match up as well as you would like, ask your property manager and creditors to change your due dates. If you set up a system right now for making sure your bills are paid on time, you can begin to build the strongest possible credit record.

Serious Financial Setbacks

Surprisingly, many mortgage lenders will more readily approve someone who has had a serious financial setback that those people who carelessly neglect their bills. Even if you have suffered a bankruptcy, foreclosure, judgement, or repossession, you may still meet the credit standards of conventional lenders, FmHA, FHA, or VA. As long as you have maintained a sterling credit record for at least the past 12 to 24 months, many mortgage lenders will consider you creditworthy. This is especially the case for home buyers whose financial setback was caused by medical expenses, unemployment, divorce, business failure, or something other than financial irresponsibility. Mortgage lenders won't always turn down all other would-be borrowers whose financial setbacks have resulted from poor judgement or credit abuse. But, if that's your Achilles' heel, you'll have to convince your lender that history won't repeat itself.

Examine Your Credit Report

Before you begin to shop for a home, get a copy of your credit report from each of the three major credit reporting agencies (TRW, Equifax, Trans Union). Then examine them closely for mistakes. Various consumer groups complain that 40 to 50 percent of all credit reports include erroneous, adverse information. While such high estimates undoubtedly overstate the problem, no one denies that serious problems do exist. Newspaper articles and television talk shows often feature people who have been denied credit because of mix-ups in names, social security numbers, addresses, merchant disputes, misreporting by creditors, out-of-date information, and computer foul-ups.

If you are the victim of an erroneous credit report, it could cost you the home you want. Real estate agent Diana Haynes says, "If a blip shows up on the buyer's credit report, I tell my sellers to get their house back on the market. If the problem is anything major at all, it could be a long time before the buyers are going to get their financing." It doesn't matter whether the "blip" is inaccurate. This agent knows that mistakes can take weeks, sometimes months, to clear up.

"If people think they're going into some type of real estate transaction in the near future," says mortgage lender Jerry Spence, "I'd advise them to get a copy of their credit report before they even start looking. It could make getting a mortgage a whole lot easier. In this case, an ounce of prevention is really worth a pound of cure. The key to smooth qualifying is to anticipate credit reporting problems. Then deal with them before you apply for your loan."

Dealing with credit problems means more than just straightening out mistakes. If you do have some credit blemishes (slow pay, overdue accounts), get back on the right track. Bring these accounts up to date and keep them current. Should you question a bill, do what you can to get it settled. Compromise, conciliate, or mediate. Consider taking the creditor to small claims court to clear your account. Hire an attorney to write nasty letters. Come up with whatever ideas you can. "If a credit bureau report shows that some bill or judgement hasn't been paid," says Jerry Spence, "we're not going to give you a mortgage." So don't apply for a mortgage until all your accounts are current and any creditor disputes are resolved. No matter what your past credit record looks like, you want your current record to show up spotless.

Errors in Your Favor

What happens if your credit report misses some serious black marks like a judgement, bankruptcy, repossession, garnishment, eviction, foreclosure, unpaid debts, tax liens, or long-forgotten unpaid student loans? Should you keep quiet? Well, there's probably no need for you to inform the credit bureau of this omission. But you should disclose any serious black marks (at least any that have occurred during the past seven years) to your lender.

For one thing, the lender may discover it even if it's not mentioned in your TRW, Equifax, Trans Union, or other credit bureau report. Today, most financial institutions don't just rely on a "credit report." Instead, they commission a broader investigation called *The Standard Mortgage Credit Report*. For these investigations, specialty credit agencies not only collect information from consumer credit bureaus, but they may also rummage through public records as well as make direct inquiries of creditors, employers, health care providers, and other data banks. In his book, *Privacy for Sale*, Jeffery Rothfeder tells "how computerization has made everyone's life an open secret." You can't assume your lender won't turn up things that consumer credit bureaus have missed. Big Brother is watching.

In addition to this more thorough credit investigation, a mortgage lender will ask you to sign various affidavits and financial statements. You must swear to the accuracy of the financial information you give the lender. To put it bluntly, material nondisclosures or misrepresentations constitute fraud. You definitely should not sign anything that intentionally gives a false or misleading impression of your past or present financial picture.

If your past is blemished, don't try to hide it. In today's world of home buying, it's not uncommon for home buyers to have had some earlier financial difficulties. At some point in our lives, most of us suffer from mistakes and misfortunes. Just do what you can to explain past difficulties. But most important of all: Make sure your current record is spotless and pay all your future accounts exactly as promised.

Too Little Credit History

Although you can have too much credit, as a general rule you can't have too little. Even if you haven't had any car loans or credit cards, you can still qualify for a mortgage. To show you're a good credit risk, provide your lender with canceled checks or other evidence that you regularly pay your utilities, telephone charges, rent, insurance, and other bills on time. It also will be a big plus to show the lender that you regularly make deposits (the larger the better) to your savings account. Contrary to popular myth, lack of previous credit is not a crime.

CASH

After getting a fix on how promptly you pay your bills, a lender will try to figure out whether you can come up with the cash you need to buy your home. To a conventional lender, adequate cash to own means (1) cash-to-close, (2) cash to make your monthly payments, and (3) cash reserves to meet temporary setbacks such as illness or unemployment.

Cash-to-Close

Nowadays, before most lenders will approve a mortgage, they're going to thoroughly investigate where you're getting your money. Your lender will probably want to know: Are the sellers paying points? Are the sellers buying down your interest rate? Are you obtaining a second mortgage, a loan from your parents, or a "gift" from relatives? Do you actually have the cash-to-close in a bank account (or other liquid assets such as stocks, government bonds, or life insurance cash values)? How long have you had these balances? What have your average account balances been during the past two to six months? Have you recently made any unusually large deposits? Where did the money come from? If you're claiming someone is giving you cash-to-close, can you prove they actually have the money and can afford to give it to you?

If all these questions make you think lenders are paranoid about cash-to-close, you're right. Statistics show that borrowers who contribute little of their own cash default more often than other borrowers. After suffering record foreclosures in the mid- to late 1980s, lenders have become gun-shy.

Although you can still finance a home using little of your own cash, lenders just don't want to be kept in the dark about what you're doing. Most financial institutions must meet various regulations that govern their cash-to-close requirements. If you're buying with little of your own cash, the lender will probably get more picky about your credit record, the type of home you're buying, and its appraised value.

As with all other mortgage underwriting guidelines, the name of the game is anticipation. Talk to Realtors. Talk to loan officers. Learn the cash-to-close rules that lenders are imposing in your area. Then plan your finances accordingly.

Monthly Payments

After securing your credit report, lenders next judge whether you earn enough income to make your monthly payments. To calculate mortgage affordability, lenders use two ratios. The first is called the *housing expense ratio* (front ratio). The second is called the *total debt ratio* (back ratio). Both of these ratios are easy to compute:

$$\text{Housing expense ratio} = \frac{\text{monthly payment}}{\text{monthly income}}$$

$$\text{Total debt ratio} = \frac{\text{monthly payment} + \text{monthly installment debt}}{\text{monthly income}}$$

Although standards differ, most lenders like to see a maximum housing expense ratio of 25 to 31 percent. A maximum total debt ratio will typically range between 33 and 41 percent. These ratios are approximate. Besides varying among lenders and loan programs, they will vary by individual borrowers. If you have a strong credit record, a good job, a promising career, and you're making a large down payment, most lenders will qualify you at the higher end of their affordability ratios—or maybe beyond. The opposite is also true. Lenders normally try to qualify weaker borrowers at the lower end of these "standard" ratios.

You can see the arithmetic of these two debt-to-income (affordability) ratios by following through an example. (You may recall that debt-to-income ratios were introduced in Chapter 2. The examples here go into greater detail and demonstrate how financial planning can strengthen your ratios and borrower profile.)

Now let's assume you would like to borrow $100,000 at 8 percent for 30 years. The monthly payment (principal and interest) for this loan amounts to $734 a month. If your property taxes, homeowner's insurance, and mortgage insurance add up to a monthly cost of $245, your monthly housing expense would total $979. Divide your monthly house payment by you and your spouse's monthly income of, say, $3,650, and you get a housing expense ratio of 27 percent.

$$\text{Housing expense ratio} = \frac{\text{monthly payment (\$979)}}{\text{monthly income (\$3650)}} = .268 \text{ or } 27\%$$

We next calculate your total debt ratio:

Monthly payment (P&I)	$ 734
Escrow (property taxes, homeowner's insurance, mortgage insurance)	245
Car payment #1	210
Car payment #2	110
Visa	80
MasterCard	45
Student loan	135
Total monthly debt payments	**$1,559**

$$\text{Total debt ratio} = \frac{\$1,559}{\$3,650} = .427 \text{ or } 43\%.$$

Now the critical question: Based on these ratios, would you qualify for this $100,000 loan? The answer: It all depends. If you are financing through an FHA, VA, or perhaps some type of liberal-qualifying first-time buyer program, you can probably locate a lender who will accept these ratios. On the other hand, if you are applying for a conventional loan, your approval may not go through. Your total debt ratio is too high. For conventional loans (especially those being sold to Freddie Mac or Fannie Mae), a total debt ratio of .35 to .40 is *usually* tops.

Possibility Analysis: Now these figures don't mean you can't get a $100,000 conventional loan. This is the kind of situation where your Realtor or loan officer could start suggesting alternative possibilities. For instance, you could switch from a fixed-rate mortgage to an adjustable-rate mortgage. This switch should save you at least $100 a month. With the ARM's lower initial monthly payments, your housing expense ratio and total debt ratio would both fall.

You also could take a hard look at your debts. Could you sell one of your cars? Not only could you eliminate a car payment, but with cash from the sale, you could pay off a credit card balance. Maybe you also could refinance your student loan at a lower interest rate or for a longer term. In this example, your long-term installment debt requires payments of $580 a month. Some creative finagling could reduce those payments by $250 a month or more.

Revamping your finances, your total debt ratio might look like this:

Monthly payment (ARM)	$ 632
Escrow (property taxes, homeowner's insurance, mortgage insurance)	245
Car payment #1	170
Car payment #2	0
Visa	0
MasterCard	45
Student loan	95
Total monthly debt payments	**$1,187**

$$\text{Total debt ratio} = \frac{\$1,187}{\$3,650} = .325 \text{ or } 33\%.$$

With your total debt ratio now less than 33 percent, you can easily qualify for a $100,000 loan. Through this example, you can see why preparing to qualify should come before prequalifying. You should plan and revise your finances as early as possible *before* you apply for your home financing. It's through planning that you can really strengthen your borrower profile.

Calculating Monthly Income: In the previous example, we assumed your income to be $3,650 per month. In practice, things

can get a little more complicated. Even after you've given a lender
your actual monthly income figures, for purposes of its
affordability ratios the lender may increase or decrease these
actual amounts. Think of all the potential sources of income you
might receive:

- Regular wages
- Self-employment
- Overtime wages
- Consulting fees
- Bonuses
- Business income
- Sales commissions
- Stock dividends
- Second job
- Rental property income
- Tips and gratuities
- Pensions
- Social Security
  (retirement)
- Welfare, food stamps,
  ADC
- Social Security
  (disability)
- Part-time work
- Alimony
- Unemployment
  Compensation
- Child support
- Workers' compensation
- Seasonal or temporary
  work
- Rents from housemates
- Insurance settlements
- Rents from rental units
- Scholarships, grants
- Partnership income
- Children's earnings
- Trust funds
- Military (retirement)
- Royalties
- Military (disability)
- Gifts

When calculating mortgage affordability, you first want to
make sure you've listed all your income. I know loan officers
who have helped buyers get qualified by reminding them of
income they had forgotten to list on their mortgage application.
Some lenders will even count potential income from a "trailing"
spouse, even though the spouse has yet to start (or find) work in
the family's new city. On the other hand, sometimes lenders will
omit income you've actually received. When some of your
income seems uncertain in amount or duration, your loan officer
may raise questions.

For example: How dependably does your ex-husband pay his

child support payments? How long are these payments scheduled to continue? This past year, you earned $6,000 working overtime. Will this income continue? If overtime remains available, do you plan to keep working so hard? What's the chance that you will be laid off or called out on strike? Your spouse has just started back to work. How safe is his or her job? How long does he or she plan to remain employed? During the past seven months, your sales commissions have averaged $4,000 a month. But what were your average earnings during the past two years? Are your sales commissions booming because buyers are pouring into the market, or because you have developed superior skills and techniques that can keep you selling through good times and bad?

Do you own your own business? Are you self-employed as a writer, artist, or consultant? How risky are your earnings? Do your tax returns understate (legally) the actual amount of cash you have available? (For example, depreciation on business property or a home office is tax deductible against business income. But depreciation doesn't require a cash outlay.) You say you plan to rent out part of your home to a roommate. Do you have a signed lease? Are you now sharing with a roommate? Or will this be something new for you?

Now you can see why figuring gross monthly income for your affordability ratios requires loan committees to judge and interpret them. To strengthen your borrower profile, you need to find out how specific lenders and loan programs are likely to count the sources and amounts of your income. To get as much counted as possible, try to assure the lender that your income is both steady and likely to go up. Letters from employers, clients, or customers can help. Industry or government studies that show increasing demand for people with your skills or education also can build a lender's confidence in you. Generally, good lenders are open to reason. Written explanations can often persuade them to count some income they might otherwise ignore.

Calculating Monthly Installment Debt: As with income, calculating monthly debts also requires judgement. Say your car loan has four months to run before it's paid off. Will the lender count your car payment as part of your monthly debt? Probably not. Most lenders exclude monthly payments that will end within a relatively short period of time.

What about payments on your Visa card? You've been paying

$125 a month. But you could pay the minimum of $50 per month. What amount should the lender include in its debt calculations? What if you pay off all your credit cards immediately before applying for a mortgage? You now have no monthly debt. Some lenders may think you're up to something. They may suspect that after your loan is approved, you will run up your credit card balances again. These lenders will assume you have some monthly debt even if you don't! A borrower with eight credit cards and no balances may be judged a higher risk than a borrower with one credit card who is up to the limit.

Exactly how lenders decide to calculate your monthly income and installment debt will vary according to their own internal underwriting guidelines, the guidelines set by secondary mortgage investors like Freddie Mac and Fannie Mae, and the guidelines that apply to specific loan products and programs (private mortgage insurers, FHA, VA, community home buyer plans, special-assistance financing, community reinvestment initiatives).

Compensating Factors: In addition, to allow for individual differences, lenders will look to see whether you have any compensating factors. All lenders maintain some flexibility and understanding. They realize there's nothing absolute about the riskiness of a 33 percent housing expense ratio or a 40 percent total debt ratio. It depends on your personal situation. So, if you need higher than typical affordability ratios, emphasize compensating factors like:

- A sterling credit record
- Simple lifestyle
- Low family living expenses
- Low or no job commute expense
- Energy-efficient house
- High net worth (for your age and home price range)
- High down payment
- Cosigner, coborrower, or co-owner
- Upward career mobility
- Advanced college or professional training
- Job stability

- A past record of high monthly savings
- Large amounts of employer fringe benefits (retirement plan, health and disability insurance, automobile, travel or living allowances)
- Handyman talents for home maintenance, repairs, and renovations
- Past record of high monthly payments for rent
- A plan to create value for the home
- Proven ability to handle high debt responsibly
- Other potential income (bonuses, commissions, royalties)
- High financial reserves

If you've really done your financial planning in detail, show the lender how you've calculated your monthly budget. When necessary, do whatever you can to explain why you can handle higher ratios. Lenders need to make loans. Chances are you can find one who's willing to listen.

Cash Reserves

Besides cash for a down payment and closing costs, most traditional lenders will want you to have two months of mortgage payments in reserve. Lenders believe this extra cash will cushion you against things like moving expenses, new curtains and blinds, and minor repairs and redecorating that go along with becoming a homeowner. Here again, though, lenders and loan programs vary. Some liberal-qualifying programs don't require cash reserves.

Nevertheless, for your own peace of mind, it's a good idea to keep cash or near cash (stocks, bonds, CDs, life insurance cash values) tucked away to help meet a financial setback like illness, accident, or unemployment. As part of becoming a homeowner, you might also review your life, property, liability, health, and disability insurance coverages. In many ways, your best financial reserve is a well-planned insurance program.

COLLATERAL

Along with checking your credit and income, a lender will appraise the home you are buying. Lenders want strong *collat-*

eral. If you don't pay your mortgage, your lender wants to be able to get its money back by selling your home (foreclosing). Yet, even though collateral is necessary, in most cases—asset-based ("hard money") lenders are the exception—your credit record, monthly income, and character will chiefly determine whether you get approved for the loan you want. Because foreclosures nearly always cost lenders money and bad publicity, most lenders won't trade strong collateral for poor credit. If your recent credit history is a wreck, you'll need to look for specialty lenders, some type of seller financing, or perhaps a nonqualifying mortgage assumption.

On the other hand, for borrowers who marginally qualify—that is, borrowers who may have a credit blemish or two, high affordability ratios, short job history, self-employment, irregular earnings, or some other potential negative—good collateral can make the deciding difference.

If you fit in one or more of these marginal categories, you can increase your chances of qualifying by improving your collateral:

1. Increase your down payment (lower your loan-to-value ratio).
2. Bring in a cosigner or coborrower.
3. Pledge additional real estate.
4. Pledge additional assets such as stocks, bonds, saving accounts, or certificates of deposit. (Remember, the real estate or pledged assets need not be yours.)
5. Buy mortgage insurance.
6. Buy at a bargain price. (This improves the lender's loan-to-value ratio just as much as increasing your down payment.)
7. Show the lender how you are going to immediately create value for your home through improvements.
8. Select a home in a neighborhood or development with strong promise of appreciation.
9. Make sure the home you've selected fits well within a lender's underwriting guidelines. Some lenders try to avoid condo or townhouse developments with a high percentage of renters, or those with pending litigation

(lawsuits by or against the complex's homeowner's association, its developer, or its contractor). Also, lenders may avoid homes because of location, construction materials, design, age, condition, size (too large, too small), environmental hazards, or purchase price (too large, too small).

10. In today's lawsuit-crazy society, many appraisers are running scared. In some cities, they are lowballing their appraisals to compensate for earlier years when they routinely inflated their value estimates. If your home's appraisal comes in low, get with your Realtor and review the appraisal. If the appraiser's facts and opinions are wrong, get him to correct his report. If he refuses, ask the lender to order another appraisal.

Although mortgage lenders primarily evaluate you, don't overlook the fact that lenders also need a security blanket called collateral. Do whatever you can do to help the lender feel warm and comfortable with the home you're financing. You will improve the chance that your loan application will go through without a hitch.

CHARACTER

"Too many of my first-time home buyers fail to realize," says mortgage banker Rosemary Steele, "mortgage lending is not strictly a numbers game. Sure, with all the laws about discrimination, we've got to be careful to treat everyone fairly. But fairness doesn't mean we treat everyone the same. Character does count.

"In every lending decision, we ask two central questions: 'Are these people *able* to pay their bills?' and, 'Are they *willing* to pay their bills?' If I've got someone in here who is a little short on credit or finances, but strong on sincerity and responsibility, I'll bend over backwards to get them approved. Just last week we accepted a young couple who had a Chapter 13 bankruptcy. But in the past 18 months, they had paid off their creditors in full and saved enough for a down payment for an FHA loan. Their front and back ratios were .31 and .41, respectively."

Character Counts

Although she may not have known it, by emphasizing character, Rosemary Steele echoed the sentiments of the great banker J.

Pierpont Morgan. In testimony before a congressional committee, Morgan was asked,

> *"Is not commercial credit based primarily upon money or property?"*
> *"No sir,"* responded J.P. *"The first thing is character." "Before money*
> *or property?"* the committee challenged. *"Before money or anything*
> *else,"* said Morgan. *"Money cannot buy credit. Because a man I do not*
> *trust could not get credit from me on all the bonds of Christendom."*

When you apply for any type of home financing, remember: Character counts. Everyone you deal with in your home-buying transaction—sellers, Realtors, loan officers, loan underwriting committees—will be judging you. Are you honest? Sincere? Responsible? Can you be counted on to do what you say you're going to do? When dealing with your loan officer, be polite, courteous, and businesslike. Meet deadlines promptly. Provide all documents and verifications as requested. Speak with self-confidence. Avoid bravado or self-boosterism. Leave your Gucci loafers and Rolex watch at home. The loan officer will be looking for sincerity, honesty, and commitment.

Loan officers and loan committees are influenced by the same human emotions and judgements as the rest of us. They will be asking themselves, "Are these borrowers the type of people we want to do business with? Do they make us feel we're doing the right thing?" Or, "Does their behavior, mannerisms, or character raise doubts and suspicions?"

So pay attention to details. Dress conservatively. Neatly print or type your loan application. Let the loan officer get to know you as a responsible, serious home buyer. Lenders love stability. If you have frequently changed jobs, point out your higher pay, greater responsibility, or opportunity for advancement. Don't blame others or come up with lame excuses ("My boss didn't like me."). Explanations are helpful, but don't try to blame others.

Just recently, a loan officer confided in me that she had turned down a man for a mortgage because he was wearing too many diamonds. In another instance, I know of a woman's mortgage application that was rejected because she never took the time to stop by and personally meet and talk with her loan officer. She had mailed her application to the bank. What the woman did do, though, was to annoy the loan officer nearly every day by complaining about how long the application process was taking.

In the end, the loan officer decided, "Enough's enough. This woman is giving me bad vibes."

Of course, neither the man with too many diamonds nor the complaining woman was told that personal characteristics influenced the loan decision. The man had high ratios, and the woman had a slight history of late payments on her car loan. For purposes of a "credit denied" form, each of these reasons could justify a rejection. But if this man and woman had paid more attention to the character issue, both would have seen their loans approved.

Put Supports in Writing

"If it's not in writing, it doesn't exist," says loan officer Jack Stubbs. "When we're trying to do all we can to get someone approved, we need letters, documents, and verifications. The more files we can create to support a loan, the more likely we can get that loan approved.

"Whether it's negatives that need explaining or positive remarks that boost a borrower's credibility, we want them in writing. If a loan goes sour, we've got to think CYA. When the regulatory honchos or executive pinstripers from upstairs come around and ask, 'Why'd you make this loan?' we want the evidence in the file. It's not going to be enough for us to answer, 'We thought they were a nice couple and just wanted to help them out.' We need reasons in writing that will pass muster."

REGARDLESS OF YOUR RACE, SEX, OR ETHNICITY, LENDERS WANT TO LEND YOU MONEY

During the past several years, major newspapers and network media have widely publicized several government studies that reveal racial and ethnic disparities in mortgage lending practices. As the statistical data show, the mortgage applications of blacks and other minorities have been turned down more frequently than the applications of whites. For example, one report showed that around 18 percent of black applications were rejected, yet only about 10 percent of whites suffered a similar fate. From these figures (and others like them), the media has jumped to the conclusion that mortgage lenders discriminate against minorities.

Unfortunately, as Disraeli pointed out more than 100 years ago, "There are lies, damned lies, and statistics." As it turns out these studies are deeply flawed. After scholarly investigation, economist Stan Liebowitz has found that "the government studies are unreliable and misleading. They were seized upon too quickly— perhaps to further political purposes, or to confirm political prejudices. . . . [Perhaps] truth is not the goal [of these studies]."

What is the Truth?

First of all, if you look on the positive side of the figures, you see that the great majority (more than 80 percent) of blacks, other minorities, and whites do receive mortgage loan approval. Clearly, mortgage lenders aren't rejecting minorities wholesale. Yet, it is also true that statistical disparities do exist. So the real question is, why?

As it turns out, careful inspection reveals that minority mortgage applications face higher rates of rejection because minority applicants are less likely to meet the standard underwriting criteria that mortgage lenders have used to judge all mortgage applications. Although no one denies that racial bigotry influences some turndowns, overt racial, sexual, or ethnic discrimination doesn't explain much of the problem. Rather, the problem of turndowns is more subtle. It's mainly the result of the standard underwriting criteria themselves.

The Good News

The good news is that the vast majority of mortgage lenders are re-evaluating their standard underwriting criteria. They're asking themselves (sometimes under threat of government penalties): "How can we change our underwriting criteria to still reject 'poor risks,' but at the same time accept good people who don't conform to stereotypical middle-class job, income, and credit standards?"

In her *ABA Banking Journal* article that addresses this question, banker Jo Ann Barefoot lists 10 criteria that lending institutions should modify to better meet the needs of minorities and low- to moderate-income individuals and families. Among those listed criteria are:

1. Increase debt ratios. Because low- to moderate-income households often pay a higher percentage of their income for housing, lenders should increase their permissible debt ratios—especially where applicants have already proved themselves by spending, say, 40 or 50 percent of their incomes for rent.

2. Eliminate arbitrary minimum loan amounts. Some lenders set their minimum mortgage amounts at say, $60,000, $75,000, or maybe even $100,000. Obviously, this standard excludes mortgages for families who want to buy smaller-sized homes, or homes in lower-priced neighborhoods.

3. Look at total job prospects and employment history—not just two years in the same job or career. Given today's tough job market for lower-skilled or less-degreed individuals, employment itself—not long-term employment in the same type of job—should be given greater weight.

4. Become more flexible as to sources and amount of down payment. Lenders should reduce down payment barriers to home ownership. Higher loan-to-value ratios, borrowed funds, gifts, sweat equity, and lease-option or lease-purchase plans should be more acceptable to lenders.

5. Look to nontraditional credit histories. Many minorities, recent immigrants, and low- to moderate-income households don't have credit cards and bank accounts. To overcome this problem, lenders should instead look at their payment records for utilities, rent, and telephone bills. In addition, lenders should assign little weight to past credit problems caused by misfortune such as medical bills, plant closings, or temporary disability.

Overall, mortgage lenders know that to grow their businesses during the coming years, they're going to have to loosen up their underwriting criteria. Emerging population demographics, the end of the 1992–1994 refinance boom, and the changing job market all signal the need to expand the market for mortgage loans to people who hoped—but never believed—they could own their own homes.

Fannie Mae Leads the Way

In the past, many mortgage lenders were reluctant to liberalize their underwriting criteria because they needed to sell their mortgages to Fannie Mae (the secondary mortgage market). And justifiably or not, Fannie Mae developed a set of rigid underwriting standards that governed the loans they bought. Lenders who violated Fannie Mae's guidelines would be shut out of Fannie's secondary market operations.

Now Fannie Mae is trying to lead the way with more relaxed standards. It has created a set of 11 initiatives called "Showing America a New Way Home." In addition to pledging $1 trillion toward this goal, Fannie has told its participating lenders, "Don't 'flat out' reject any mortgage loan application. Before you say no, give that application a second review. If your answer is still 'No,' give the application a third review. If the answer is still 'No,' get the applicant into high-quality home buyer counseling." Fannie Mae chairman James A. Johnson says, "Every American who wants to get a mortgage will either have their loan approved, or be put on a path that can lead to approval."

PLAN TO QUALIFY

As you can now see, regardless of your race, sex, ethnicity, or income level, mortgage lenders want to help you finance your home. Yet, that doesn't mean lenders are going to shovel out money to anyone who rolls in a wheelbarrow. You may still need to act with self-discipline, determination and creativity. So, take time to sit down with your Realtor, a mortgage loan advisor, or a home buying counselor. Work through the numbers. Create ways to improve your finances. Evaluate your ratios. Get your employer to give you a strong letter of recommendation. Emphasize your roots in the community. Tell how your career's on an upward path. Explain credibly any slip-ups in your credit or employment history. Point out how you're improving your job skills or credentials through education.

Come up with ideas to increase your income, spend less, save more, and reduce your outstanding debts and monthly payments. Can you consolidate your bills? Can you refinance your student loans to get lower payments? Can you replace your late-model car with an older model to get rid of those high car payments? Can you get a second job? Ask for a raise? Seek a promotion? Increase your tips? Generate some consulting revenues? Start a business? Put your spouse to work?

Whatever you do, don't accept your present income, spending, and saving as the best you can do. Even if you have misstepped in the past, from now on vow to pay your bills on or before their due dates. When you strengthen your borrower profile, you move yourself closer to home ownership.

DISCOVER THE RIGHT LENDER

Who is the right lender for you? It's not necessarily the lender who offers the lowest interest rate, the lowest fees and points, the easiest qualifying, the least documentation, or the quickest closing. The right lender is the one whose total package of costs, loan products, qualifying standards, timeliness, convenience, and overall underwriting philosophy best matches your borrower profile (as strengthened). For most first-time home buyers, it's the discovery of a good match that stands most important.

Where to Look for Financing

It's impossible to survey all sources of home loans. Even a computer data bank can't keep track of the thousands of potential lenders and hundreds of finance plans (in all their variations) available on any given day. That's why you need to think through a buying and home finance strategy. A strategy narrows your search to neighborhoods, homes, and finance plans that fit your budget and credit record.

The large number of lenders, finance plans, and homes available also helps to explain why most experts advise you to consult a knowledgeable Realtor about financing. A real estate professional can help you locate the lenders or property owners who might be right for you. Here's a description of the types of mortgage lenders you have to choose from.

Conforming Lenders: Many banks and savings institutions originate mortgages that conform to the underwriting guidelines of Fannie Mae and Freddie Mac. Although conforming lenders enjoy some flexibility, they generally impose the most restrictive qualifying criteria. However, as just mentioned above, Fannie (and Freddie) are now actively promoting a variety of easier-qualifying first-time buyer programs. Both of these suppliers of mortgage money are pushing to make millions of mortgage loans to low- to moderate-income households during the next five years. Fannie and Freddie want you to become a homeowner. Ask your local lenders about the "Showing America a New Way Home" initiative, as well as other similar affordable or first-time buyer loan programs. (One initiative by Freddie Mac, for example, is called "Discover Gold through Expanding Markets.")

Portfolio Lenders: Lenders who don't sell their loans in the secondary mortgage market are called *portfolio lenders.* Since portfolio lenders set their own lending guidelines (subject to some broad government regulations), they tend to be flexible in the types of loans they offer and their qualifying criteria. If you can't qualify according to the underwriting standards of conforming lenders, ask your Realtor to help you locate a bank or S&L that's a portfolio lender. Also, some portfolio lenders will give low-down-payment (3 to 15 percent down) loans without requiring borrowers to buy mortgage insurance.

Credit Unions: Many large credit unions provide home financing on quite favorable terms. Although you must be a member to borrow, rules for joining credit unions have been liberalized. Look to see whether any credit unions in your area offer mortgage loans.

Mortgage Bankers: Often, mortgage bankers are wholly owned subsidiaries of large financial institutions. Sometimes they also make loans for other institutions such as life insurers and pension funds. Many mortgage bankers provide a wide variety of loan products. But some focus on FHA, VA, or other loans that conform to the guidelines of secondary market investors like Freddie Mac and Fannie Mae.

Mortgage Brokers: Mortgage brokers have become the fastest-growing source for home financing. Unlike mortgage bankers, mortgage brokers rarely lend their own money. A mortgage broker can discuss your needs, look at your borrower profile, take your application, and then search for a lender who will make the kind of loan you want. Although to a certain extent, all good loan officers are problem solvers, mortgage brokers are frequently the problem solvers *par excellence.* If your financial problem can be solved, a good mortgage broker might be the lender you need to get the job done. (Beware, though, that the reputations of mortgage brokers in some areas have been sullied by those who promise and charge for far more than they can deliver. Before you pay fees to a mortgage broker—or any other lender, for that matter—check out their reputation and references.)

Employers: The *Harvard Business Review, Business Week, Fortune,* and other leading business magazines have featured articles to encourage employers to help their employees buy homes. Can you persuade your employer to help you? Even if your employer can't lend you the money, it may have the economic clout to get a lender to offer you (and its other employees) home financing on favorable terms.

Lenders with REOs: Nearly all lenders own homes they have acquired because of borrower defaults, abandonments, and fore-closures. Often lenders just want to get these properties off their books. They are frequently willing to sell them with favorable financing. On occasion, lenders will sell directly to home buyers, but more frequently they list their REOs with Realtors.

Parents, Relatives and Friends: As many as 50 percent of all first-time home buyers raise at least part of their home financing from parents, relatives, or friends. Since home buying is such a desirable goal, your relatives or friends might be glad to help you out. Ask them.

New-Home Builders: During the past several years, I've seen builders advertise virtually every type of home finance plan. To name just a few: lease option, nothing down, shared equity, sweat equity, FHA/VA, community home buyer programs, state finance agency programs, mortgage credit certificates, below-market interest rates, discount pricing, and interest-free second mortgages.

Sellers: No one knows for sure how many sellers help their buyers with financing. From my own experience, I would say the percentage ranges between 20 and 40 percent. In this figure are included lease options, nonqualifying assumptions, cosigning, seller first mortgages, seller second mortgages, wraparounds, land contracts, and interest rate buydowns. Sellers also frequently help by paying some (or all) of their buyers' mortgage points and closing costs. In periods of tight qualifying standards and high interest rates, seller-assisted financing often occurs in more than 50 percent of all home buying transactions. Sellers can provide a great source of financing because they set their own qualifying criteria. No sellers' agent is going to advise their seller to lend to a deadbeat. But if you are strong on character and can show your ability and willingness to pay, you can nearly always find a seller who will accept a seller mortgage or contract-for-deed.

Realtors: As emphasized earlier, a real estate professional should be one good primary source of market information about sellers and lenders who can meet your financing needs. On occasion, though, the realty firm (or the agent) you're working with might be willing to directly arrange some or all of your home financing. In fact, some real estate offices are now hooked into computer networks of mortgage lenders. Some realty firms even operate their own mortgage banking subsidiaries.

Other Sources: Anywhere you can find cash can serve as a potential source of financing for your home. Retirement accounts, union pension funds, life insurance cash values, personal loans, selling off assets (furniture, jewelry, electronics, cars, boats, stocks, investments), credit card cash advances, and cash-out refinancings of other property (real estate, car) have all been used by first-time buyers. Put your mind to work. Ask yourself, "How can I raise additional cash?"

LOOK BEYOND INTEREST RATES

Many first-time home buyers mistakenly set out to find home financing by shopping for the lowest interest rate, mortgage points, and fees. It's called *dialing for dollars.* They telephone 10, 20, maybe 30 lenders. They faithfully record all this cost information. Next, these buyers choose the three or four lowest-cost lenders and schedule appointments for application interviews. Since mortgage payments can take a large chunk out of your monthly income, shopping for lower-cost loans certainly makes sense. But there are at least six problems that may arise with this approach:

1.   Mortgage rates change daily. The lender that quotes the lowest rates and fees today may not offer the lowest rates and fees tomorrow.

2.   On occasion, an oral rate quotation isn't worth the paper it's printed on. With some lenders, you won't know the real cost of your loan until the day of closing.

3.   It does little good to locate the lowest-cost lender if that lender won't qualify you for the loan you want.

4.   Loan costs themselves may be difficult to rank. Which is better—a 7.9 percent interest rate and three points, or an 8.75 percent interest rate and no points? You can't answer that question unless you know how many years you plan to keep the loan. Also, your answer would depend on how much cash you have available to close and whether the seller is willing to pay part of your mortgage points and fees. (See mistake number 10 on page 243.)

5.   Lenders differ substantially in both their ethics and their quality of service. Some lenders have hidden costs. Some lenders will drag out your application while anticipating an uptick in interest rates. Others will use bait-and-switch tactics to move you from a highly touted low-cost loan to one with higher costs.

6.   Lending terms and loan agreements themselves differ among various lenders. Here are just a few: ARM indexes, late fees, grace periods, default remedies, forbearance practices, escrow requirements, private mortgage insurance costs and requirements, ARM adjustment periods, prepayment penalties, assumption (due-on-sale clauses), when and if rate quotations are "locked-in," and fixed-rate conversion rights.

Most definitely, you want to shop for home financing and gather enough information to learn which lenders price their loans competitively. But don't apply for a mortgage simply because a lender has quoted low-cost interest rates, points, and fees. Seek advice on other important terms of the loan agreement. Choose a lender who has a good reputation for fair dealing. You want a lender who faithfully honors the spirit of its oral and written promises.

That's why you can benefit by relying on a Realtor (or other mortgage advisor) who knows the ins and outs of mortgage lenders and lending practices in your area. You want to locate a lender who will process your financing competently, smoothly, timely, and in some cases, creatively.

AFFORDABILITY DEPENDS ON YOU: HOW MUCH HOME DO YOU WANT?

Real estate author Joan Meyers writes, "No longer is figuring how much home you can afford a simple process of coming up with a monthly payment figure and then translating it into a price with a set of mortgage tables." Joan's right. But even in the past, affordability should never have been a simple process of, "Go to the bank, order a credit report, plug in the numbers—do I qualify?" Unfortunately, that game has been played too often. As a result, millions of Americans who could have become homeowners years ago never realized their actual opportunity to own. Don't make this same mistake. How much home you can afford depends on you. It's not an unchangeable fact of life.

Are you willing to develop a "can do, will do" attitude? Have you educated yourself about all the home finance options available in your area? Are you willing to use one or more of the many techniques that make borrowing or buying easier? Have you discovered affordable neighborhoods or low-cost new-home developments? Would you consider buying a duplex, triplex, fourplex, or maybe a fixer-upper? What about a condo, co-op, loft, or townhouse? Can you take in housemates or create an accessory apartment? Are you willing to put a financial plan into action to cut expenses, increase your income, and build your savings? Are you working to strengthen your credit record and borrower profile? Have you established a loyal working relationship with a sharp Realtor who appreciates the challenges and rewards of helping first-time buyers?

Never forget: Today many Realtors, as well as home-buying counselors and mortgage lenders, are eager to help you. Affordability does depend on you. But you don't have to do it alone. Go out and get the advice you need. Ask a real estate or mortgage professional which techniques can work for you in your local area. But most important, firmly make the decision to own.

Tony Robbins (*Awaken the Giant Within*) writes, "More than anything else, I believe our decisions, not the conditions of our lives, create our destiny. . . . Life is cumulative. Whatever results we're experiencing have accumulated from a host of small decisions we've made. . . . They're not the result of one cataclysmic event or earth-shaking decision. . . . Rather, success or failure is determined by the actions we take every day." According to Tony, the best question to ask ourselves is, "'What action can I take each day to shape my ultimate destiny?' When you truly decide to, you can do almost anything."

To achieve home ownership, Tony Robbins's advice hits pay dirt. How much home you can buy is not a straightforward question of affordability. It's a question of decision-making and taking action. Decide to own. Choose priorities. Put a financial plan into action. Follow that strategy and you can own the home you want.

10 START BUILDING WEALTH

Have you heard these predictions? According to many popular journalists, economists, and even some home buyers, you should buy a home as a comfortable place to live, but not as a solid investment for your future. Here's what they're saying:

"If you bought your home recently," says housing economist John Dean, "you have made your purchase at what in the long run may turn out to be the top of the market. . . . The days when you couldn't lose in a home purchase are no longer with us."

Forbes columnist William Flanagan seems to agree. "It was the accepted wisdom," writes Flanagan, "the best investment you could make was the roof over your head. . . . [But home ownership] is no longer a sure thing."

Some home buyers have reflected this same belief. Catherine Gowing writes, "Many people . . . are afraid they may lose some of their savings if they invest in a home at today's prices. In the meantime they are doing irreparable damage to themselves—damage that can't be measured in terms of money. . . . We didn't buy our home as an investment. We knew that for our child's good we must get a house. . . . [At first] we hated risking our small savings . . . but we made up our minds the money should be used, rather than saved for some unpredictable future. We're glad we bought a home."

In San Diego, Lyn and Rick Edwards moved from a one-bedroom apartment to their own new three-bedroom home because, "We needed a safer neighborhood and more room for our daughter. We even got financing where our house payments run just slightly more than our rent. We didn't buy for investment. Californians are getting away from the idea of homes as a way to make money. We simply wanted a place to call home."

* * * * *

For the past several years, in many parts of the country and in much of the national media, there's been much ballyhoo about homes no longer being a good investment. Sadly, many renters and home buyers have come to accept this view. But this mistaken belief today is just as wrong as it was in 1948 when economist John Dean and home buyer Catherine Gowing complained of high housing prices. That's right! The preceding quotations of housing economist Dean and home buyer Gowing aren't from the pages of today's newspapers and magazines; they're from 1948. The outrageously high home prices of that era typically ranged between $5,000 and $10,000. At those prices everyone knew homes were no longer a good investment.

Although they may not realize it, when today's journalists or home buyers (like the above-quoted Flanagan and Edwards) lament that homes are not the sound investment they once were, they're saying nothing new. Off and on since at least the 1940s, Americans have alternated between the views that homes are no longer affordable and homes are no longer a sure-thing investment. At present, with increased affordability, media experts have been giving most attention to the "no longer a good investment" theme. But over time, we've seen only one constant. Regardless of the recurring complaints of unaffordability and "no longer a good investment," the great majority of Americans do find ways to buy their own homes, and those who do buy accumulate far more wealth than those who don't.

HOMEOWNERS BUILD WEALTH

This past year, the Joint Center for Housing Studies of Harvard University published its annual *State of the Nation's Housing* report. "Lack of home ownership blocks access to an important savings vehicle," says the study. "Home equity accounts for the majority of all net worth. . . . The wealth of young homeowners is over 14 times that of young renters. . . [and] from age 35 to 64, homeowners build nearly 40 times the net wealth of renters."

The Harvard study does point out that "buying at the peak of any housing market" may not appear to be a good investment in the short run. But over time, "even small [annual] gains in house prices produce substantial growth in home equity." The reason is *leverage*. You can buy a home with just a relatively small percentage of the purchase price as your initial cash investment. However, your appreciation gains are based on the total value of your home.

The Harvard researchers, for example, calculated the equity gains of homeowners in 12 major American cities. Looking at homeowners who bought in 1974, 1983, or 1987, the study found that by the early 1990s, with only two exceptions, all homeowners experienced large gains in wealth through home equity. The exceptions were home buyers in Boston in 1987 and home buyers in Houston in 1983, and as of spring 1995, home prices in both these cities were experiencing an upswing.

HOMES WILL APPRECIATE

To Catherine Gowing and her family in 1948, their home price of $10,000—up from $5,000 in 1939—seemed outrageous. To Lyn and Rick Edwards in 1994, their $156,900 purchase price—up from $119,000 for a similar new home in 1986—seemed impossibly high. But whenever we look back in time, we'll find people who thought that home prices in their day were too high.

In 1976, *The Wall Street Journal* complained, "The American dream may be dying. . . . In many cities it's tough to find any single-family house priced at less than $30,000." In 1977, *Nation's Business* reported, "We've reached the limit of what families can set aside for housing. Housing experts agree price rises in the future won't be that great." And in 1985, just before housing prices on both coasts began their double-digit appreciation rates, *Money Magazine* advised its readers, "Get used to the fact [that] the easy-come atmosphere of steep housing price increases is gone. . . . Besides, even if inflation re-ignites, too many buyers would be priced out of the market to push housing prices up."

These recurring predictions that housing prices had reached their limit all have one thing in common. They've all been wrong. So when *Forbes* financial writer William Flanagan joins the age-old chorus and says, "Don't be so quick to buy a house. Renting your next home could be a much smarter move," remember the similar and mistaken forecasts of the past. Rather than price stability or decline, today's market fundamentals point to another round of appreciation in home values. Here's why:

1. Homes are more affordable. In 1980, a median-income family who brought a median-priced home needed to spend 36 percent of their income to cover mortgage payments. Today, the comparable figure is around 20 percent.

2. Population is growing. Population forecasts by the U.S. Bureau of the Census show that between now and the year 2000, the U.S. population will grow by 20 million, from 255 million to 275 million.

3. Population demographics favor home buying. The great majority of homes are bought by individuals and families within the 18 to 44 age group. In 1970, this group counted 70 million; in 1980, 91.3 million; and in 1990, 105.1 million people were in this prime home-buying age group.

4. Population demographics favor home ownership. At age 25 or less, only 15 percent of households own their own home. By age 50, nearly 80 percent of all Americans have become homeowners. As baby boomers approach their 40s and 50s during the coming 10 years, their currently lagging rates of home ownership should shoot up dramatically.

5. Incomes are increasing. Between 1989 and the end of 1994, the total personal income of Americans increased from $4.3 trillion to $5.8 trillion. Per capita disposable income increased during these years from $15,307 to more than $18,600.

6. New-housing supply is down. Between 1983 and 1989, home builders constructed an average of 1.64 million new single-family houses and apartments each year. During the first three years of the 1990s, builders built just 1.1 million housing units each year. For 1993 and 1994, the numbers were around 1.3 million each year.

7. The costs of home building are increasing. Environmental controls, zoning regulations, lumber prices, taxes, impact fees, assessments, ADA (Americans with Disabilities Act) requirements, and other costs are forcing many builders to raise prices.

8. Financial institutions have tightened their lending for subdivision development and new-home building. Many developers and home builders can't get the financing they need for site acquisition, development, and construction.

Taken together, these market fundamentals—increasing demand, increased building costs, and lower levels of new construction—spell opportunity for home buyers. Some cities and neighborhoods will experience greater rates of appreciation than others, but wealth building doesn't require double-digit runaway inflation. Over a period of years, even modest increases can produce large gains.

As you can see from the wealth-building home equity amounts in Figure 10–1, even at just a 3-percent rate of appreciation, your home equity triples from $10,000 to $30,772 after just five years of ownership; by year 10, it's up to $56,279; and by year 30, an original $10,000 down payment will have grown to nearly $250,000. If your home grows in value at an average rate of 7 percent a year, you will hit $55,000 in equity after just five years; after 20 years of ownership, you will have accumulated home equity wealth of $333,951; and by the time your mortgage is paid off after 30 years, your original $10,000 investment will have grown more than 75-fold and will exceed $750,000.

With numbers like these, it's no wonder Peter Lynch, one of the most successful stock market investors in the United States, encourages Americans to begin their wealth building with home ownership. In his best-selling and highly regarded book, *One Up on Wall Street*, this director of the Fidelity Magellan group of mutual funds writes, "Before you invest anything in stocks, you ought to buy a house. A house, after all, is the one good investment that almost everyone can make. . . . It's no accident that people who are geniuses in choosing their home are idiots in picking stocks. A house investment is entirely rigged in the homeowner's favor." As Peter Lynch knows, home ownership remains your surest and safest way to build wealth.

RENTERS BECOME POORER

As homeowners build wealth throughout their lives, renters often become poorer. A recent study by the U.S. Department of Housing

FIGURE 10–1 Building Wealth Through Increasing Home Equity*

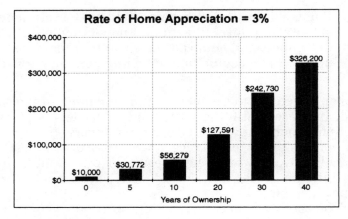

Rate of Home Appreciation = 3%

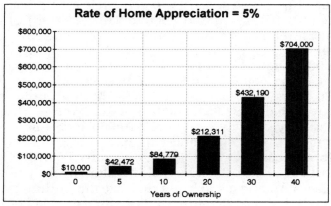

Rate of Home Appreciation = 5%

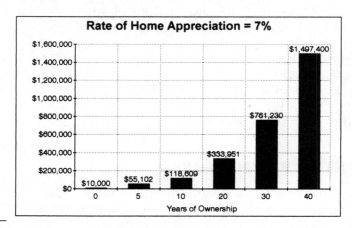

Rate of Home Appreciation = 7%

*Assumes a $10,000 down payment on a $100,000 home financed over 30 years at an interest rate of 7.5 percent. Home equity is created both by paying down the mortgage balance and by price appreciation of the home.

and Urban Development and the U.S. Bureau of the Census has discovered that renters pay a much larger share of their incomes for rent than homeowners pay for their homes. In fact, 20 percent of renters hand over more than one-half of their incomes to their landlords. In contrast, only 6.6 percent of homeowners have to part with so much of their cash each month just to keep a roof over their heads.

Once you think about it, the reason for this surprising statistic becomes obvious. As renters get older their rents keep going up, but due to ill health, layoffs, plant closings, retirement, or other causes, their income seldom keeps pace. (A layoff at age 30 can create temporary hardship; a layoff at age 52 can create economic disaster.) So over time, as rents go up and individual incomes level off or decline, renters must either switch to lower-cost apartments or cut back on spending for food, travel, clothes, entertainment, or other expenses. They become poorer.

For most of us, it's nearly impossible now to think about how high rents will be in the future because the numbers look so ridiculously large. Yet, in the late 1940s and 1950s, renters could find many houses to rent for $25 to $75 a month. Today, comparable houses might go for $500 to $1,500 a month. Who could have imagined in those earlier years that rents would head up by multiples of 20 or 30?

Over the next 10, 20, 30 or 40 years, on average, how much do you think rents will go up? What seems reasonable—3 percent a year, 5 percent, maybe 8 percent? Table 10.1 shows what future rents will look like at these relatively modest yearly increases.

As you can see, over a period of years, the multiplier effects of compound interest on rents can be overwhelming. Although you might be able to afford rent increases of 3 percent a year, do you think you could easily pay yearly rent increases of 5 or 8 percent? Do you really want to leave your future financial well-being to chance?

According to the Consumer Price Index, rents have gone up during the past 12 years by almost 6 percent a year. Renters who paid $600 a month in 1980 could easily be paying more than $1,000 a month for rent today. On the other hand, 1980 home-owners who then paid around $750 a month (pre-tax) for principal, interest, property taxes, and insurance (PITI), would now pay around $550 a month, after a 1990s refinance. After

TABLE 10-1
Effects of Yearly Increases on Future Rents

Today's Rent	Years/Future Rent Levels			
	10	20	30	40
Monthly Rents with Annual Increases @ 3%				
$ 600	$ 805	$1083	$1456	$1957
900	1209	1625	2184	2936
1200	1612	2167	2912	3915
Monthly Rents with Annual Increases @ 5%				
$ 600	$ 974	$1592	$2593	$4224
900	1461	2388	3889	6336
1200	1948	3184	5185	8448
Monthly Rents with Annual Increases @ 8%				
$ 600	$1295	$2797	$ 6038	$13,035
900	1943	4195	9057	19,553
1200	2591	5593	12,076	26,070

income tax deductions, the actual cost of their mortgage payments probably would drop to somewhere between $425 and $475 a month. If these typical homeowners had earned $27,000 a year in 1980, their monthly payments would have taken 33 percent of their income. If, over the years, their income went up 6 percent a year, they would now be earning around $57,000 a year. Their mortgage payments would have dropped to less than 10 percent of their income.

Wasting Money on Rent

Often you see figures showing how much you really pay for a home after you factor in 30 years of interest. But how much do you think you will pay for rent? Here's how the numbers compare: Let's say that after allowing for income tax deductions, you pay $1,000 a month for your home during the next 30 years. That comes to total payments of $360,000.

Now let's say you could rent a similar house today for $900 a month. So (excluding gains from appreciation) it seems like renting costs less. But if your rents go up by just 5 percent a year, over a period of 30 years your total rent payments will add up to more than $700,000. You will have wasted nearly three-quarters of a million dollars. And, of course, after this 30 years has passed, you still will have to pay rent for the rest of your life, whereas homeowners will not only be relieved of making monthly mortgage payments, they will own a home free and clear worth hundreds of thousands of dollars.

There's still another reason renters nearly always end up poorer than homeowners. As we just saw, due to increasing earnings, homeowners pay a decreasing percentage of their incomes for housing. This means that over time, homeowners enjoy larger discretionary incomes, which they can use to accumulate stocks, bonds, more real estate, or other investments.

Renters Build Less Wealth with Other Investments

Let's look once again at a renting versus owning example. Consider two average families who in 1980 both earned $25,000 a year. One family bought a home and had to pay $750 a month (after tax deductions) to cover their mortgage payments, property taxes, and homeowners insurance. The other family chose to rent. They paid $600 a month for their house. Today, both families have gross incomes of $50,000 a year, or about $4,160 a month.

Our homeowners recently refinanced their mortgage. Their monthly payments dropped from $750 to $560 a month. They now pay just 13.5 percent of their monthly income for housing. On the other hand, facing 6 percent yearly rent increases over the past 15 years, the renting family now pays around $1,380 a month, which takes 33 percent of their monthly income.

The renting family currently pays $840 a month more to rent than the family who bought pays to own. The homeowners enjoy far more discretionary income to invest. During the coming 10 years, the situation will get much worse for the renters. Even with only 4 percent yearly increases in rents, by the year 2004 this family will be paying close to $2,000 a month for rent—$1,400 a month more for housing than the owners have to pay. (As a bonus, of course, in 2004 the owning family will just about have their home mortgage paid off.)

It's easy to see why homeowners build more home equity wealth than renters. But the fact is often overlooked that owners also accumulate more wealth through other investments. Over time, as homeowners pay less and less of their income for their home, they can put increasing amounts into stocks, bonds, and other investments. On the other hand, not only do individuals and families who fail to own waste their money on rent, but because rents keep going up, these people generally fail to build wealth and financial security through savings and other investments. They end up poorer two ways.

START BUILDING WEALTH:
BECOME A HOMEOWNER

Do you ever debate with yourself whether you should buy a home? One day you think you should. The next day you change your mind. So it goes, and you never commit to a firm decision. You drift. Some renters waste years struggling through this imagined dilemma.

Now, here's what may come as a surprise: The question of whether to buy poses a false debate. For even when you pay rent, you *are* buying. That's already been decided. The only question is, Who's going to own the property you do buy? You or your landlord? Choosing to rent means that you're buying a house or apartment not for yourself, but for someone else.

The question for you to answer is: "Do I want to own *my own* home?"—not just, "Do I want to *buy* a home?" You must choose: Will you continue to build wealth for a series of landlords? Or will you start building wealth and financial security for yourself?

From earlier chapters, you've learned that with the right attitude, education, and financial planning, you can bring the dream of home ownership within your grasp. When you want to own, when you plan to own, you can own. In this chapter you've seen how through the magic of leverage and compound interest, even a low rate of appreciation can grow a small down payment into hundreds of thousands of dollars of home equity. Wouldn't you rather see this fortune belong to you instead of your landlords? Without a doubt, your home will stand as far more than just a comfortable place to live. It's still the best investment you can make. Owning your own home will set you on the surest path to achieving long-term emotional and financial security.

This year between four and five million individuals, couples, and families will buy homes. What do you think? Wouldn't you like to join them? Isn't it time for you to get out of a rental, move up to home ownership, and start building wealth?

Then choose your Realtor, create an affordability strategy, and put your plan into action now. You'll be glad you did.

THE NATIONAL HOMEOWNERSHIP STRATEGY

THE WHITE HOUSE

WASHINGTON

May 2, 1995

Our nation's greatest promise has always been the chance to build a better life. For millions of America's working families throughout our history, owning a home has come to symbolize the realization of the American Dream. Yet sadly, in the 1980s, it became much harder for many young families to buy their first homes, and our national homeownership rate declined for the first time in forty-six years. Our Administration is determined to reverse this trend, and we are committed to ensuring that working families can once again discover the joys of owning a home.

This past year, I directed HUD Secretary Henry G. Cisneros to work with leaders of the housing industry, with nonprofit organizations, and with leaders at every level of government to develop a plan to boost homeownership in America to an all-time high by the end of this century. *The National Homeownership Strategy: Partners in the American Dream* outlines a substantive, detailed plan to reach this goal. This report identifies specific actions that the federal government, its partners in state and local government, the private, nonprofit community, and private industry will take to lower barriers that prevent American families from becoming homeowners. Working together, we can add as many as eight million new families to America's homeownership rolls by the year 2000.

Expanding homeownership will strengthen our nation's families and communities, strengthen our economy, and expand this country's great middle class. Rekindling the dream of homeownership for America's working families can prepare our nation to embrace the rich possibilities of the twenty-first century.

Bill Clinton

Source: The National Homeownership Strategy: Partners in the American Dream (Washington, DC: U.S. Department of Housing and Urban Development, May 1995).

Foreword

I am honored to present *The National Homeownership Strategy* for the consideration of the American people. The strategy was prepared in response to a request from President Clinton. On Nov. 5, 1994, the President called for a national effort to lift America's homeownership rate to an all-time high by the end of the century. He directed me to develop a National Homeownership Strategy to reach this goal and to form a national partnership of the private, public, and community sectors to carry out the strategy.

Homeownership is the American dream, but the dream has been fading since 1980, when the national homeownership rate slipped into decline after 46 years of steady growth. Although the homeownership rate has risen over the past 2 years, it is still well below its historic peak. Reviving the trend toward greater homeownership is vital to our Nation's families, communities, and economic prosperity.

The goal of this strategy is ambitious: to generate up to 8 million additional homeowners from 1995 through the year 2000. The strategy recommends a series of concerted actions to help middle-income and low-income families, racial and ethnic minorities, families with children, and young adults overcome current barriers to homeownership. These actions will be undertaken by private industry, national nonprofit organizations, nonprofit community groups, and Federal, State, and local governments working in cooperation at the national, State, and local levels.

Working as partners in this way, we can translate strategy into achievement, making the dream of homeownership a reality for millions of hard-working people and building a better future for all Americans.

Henry G. Cisneros
Secretary of Housing
and Urban Development

OVERVIEW

This appendix reiterates the theme and many of the topics covered in the earlier chapters of this book. In the following pages I have summarized the National Homeownership Strategy so you can see for yourself that we are truly entering a new era for home buying and home financing. Because of a national commitment to this Strategy, renters who believed they were years away from owning are finding that they can become homeowners now.

WHAT IS THE NATIONAL HOMEOWNERSHIP STRATEGY?

As President Clinton and HUD Secretary Cisneros point out in their letters, the overall purpose of the National Homeownership Strategy is to raise the number of homeowners in the United States to a record high by the year 2000. To achieve this goal, an enormous effort will be put forth by federal, state, and local government agencies; not-for-profit neighborhood housing groups; and thousands of men and women who work in real estate sales, home building, home financing, and related services (insurers, title companies, appraisers). In other words, all of these "partners" want to make it easier for you to own your own home. That's the bottom line.

WHY HOME OWNERSHIP?

Those who have committed to this public–private partnership believe that private property rights are basic to the American Way of Life. Naturally, then, the larger the number of individuals and families who can own their own homes, the greater the number of Americans and recent immigrants who can, in the words of President Clinton, "try to build their own personal version of the American Dream."

More specifically, those who support the Strategy's goals firmly believe home ownership will benefit you and your community, state, and nation in four major ways:

1. Home Ownership Builds Personal Financial Security

As is illustrated in Chapter 10, home ownership will lead you to build home equity both through paying off your mortgage and through long-term increases in your home's value. In addition, because your maximum mortgage payment is fixed, over time, your housing costs will require a smaller and smaller percentage of your monthly earnings as you advance in your career and job opportunities.

This declining real cost of housing will leave you more money to make other types of investments. Also, the equity you build in your home might later provide the money you need to start your own business, pay college tuition for your children, or perhaps trade up to a larger or more expensive home or neighborhood. Through the use of a reverse annuity mortgage, you might also choose to use your home equity to boost your retirement income. As history has repeatedly proven, most homeowners build wealth, while most renters become less able to meet their housing needs.

Which would you rather experience: watching the value of your home increase or watching your rent go up?

2. Home Ownership Strengthens Families and Promotes Good Citizenship

When people own their own homes, they develop a more responsible attitude toward the property rights of others and they take on more responsibility for keeping their own homes well maintained. In terms of social problems, studies show that children of homeowning families are less likely to be tempted into drugs or gangs and they are more likely to stay in school and make better grades.

As a result of home ownership, families feel more in control of their lives and become more confident that they can achieve other important life goals. Although no one would claim that home ownership is the cure-all for personal or social difficulties, the partners of the National Homeownership Strategy believe it's an excellent start.

3. Home Ownership Helps to Build (Rebuild) Neighborhoods and Communities

Walk through a neighborhood of homes where most people rent. Then walk through a neighborhood where the great majority of residents own their own homes. At all income levels and price ranges, it's nearly always true that predominantly owner-occupied neighborhoods are better kept, more attractive, safer, and more desirable than their renter-occupied counterparts.

When people own their own homes, they are "stockholders" in their neighborhood. These people know that one of the best ways to create appreciation for their homes is to join together in neighborhood action groups, and pitching in to eliminate a neighborhood's negatives and build up its positives. Home ownership leads to revitalized communities.

4. Home Ownership Stimulates Job Growth

The largest industry in this country is home ownership: home building, home improvement, home financing, and home marketing. "When we boost the number of homeowners in our country," says President Clinton, "we strengthen our economy, create jobs, build up the middle-class, and build better citizens. . . .

"When a family buys a home, the ripple effect is enormous. [People] need more durable goods like washers and dryers, refrigerators, and water heaters. If more families could buy new homes—or even older homes—more hammers will be pounding, more saws will be buzzing. Home builders and home fixers will be put to work."

Agreeing with Mr. Clinton, Gill Woods, the president of the National Association of Realtors, says, "This effort will be good for housing, and more importantly, good for America. Any plan to increase home ownership is a step forward, and we are very pleased to be a part of this initiative." Echoing President Clinton and Mr. Woods, the *San Francisco Chronicle*, like other members of the media, has given the National Homeownership Strategy a big "thumbs up."

"The administration's thoughtful new plan to increase home ownership in America is overdue," announces the *Chronicle*. "It costs the taxpayers nothing, yet its implementation will bring benefits to individuals and the nation alike. It represents the best kind of private–public partnership. . . . A boost in home ownership strengthens the economy by creating jobs and increasing the need for more durable goods. It gives people a greater stake in their communities, making them better citizens. . . . Working together [the partnership's strategy] is to make it less expensive to buy, rehabilitate, or build homes, make it easier for people to get mortgages, and increase the production of affordable homes."[1]

LEARN ALL YOU CAN ABOUT THE NATIONAL HOMEOWNERSHIP STRATEGY

President Clinton announced this partnership initiative to expand home ownership in a speech delivered in November of 1994 at the National Association of Realtors annual convention. He told the 17,000 attendees that, "Most people don't start saving for a home until they believe they can actually buy a home . . . [but] I want to say to the American people, and especially to young families, if that is what you think, you ought to start saving now because I am determined to see that you have this opportunity."

That statement sums up the president's mission and the mission accepted and endorsed by all of the partners to this initiative. It's also the basic theme of this book: "If you want to own your own home, you can own your own home."

But you should realize that even though the National Homeownership Strategy was announced in November of 1994, it was not officially put into effect until the White House Homeownership Event was held on June 5, 1995.

During the intervening months hundreds of volunteers worked to come up with 100 "action items" that form the core of this Strategy. Yet, much more work still needs to be done. Experiments will be tried. Successes will be expanded. Things that aren't working will be revamped.

So, consider this book as a primer. It gives you the basic knowledge you need. But (regardless of what happens in the 1996 presidential elections) the partners in this initiative are committed to positive and continuous changes until at least the year 2000.

Therefore, over the next several pages of this appendix, I identify the current partnership organizations as well as list and briefly discuss the National Homeownership Strategy's 100 action items. As this Strategy continues to unfold, follow up on

---

[1]Editorial. The *San Francisco Chronicle* (June 6, 1995):A18.

what's happening in your area. Contact local chapters of partnership organizations. Talk to Realtors, mortgage lenders, home builders, and not-for-profit housing groups. Or, please call me at (800) 942-9304 (extension 20691). By staying alert and learning all you can about new home finance programs and new home buying techniques, you're sure to find that, *Yes! You Can Own the Home You Want.*

56 ORGANIZATIONS THAT HAVE SIGNED PARTNERSHIP AGREEMENTS BY 6/1/95[2]

American Bankers Association
American Institute of Architects
American Land Title Association
American Planning Association
America's Community Bankers
Appraisal Institute
Association of Community Organizations for Reform Now (ACORN)
Association of Local Housing Finance Agencies
Center for Neighborhood Technology
Community Development Financial Institutions Fund
Corporation for National Service
Council of American Building Officials

Council of State Community Development Agencies
Enterprise Foundation
Fannie Mae
Federal Home Loan Bank System
Freddie Mac
Habitat for Humanity International
Housing Assistance Council
Local Initiatives Support Corporation (LISC)
Manufactured Housing Institute
Mortgage Bankers Association of America
Mortgage Insurance Companies of America
National American Indian Housing Council
National Association for the Advancement of Colored People (NAACP)

---

[2]*Source: The National Homeowner Strategy: Partners in the American Dream* (Washington, DC: U.S. Department of Housing and Urban Development, May 1995).

National Association of Affordable Housing Lenders

National Association of Counties

National Association of County Community and Economic Development

National Association of Home Builders

National Association of Real Estate Brokers

National Association of Realtors

National Bankers Association

National Community Development Association

National Community Reinvestment Coalition

National Conference of States on Building Code Standards

National Congress of Community Economic Development

National Cooperative Bank

National Council of La Raza

National Council of State Housing Agencies

National Fire Protection Association

National Foundation of Consumer Credit

National Foundation of Manufactured Home Owners

National Hispanic Housing Council

National Low Income Housing Coalition

National Neighborhood Coalition

National Trust for Historic Preservation

National Urban League

Neighborhood Reinvestment Corportion

Resolution Trust Corporation

Social Compact

U.S. Department of Agriculture

U.S. Department of Housing and Urban Development

U.S. Department of Veterans Affairs.

United Homeowners Association

United States Conference of Mayors

Urban Land Institute

NATIONAL HOMEOWNERSHIP STRATEGY
LIST OF PROPOSED ACTIONS[3]

Production

Action   1:   Assessing Regulatory Impacts on Affordable Home-ownership

Action   2:   Modernizing Planning, Zoning, and Subdivision Laws

Action   3:   Education and Technical Assistance for Regulatory Reform

Action   4:   Consensus Building and Mediation Techniques for Affordable Homeownership

Action   5:   Statewide Standards for Impact Fees

Action   6:   Models of Regulatory Flexibility and Development Controls

Action   7:   Expanded Research on Regulatory Reform

Action   8:   Building Code Reform

Action   9:   Education and Outreach for Higher Density Home Construction

Action 10:   Fast-Track Administrative Review Procedures for Starter Homes

Action 11:   Removing Barriers to Mortgage Financing for Starter Homes

Action 12:   Stock Plans and Guidance Materials for Starter Homes

Action 13:   Flexible Regulations to Accommodate Home Rehabilitation

Action 14:   Home Rehabilitation Research

Action 15:   Technical Evaluation and Guidance Materials for Energy Conservation

Action 16:   Affordable Home Technology Program

Action 17:   Information, Training, and Technical Assistance for Innovative Technologies

Action 18:   Affordable Home Design and Construction Awards

Action 19:   Stock Plans for Building Affordable Homes

Action 20:   Enhanced Homebuilding Product Evaluation

Action 21:   HUD Technical Evaluations of Homebuilding Products

---

[3]Source: *The National Homeowner Strategy: Partners in the American Dream* (Washington, DC: U.S. Department of Housing and Urban Development, May 1995).

Action 49: Continuation of the Mortgage Revenue Bond Program and Mortgage Credit Certificates
Action 50: Energy Efficiency and Home Mortgage Underwriting
Action 51: Cooperative Homeownership

Building Communities

Action 52: Homeownership Education and Technical Assistance for Communities
Action 53: Spotlight on Successful Local Partnerships
Action 54: Employer-Assisted Homeownership
Action 55: Location-Efficient Home Mortgages
Action 56: Comprehensive Community Revitalization
Action 57: Homeownership Zones
Action 58: Federal and State Resources for Affordable Homeownership
Action 59: Promoting Mixed-Income Neighborhoods
Action 60: Redeveloping Vacant Properties
Action 61: Mortgage Credit for Rural Areas
Action 62: Rural Home Financing Demonstration Program
Action 63: Expanding Rural Home Financing
Action 64: Homeownership Capacity Building in Rural Areas
Action 65: Rehabilitating Rural Homes
Action 66: Homeownership Opportunities for Native Americans

Opening Markets

Action 67: The President's Fair Housing Council
Action 68: Voluntary Fair Housing Self-Enforcement and Affirmative Marketing by Homeownership Industry Organizations
Action 69: Metropolitan Regional Fair Housing Initiatives
Action 70: Voluntary Self-Enforcement and Affirmative Marketing by Mortgage Lending and Homeowners Insurance Industry Organizations
Action 71: Access to Home Mortgage Lending Data
Action 72: Research on Fair Lending and Insurance Issues
Action 73: Market Review of Underserved Groups and Communities

Action 74: Workplace Diversity in Hiring and Promotion
Action 75: Research on the Homeownership Impacts of Diversity
Action 76: Mentoring Minority-Owned Homeownership Businesses
Action 77: Marketing Homeownership Products and Programs in Foreign Languages
Action 78: Tailoring Home Design and Construction to Diverse Populations
Action 79: Homeownership Models That Work
Action 80: "One-Stop" Home Financing Catalogue

Homeownership Education and Counseling

Action 81: National Institute for Homeownership Education and Counseling
Action 82: Federal Efforts to Build Local Homeownership Counseling Capacity
Action 83: Research on Homeownership Education and Counseling
Action 84: Clearinghouse for Homeownership Education and Counseling
Action 85: Curriculum Development for Homeownership Education and Counseling
Action 86: Training and Accreditation for Homeownership Education and Counseling
Action 87: Cultural Sensitivity and Diversity in Homeownership Education and Counseling
Action 88: Education on Alternative Forms of Homeownership
Action 89: Task Force on Long-Term Funding of Homeownership Counseling
Action 90: Nonprofit Business Planning for Homeownership Counseling Organizations
Action 91: HUD Allocation of Counseling Funds
Action 92: Showcasing Successful Collaborative Homeownership Counseling Programs
Action 93: Local Homeownership Counseling Roundtables

Raising Awareness

Action 94: Publicizing Homeownership Opportunities and Achievements

Action 95: Homeownership Site Visits
Action 96: Successful Transitions to Homeownership
Action 97: Homeownership Educational Centers and Special
             Events
Action 98: Educating Homebuyers and Homeowners Through
             Technology and the Media
Action 99: Homebuyer Access to Government-Owned Homes
Action 100: Research Networks and Information Clearinghouses
             on Homeownership Data

HOW YOU CAN BENEFIT FROM THE
NATIONAL HOMEOWNERSHIP STRATEGY

As you can see from the previous listing, the 100 action items of
the National Homeownership Strategy are categorized into six
topic areas:

1. *Production:* Reducing the costs of new construction and
    rehabilitation.

2. *Financing:* Increasing the availability of home financing
    and lowering its costs.

3. *Building Communities:* Working locally to identify and
    revitalize home ownership opportunities in underserved
    geographic communities.

4. *Opening Markets:* Reaching out to minorities, immigrants,
    single-parent households, and other people whose rates
    of home ownership fall below national averages.

5. *Home Ownership Counseling:* Providing a critical link
    between individual first-time home buyers and what often
    seems to be a complex and perplexing home buying
    process.

6. *Raising Public Awareness:* Informing members of the
    general public and target audiences of the Strategy and
    encouraging and promoting the idea of home ownership
    as an achievable goal.

Although space does not permit me to discuss each of the 100
action items individually, I have summarized many of the most

important points. For further information as to what's happening
in your area, I again remind you to talk with local affiliates of
the partnership groups.

Production: Lowering Construction Costs

Today, the average price for a newly constructed home in the
United States is approaching $130,000. Obviously, this price is
outside the affordability range of many low- to middle-income
families. So, the National Homeownership Strategy is searching
for ways to reduce the costs of construction. One important
solution is reduced government regulation.

Reducing Regulations

Would it surprise you to learn that current government regulations add 20 to 35 percent to the costs of a new home? Restrictive
zoning laws, minimum lot sizes, health and safety codes, environmental restrictions, architectural review boards, multiple and
contradictory government approval processes that can delay a
subdivision development for years and run up hundreds of
thousands of dollars in legal fees, land holding costs, and interest
expense all combine to push home prices up.

In addition, in many cities and suburbs, home builders must
pay the government anywhere from $3,000 to $30,000 in "impact
fees" for each house they build. Although ostensibly these fees
are supposed to reimburse governments for necessary public
services, quite often they are used to raise home prices and
unfairly shift the tax burden to the purchasers of new homes.

Of course, no one argues that new housing developments
shouldn't pay their fair share for government services, nor that
home builders should be able to build free of all regulation. But
the National Homeownership Strategy does call for "the reinven-
tion of state and local housing development approval processes
. . . and eliminating unnecessary, excessive, and duplicative
regulatory barriers to the production of affordable homes." It also
encourages statewide standards for impact fees that require a
direct relationship between the amount of fees levied and the
government benefits that buyers of new homes will receive.

What This Means to You: Talk to local home builders and
government planning offices. See whether any reduced-cost, less

regulated new home developments are planned or under construction in your area.

More Starter Homes

Between 1970 and the early 1990s the average home size grew from 1,385 square feet to 1,920 square feet. Homes also grew in terms of amenities: fireplaces, vaulted ceilings, decks, double- and triple-car garages, built-in appliances, and other extras have now become commonplace. While these increased square-footages and amenities are certainly appreciated by many home buyers, they also add significantly to new home prices.

So as part of the National Homeownership Strategy, home builders, government planners, and regulatory officials have agreed to "go back to basics." They have promised to build more starter homes of 900 to 1,300 square feet with fewer amenities. The idea is to build a low-cost house. Then, later, buyers can add on space or perhaps finish off previously uncompleted rooms to expand and upgrade their homes as their incomes increase.

Other parts of the starter home strategy include relaxed regulations for homes with a second unit (duplex) or an accessory apartment. At one time, it was common for home buyers to help meet their mortgage payments with income from extra living units or by taking in boarders (now called *housemates*—see Chapter 5). It's now time to again make this affordability strategy more widely available.

What This Means to You: Check with your local planners, regulatory officials, and home builders. See whether you can locate any starter home developments in your area. Also, learn which neighborhoods have been zoned (or rezoned) to legalize homes with extra income units.

Making Home Financing Easier and Less Costly

The National Homeownership Strategy clearly recognizes that to help renters move up to home ownership, lenders must lower the costs of home financing and make sure all good people who want home loans can obtain them. Of course, you may still have to take steps to strengthen your borrower profile, but the partners to the Strategy have pledged themselves to:

1.   Cut loan transaction costs and speed up loan processing.

2.   Expand the number of ways cash-poor renters can safely buy with little (or no) down payment.

3.   Increase the availability of home financing for underserved markets and non-conforming or non-traditional types of properties and living arrangements.

Cut Transactions Costs

With some loan programs, closing (settlement) costs can amount to nearly as much as your down payment. On a $100,000 loan, transaction expenses of $4,000 to $8,000 (not including the real estate sales commission) are not out of the ordinary. These expenses may include application fees, origination fees, mortgage points, mortgage insurance, home inspection, home warranty, title insurance, lawyer bills, appraisal, survey, pest inspection, environmental inspection, credit report, escrow for homeowners insurance and property taxes, courier services, documentary stamps, recording fees, and a variety of other miscellaneous charges. In addition, just to collect and put together piles of "necessary" documents, forms, and verifications, lenders can frequently require four to twelve weeks of loan processing time.

The Strategy's partners believe there's got to be a better, faster, and less costly way to handle all of this paperwork. Moreover, they are questioning whether much of it is even necessary.

What This Means to You: To get faster, less expensive closings, look for lenders who are traveling the fast lane along the information highway. These lenders are more fully automating their loan processing, underwriting, and appraisals. Some lenders, too, are "bulk purchasing" various types of services (appraisal, property inspections, title insurance, etc.) and passing these savings on to home buyers. When comparing lenders, don't just shop interest rates; also check out closing costs and loan processing procedures.

Reduce Down Payments

The down payment poses a big obstacle to many renters who would like to own their own homes. To meet this need, mortgage lenders are developing and promoting various types of low- (and even no-) down-payment mortgages. (Fannie 97 is just one example.) Beyond the *amount* of down payment, though, lenders frequently set rules concerning the *source* of the down payment.

In this respect, the Strategy partners are encouraging lenders to accept nontraditional sources of down payment money. Gifts or loans from relatives; pooled funds of family members; retirement funds; rent credits from lease-option/lease-purchase agreements; sweat equity; employer, government, or not-for-profit down payment assistance; and even "mattress money" (if verified) are now permitted in some loan programs.

Still, even though lower down payments are becoming more popular, the more cash you can save on your own, the better. To assist in this respect, some lenders are sponsoring various incentive savings plans especially designed to encourage renters to accumulate money for a down payment. Also, Realtors, lenders, and other partners in the Strategy might be able to refer you to a "home buyer club" where members motivate each other and swap information about homes, neighborhoods, lenders, and loan programs.

What This Means to You: The field of low- (or no-) down-payment home finance plans is expanding and changing rapidly. Keep informed and stay alert and you're nearly certain to find a plan that can work for you.

Broaden the Availability of Mortgage Financing

Although mortgage money is widely available to purchase a nice, three-bedroom, two-bath ranch home in the suburbs, it can be more difficult to locate lenders who will finance a run-down, three-family house located in a central city neighborhood of marginal quality. Yet, to bring these properties and neighborhoods back to prosperity requires large infusions of cash.

Fortunately, the National Homeownership Strategy recognizes this difficulty. As a result, mortgage lenders are developing a variety of loan products that home buyers (and homeowners) can use to rehabilitate houses and revitalize neighborhoods. (The newly streamlined FHA 203[k] is one example.) Also, because many low- to moderate-income individuals and families need the income from multiple-unit properties to help them meet their monthly mortgage payments, some lenders are becoming more flexible in how they incorporate rental unit income into a borrower's qualifying income.

What This Means to You: Mortgage lenders are re-evaluating their underwriting, appraisal, down payment, and qualifying ratio guidelines for previously nonconforming or nontraditional neighborhoods, properties, and borrowers. They are trying harder, too, to give greater weight to compensating factors. They are also combining efforts with not-for-profit housing groups and government agencies. So, if you would like to rehab a home to enhance its value, or work to help turn around and revitalize a neighborhood, the chances are good that you can locate a lender and other "partners" to support your efforts to achieve this goal.

Building Communities

The "Building Communities" initiative of the National Home-ownership Strategy encourages individual partners in the Strategy to join with other partners to create team projects. These projects will be designed not only to help individuals, but also to give more "oomph" to rebuilding and revitalizing entire neighborhoods and communities. Specifically, this part of the action plan will consist of four general goals:

1. Build local capacity.
2. Expand home ownership opportunities close to job centers.
3. Revitalize the infrastructure of urban neighborhoods.
4. Improve housing and home ownership in rural areas.

Build Local Capacity

To revitalize and strengthen neighborhoods and communities will require large numbers of local service providers who have knowledge and experience in the areas they serve. It also will require money.

Thus, the Strategy is bringing in human and financial resources from local Realtors; Realtists; home builders; loan officers and bank executives; insurance agents; suppliers of building materials; not-for-profit employees and volunteers; city, county, and state housing finance officers; redevelopment agencies; church members; business owners and employers; and everyone else who wants to improve the quality of life in targeted areas.

By fostering cooperation among many different businesses,

churches, government agencies, financial institutions, and of course, community residents themselves, much more can be accomplished than if individual partners to the Strategy set out on their own. While it takes an entire village to raise a child, it also takes an entire community to revitalize a neighborhood and replace the absentee landlords (including the U.S. Government) with owner-occupied homes and resident-owned apartment buildings and cooperatives.

What This Means to You: In the past, scattered and uncoordinated efforts of individual citizens, service providers, and government agencies frequently have not been enough to reverse neighborhood decline. Now, with the Strategy's emphasis on teamwork and building local capacity for revitalization, you've got a much greater opportunity to take part in and profit from owning a home in a turnaround neighborhood.

Expand Home Ownership Opportunities Close to Job Centers

In many higher cost cities throughout the country, low- to middle-income individuals can't afford to live within a close commute of their jobs. Or, if they can find lower-cost home ownership possibilities nearby, more than likely they're not in neighborhoods that present an appealing quality of life. Of course, that's one reason neighborhood revitalization is so important.

But, in addition, the Strategy is working with government agencies, private lenders, and employers to help find other ways to overcome this difficulty. Down payment assistance, cut-rate interest on mortgages, and low (or no) closing costs on home loans are three possibilities that are being promoted. Other efforts include "location-efficient" mortgages (i.e., a lender will qualify you for a much larger mortgage if you live close enough to work to avoid any significant commuting expenses), in-fill development on city owned-lots, and rehabbing city-owned abandoned houses and apartment buildings.

What This Means to You: If you can't afford to buy a home close to your job, check with local lenders, city housing finance agencies, redevelopment agencies, and not-for-profit housing groups to learn about special home finance and home buying programs for which you might be eligible.

These types of programs especially are becoming more common for teachers, policemen, firefighters, social workers, and other government employees who otherwise are priced out of the housing markets in the cities where they work. Also, don't forget to investigate any help that your employer or your employer's credit union might offer.

Revitalize the Infrastructure of Urban Neighborhoods

Rehabbing houses and converting renters into homeowners is only part of the job that needs to be done to revitalize neighborhoods. The Strategy also recognizes that partners must operate politically to enhance the quality of community police and fire protection, schools, parks, streets, and other municipal services.

A desirable community doesn't just mean homeowners. It means a safe, clean, and pleasant environment that's attractive for those business people who create jobs as well as the grocers, restaurants, dry cleaners, hardware stores, pharmacies, and other merchants that every neighborhood needs to prosper.

The National Homeownership Strategy is promoting the revitalization of Urban neighborhoods through Empowerment Zones, the Enterprise Communities Program, the new Community Development Financial Institutions Fund, and Homeownership Zones. With such concentrated local impact, according to the Strategy, these efforts "can help spawn genuine neighborhood revitalization, civic spirit, and community involvement that goes beyond the scope of the initial number of homes sold."

What This Means to You: To really boost your ability to pick a winner in the neighborhood turnaround sweepstakes, look for areas that are likely candidates for "Homeownership Zone" designations. In addition, homes in these areas often qualify for lower interest mortgage bond financing and mortgage credit certificates (MCCs).

Homeownership in Rural Areas

The poor quality of many houses in rural areas combined with generally low to moderate family incomes has made it difficult for many noncity people to obtain loans to buy their own homes. To meet this challenge, the National Homeownership Strategy plans to increase the amount of mortgage money flowing into rural areas and to rewrite loan underwriting criteria to better match the realities of life in America's small towns and farm country.

Fannie Mae, for example, is circulating a newly revised version of its more flexible *Guide to Underwriting Rural Properties* to rural lenders. Also, Strategy partners are working to better publicize the rural lending programs of FHA, FmHA, and various state housing finance agencies. Plus, 40 percent of HUD's proposed Affordable Housing Fund will be earmarked for rural areas. The Strategy is also pushing to widen the rural availability of rehab loan products such as the FHA 203(k) program.

What This Means to You: Even if in the past you've been unsuccessful in trying to buy and finance a home in a rural area, prepare yourself to try again. Within the coming year or two, lenders will be making available an increasing variety of easier-qualifying "rural responsive" home mortgages and property rehabilitation loans.

Opening Markets

U.S. homeownership statistics clearly show that African Americans, Hispanics, recent immigrants, single-parent households, and persons under age 35 are much less likely to own their own homes than other Americans. In acknowledging this fact, the partners of the National Homeownership Strategy have agreed to reach out and break down barriers that may block members of these groups from even trying to become homeowners. As I point out in Chapter 9, "lenders want to loan you money regardless of your race, sex, ethnicity, or any other irrelevant personal characteristic." More specifically, the Strategy, itself sets the following goals:

1. Promote fair housing by removing barriers to purchasing a home. This includes more flexible underwriting, greater use of "testers," and affirmative marketing agreements between HUD and Strategy partners.

2. Promote fair lending and fair access to homeowners insurance. Essentially, this means "greenlining" (putting money into turnaround neighborhoods) rather than "redlining" (keeping certain neighborhoods off limits to mortgage loans and property insurance).

3. Increase minority employment as real estate agents, mort-

gage loan officers, appraisers, and other service providers within the home ownership delivery system.

4. Increase marketing and promotion efforts in underserved communities. Set performance targets (rather than "spending budgets") to measure results and continually enhance and broaden efforts that prove successful.

"Our reaching out to these potential homebuyers is not only the law, it's the right thing to do," says Joe Pickett, president of the Mortgage Bankers Association of America. "It's those mortgage companies who reach out to potential homebuyers," Joe adds, "who will write our industry's success stories in the years ahead. . . . We need to make home ownership something all renters believe they can achieve, rather than something they assume they can't."

What This Means to You: Don't hold back from trying to buy a home out of fear of discrimination. Throw away any ideas that tell you loan officers and real estate agents don't want or don't appreciate your business. It's tough to make a living out there. Real estate agents and loan officers need all of the customers they can get. Also, don't believe that to qualify for a mortgage you must fit perfectly into some cookie-cutter mold. Mortgage lenders really are breaking down barriers to make qualifying for a mortgage more accessible to all potential home buyers.

Home Ownership Counseling

If, after reading this book, you still need help to prepare yourself for home buying and home financing, see if you can locate a home buyer counseling service in your area. The National Homeownership Strategy is placing great emphasis on personal counseling, especially to help low- to moderate-income households budget their finances. If you can't locate a home counseling service, call the Fannie Mae Home Path line at (800) 832-2345. They can put you in touch with a counseling service that's near you.

Also, don't forget, your Realtor, too, can help you develop a budget. In addition, even if you can't get your credit and finances in shape to qualify with a financial institution, a Realtor might be able to find you a non-qual assumable mortgage, owner-will-carry mortgage financing, a contract-for-deed installment pur-chase, or a lease-option/lease-purchase agreement.

What This Means to You: A current lack of education, credit, or cash need not block you from becoming a homeowner. Many dedicated people are willing to help you get prepared—if you will only ask them.

Raising Public Awareness

The sixth major goal of the National Homeownerhip Strategy is to raise public awareness of the Strategy and to promote the following messages:

1. Over time, renting will cost far more than owning. While tenants file away rent receipts, homeowners build wealth.

2. Home ownership is an achievable goal for all who plan for it.

3. Home ownership strengthens and revitalizes neighbor-hoods and communities.

4. As with any long-term investment, the sooner you get started, the better off you will be.

What This Means to You: Since you have no more excuses, isn't it time for you to stop renting now?

NEIGHBORHOOD CHECKLIST

I. How convenient (in time and distance) is the neighborhood?
   A. schools (public, private)
   B. restaurants and cafes
   C. your job
   D. your spouse's job
   E. shops and convenience stores
   F. shopping centers, supermarkets
   G. recreational facilities (parks, health clubs, tennis courts, library, bookstores, beaches, etc.)
   H. friends and relatives
   I. places of worship
II. What are the sources and costs of public or private transportation?
   A. buses
   B. commuter trains
   C. freeways, tollways
   D. ferries
   E. taxi or limousine service
   F. airport(s)
III. What legal restrictions apply?
   A. zoning laws (use, height, setback, floor area ratios, etc.)
   B. deed restrictions
   C. homeowner association rules and regulations
   D. environmental laws
   E. health and safety codes
   F. architectural review boards
IV. How good are the government (or private) services for the amount of taxes and fees you'll pay?
   A. schools

B. police and fire protection
C. utilities (water, sewage disposal, electric, gas, cable T.V., etc.)
D. trash pick-up, snow removal
E. parks, libraries, streets
F. cultural facilities
G. county, city, or other jurisdictional bond rating and indebtedness

V. What's the neighborhood like?
A. people (ages, occupation, family size, sociability, income level)
B. esthetics (cleanliness, upkeep, landscaping, quiet)
C. natural disaster potential (earthquake, flood, mudslide, windstorm, sinkholes)
D. microclimates (wind, sun, clouds, rainfall, snowfall, heat, cold)

VI. Is there good potential for appreciation?
A. civic and community spirit
B. community action
C. turnaround in process
D. new construction increasing
E. rehabs, remodeling, and renovations increasing
F. effective Neighborhood Watch and reduced crime
H. good relative value
I. close to job centers or other attractions
J. increasing demand for homes

HOME SELECTION CHECKLIST

I.   What are your top home buying goals?
    A.   first, choose ownership
    B.   affordability
    C.   neighborhood
    D.   bargain price
    E.   creation of value
    F.   appreciation potential
    G.   emotional appeal
    I.   a comfortable (convenient) place to live

II. What are the important site features?
    A.   site size, shape, and boundaries
    B.   soil quality
    C.   on-site amenities (fencing, swimming pool, side-
        walks, driveway, landscaping)
    D.   site grade
    E.   unique features (view, waterfront, cul-de-sac, private
        setting)
    F.   environmental quality (well water, underground stor-
        age tanks, radon, drainage)

III. What are the home's exterior features?
    A.   esthetics (design, color, cleanliness, visibility)
    B.   extras (hot tub, deck, patio, garage, porch)
    C.   construction materials (roof, siding)
    D.   maintenance requirements (time, effort, costs)
    E.   condition
    F.   site placement

IV. What are the home's interior features?
    A.   size (number and kind of rooms, square footage)
    B.   livability (floor plan, zones of privacy, closets and
        storage areas, soundproofing between rooms and
        other areas of the house)

    C.   esthetics (color, design, materials,)

    D.   physical condition (plumbing, HVAC, electrical, structural, ceilings, walls)

    E.   natural light (windows, skylights)

    F.   quality of finishing materials (doors, woodwork, carpeting, tile, plumbing fixtures, light fixtures)

    G.   personal property included (drapes, blinds, ceiling fans, storage shed, porch furniture, barbecue grill, wall mirrors, chandeliers, carpets or rugs, bar, other furniture)

V.   What is the home's profit potential?

    A.   accessory apartment (actual or possible)

    B.   fixer-upper (repair, remodel, redecorate)

    C.   located in an increasingly popular neighborhood

    D.   add-on potential (second story, extra bedroom, den, deck, etc.)

    E.   suitable for homesharing

    F.   more effective use of space

    G.   save money with owner financing or low rate assumable mortgage

THE MOST COSTLY MISTAKES IN HOME BUYING

Recently I was giving a radio interview to publicize my book, *The 106 Common Mistakes Home Buyers Make* (John Wiley & Sons, Inc.). The host of the show said he would like to discuss all 106 mistakes, but time wouldn't permit. So, as a start, could I tell the listening audience the 10 most costly mistakes that I have seen home buyers make over the years?

Naturally, as I told the interviewer, any mistake can be costly if it's the mistake you make. But, here are 10 that I've frequently witnessed. Yet, even though they can be costly, they're also among the easiest to avoid.

1. Waiting Too Long To Buy

Although exceptions do occur, buying now nearly always proves wiser than buying later. Even when you might live in an area for only a year or two, before you decide to rent, look into the possibilities of a lease-option, buying at a bargain price, buying a home where you can quickly create value, buying a home that has an easily assumable mortgage, or buying a home that would make a good rental property investment.

2. Waiting for Interest Rates to Come Down

If you think you're good at forecasting the direction of interest rates, go speculate in the bond market. You can make a killing. Then, you won't have to concern yourself with home financing. On the other hand, if you can't accurately predict interest rates, buy now and refinance when rates fall lower. If you hesitate and interest rates (or home prices) go up, then you're going to be either out of the home buying game or out-of-pocket thousands of additional dollars.

3. Buying with Your Eyes Focused on a Rearview Mirror

Most home buyers ask, "Which neighborhoods have appreciated the fastest?" Wrong question! You will be owning in the future, not the past. So investigate value signals. Don't simply assume that past rates of neighborhood appreciation will continue. Look for those neighborhoods that will be "hot" tomorrow, not necessarily those that were hot yesterday.

4. Relying on a Lender or a Real Estate Agent to Tell You Exactly How Much Home You Can Afford

How much home you can afford depends on how well you shape up your finances, what types of properties you're considering (duplex, fourplex, larger?), the type of financing (ARM, fixed-rate, GPM), the loan program (FHA, PMI, OWC, VA, non-qual assumable, first-time buyer, other), and myriad other details. A loan officer will tell you approximately how much money his or her bank will loan you. But you won't know how much home you can buy until you explore all of your possibilities.

5. Centering Negotiations on Price

Today, some real estate agents are advertising that they can help you buy a home at "the lowest possible price." Beware. When you offer to buy a home, you've got many items to negotiate. By focusing on "low price" you not only can antagonize the sellers, you may actually be passing up other goodies that can yield larger benefits. Instead of a single-minded pursuit of the lowest price, consider asking for seller-paid closing costs and/or buydown, owner-will-carry financing, escrow credit for repairs or renovations, or maybe that beautiful dining room set that's too large for the sellers' next home.

6. Comparing Homes on the Basis of Purchase Price Rather Than Monthly Costs of Ownership

You might like a three-bedroom, two-bath ranch home in Suffolk Heights that you can buy for $119,500. However, you favor a contempory in Pleasantown priced at $130,000. To choose between these two houses, it seems that you must decide whether the contemporary is worth $10,500 more than the ranch. But this type of comparison isn't enough. Besides price, these homes may differ in property taxes, homeowners' insurance premiums, homeowner association fees, commuting costs, utility bills, cost of upkeep, profit potential (appreciation, creation of value, income), costs of financing, and other items. As a result, when you really get down to comparing home economics, move beyond price. Estimate and compare your expected total average monthly costs of ownership.

7. Failing to Plan for Home Ownership

In survey after survey, renters claim they "can't afford" to buy because they lack enough money for a down payment. Often this belief reveals a lack of education about low- (or no-) down-payment home finance possibilities. But just as often, it reveals a failure to plan. Mortgage loan officers repeatedly point out that high monthly bills (car payments, furniture payments, credit card debt) block people's ability to save. Don't fall into this trap. Make saving for home ownership a number 1 priority. As long as you tell yourself you don't have enough for a down payment, you'll never break those borrow-and-spend habits that keep you broke.

8. Changing Your "Loan Status" Before Your Loan Closes

When you apply for a mortgage you'll have to detail your complete financial picture: your job, income, bills, savings, assets, liabilities, and a dozen other things. Until your loan closes, don't change anything without first getting your lender's approval. Don't buy a new car; don't change jobs; don't take a maternity leave; don't open a new charge account; don't take a vacation and charge it to your Visa card. Anything you change in your "loan status" may cause your lender to delay or deny approval of your loan.

9. Failing to Accurately Estimate Repair, Renovation, and Redecorating Expenses

Make sure you get your home professionally inspected by appropriate specialists (roofing, structural, pest infestation, electrical, plumbing, HVAC, etc.). Don't rely on a friend, relative, or Realtor. If you do plan to spend money for repairs, renovations, or redecorating, don't rely on ballpark estimates. Get as firm a grasp on the figures as you can. Also, remember that expenses can accumulate rapidly. It doesn't take long for a few "minor" items to add up to major dollars. Know what you're getting into before you buy.

10. Failing to Accurately Compare the Costs, Risks, and Benefits of Various Mortgages

When you shop for a home loan, you'll find a near infinite variety of loan-to-value ratios, points, fees, closing costs, annual caps, lifetime caps, mortgage insurance premiums, and interest rates along with terms ranging anywhere from 10 to 40 years. Given this wide variety of variables, it's virtually impossible for you to accurately figure out the best home loan for your needs. The calculations are too complex unless you have a computer software program that can easily handle all of the data. As a result, most home buyers "eyeball" the numbers, or maybe work through some relatively simple calculations.

However, mistakes here can cost you many thousands of dollars over the period you hold your loan. The solution is to buy a mortgage comparison software program; work with a Realtor, lender, or home buyer counselor who has such a program; or, give me a call at (800) 942-9304 (extension 20691). I find it somewhat perplexing that home buyers will haggle to the death to get another $1,000 or $2,000 off their home's sales price and then choose their home financing with little technical comparison of costs, risks, and benefits. (Note: lenders will provide you a government-mandated interest calculation called APR. However, no matter what anyone tells you, this basic "one size fits all" figure is of little practical use for individual decision making.)

INDEX